# The Couscous Chronicles

## A PEACE CORPS MEMOIR

### Richard Wallace
with a Foreword by Ambassador Paul J. Hare

**The Couscous Chronicles — A Peace Corps Memoir**
Copyright © 2020 by Richard Wallace

All rights reserved. No part of this book may be reproduced or transmitted in any form or by any electronic or mechanical means, including photocopying, recording or information storage and retrieval systems, without written permission of the author, except for the use of brief quotations in a book review or where permitted by law.

The author has recreated events, locales and conversations based upon his memories of them. The full names of persons mentioned in this book, other than government employees, public officials and those deceased, are used with their permissions. Some persons identified by their first names only are fictitious or have been changed in the interest of privacy.

ISBN: 979-8-6512-8589-1

First Edition, July 2020, Ponchatoula, Louisiana USA
Library of Congress Control Number: 2020910746

10 9 8 7 6 5 4 3 2 1

Cover Design Art & Map: Allison Behan, artbyallie.com
Back Cover, Title Design & Interior Formatting: Rachael Ritchey, rachaelritchey.com

To the loving memory of
my parents
Charles W. and Winifred K. Wallace,
and my very special correspondent
Mary Catherine "Aunt Kaki" Wallace

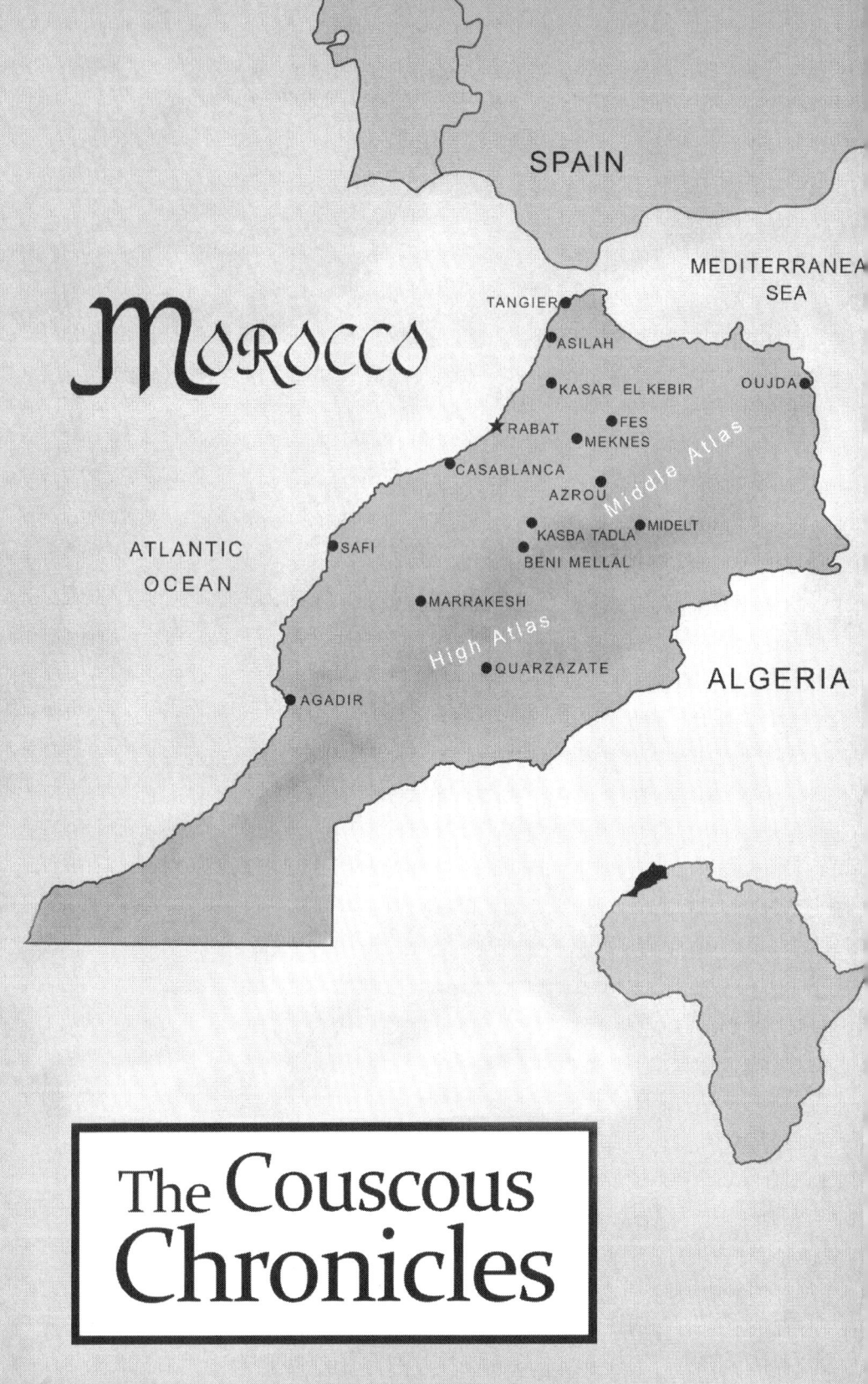

# CONTENTS

## Part One
*This Land Was Made for You ... and (Hopefully) Me*     1

## Part Two
*Into September ... and Beyond!*     57

## Part Three
*A Changing of the Guard*     163

## Part Four
*... and the Job Came Tumblin' Down*     197

*Epilogue*     237

*Acknowledgments*     245

*About the Author*     246

# FOREWORD

Richard Wallace either has a prodigious memory or is a diarist in the grand tradition of Pepys and Boswell. He recalls a seemingly infinite number of places visited in Morocco from remote Berber villages in the Middle Atlas to famed imperial cities, persons encountered of all classes, conversations and meals consumed (often with a glass or more of Moroccan wine, quite cheap and not bad at all) during his tour as a Peace Corps Volunteer in Morocco in the late 1970s.

His attention to the details that transpired 40 years ago is uncanny. Among many other things that I have long forgotten, he recalls the name of my cat, Zany, and the number of turkeys I procured for the traditional Thanksgiving meal for the volunteers. And that is just a start.

Richard was based in Rabat, worked at the Ministry of Agriculture in the film section and shared an apartment with his co-worker, Becky. Their residence very quickly became a point of destination for other volunteers who served in all parts of Morocco and came to Rabat where the Peace Corps office was located. Out of this cauldron of visitors and friends many stories were spun – some inspiring, others less so – but they also revealed in graphic detail the daily lives of the volunteers and the bonds of camaraderie that existed between them. The apartment became known as the "Ocean Hotel" because of the neighborhood's proximity to the Atlantic.

While the hotel is one of the focal points in the chronicles, interspersed throughout are stories told by other volunteers about their experiences. I particularly enjoyed the story of the women volunteers who found temporary lodging in Beni Mellal, their town of assignment, only to find that their place of abode was the local brothel! In another, a volunteer in Kasba Tadla went to the local shop to buy a Coke and was accosted by an elderly gentleman who thought he was the son of his good friend, Hussein. When the volunteer replied in perfect dialect that he was not in fact the son in question, the whole shop burst out in laughter. The stories are endless and priceless.

While a common theme throughout concerns the generosity and hospitality shown by the Moroccans, Richard does not gloss over his experiences or that of other volunteers. He talks about women volunteers being harassed and those who are despondent about their work or inability to function in admittedly difficult circumstances. His honesty is refreshing and sheds a sharp light on the daily existence of life in Morocco with little money in one's pocket. In the same spirit of speaking honestly, he describes the reasons why he decided to leave the Ocean Hotel – the inundation of visitors was becoming a bit too much – and subsequently to terminate his two-year assignment early (absence of meaningful employment). Neither decision was easy.

Does that mean that the Peace Corps experience was wasted time? Hardly. It is unlikely Richard would have embarked on this journalistic journey and sought out the memories of other volunteers if it were. The good clearly outweighed the bad. It is best summarized by Richard himself who concluded at the end of the chronicles: "The experiment was over. The experience and productivity of my future would be the only measure of the worth, in knowledge gained, of this treasured past. *Kulshi la bes!* (Everything is fine!)"

In closing, I would like to thank Richard for his friendship and his creativity and determination in producing *The Couscous Chronicles*. It is a very special undertaking which brings back a flood of memories. I would like also to thank his fellow volunteers for their dedicated service which made my all-too-brief time in Morocco a high point of my career in the Foreign Service.

- Paul J. Hare
*Country Director, Peace Corps Morocco, 1977–1979*
*U.S. Ambassador to Zambia, 1985–1988*

# PREFACE

President John F. Kennedy created the Peace Corps in 1961 to "promote world peace and friendship," among other goals. Volunteer ranks peaked in 1966 with more than 15,000 serving worldwide. By the late 1970s, this government agency for volunteer service struggled to remain relevant. By 1977, some 6,000 volunteers served in 62 developing countries, operating on a budget barely one-third of that allocated 10 years earlier. The Peace Corps lost much of its identity during the Nixon years when it was merged with ACTION, the umbrella agency that included VISTA (Volunteers in Service to America) and other domestic volunteer programs. By 1977, recruiters tasked with reviving the Peace Corps searched for liberal arts generalists who could be thoroughly trained to become successful in a wide variety of assignments.

Peace Corps life is called volunteering. Or, it could be considered surrendering oneself to the U.S. government and simply hoping to be kept safe, housed and fed for a two-year period in a faraway land while sharing one's skills and personality with people who don't speak English. As clearly stated in the 1977 edition of the *Peace Corps Handbook,* "Peace Corps Volunteers are not officers or employees of the United States Government ...," though their daily lifestyle may occasionally be at the mercy of the bureaucracy and politics of Washington, D.C. Completing a mountain of paperwork (and possibly a personal interview) and signing those final forms authorized Uncle Sam to ship us off to territories we had never heard of, much less visited.

The Peace Corps experience might be considered a long trip, a journey: not a vacation. It was hard work – maybe not physical, but certainly emotional. Two years seemed a long time to be away from family and close friends; but the weeks and months flew by, filled with many ups and downs and relationships formed, all punctuated by hilarious frivolities and once-in-a-lifetime happenings.

# INTRODUCTION

Do memories have a lifespan or an expiration date? My memories of a special period in my life are well-preserved, thanks to a collection of letters, cassette tapes, assorted papers and postcards – all now more than 40 years old.

Step back to 1977 through 1979 ... quite a different era. You could buy a new car for $4500 and fill it up at 65 cents a gallon. You could mail a letter for 13 cents. Jimmy Carter occupied the White House, facing an inflation rate of 11 percent plus unemployment just under 8 percent (both rising). *Star Wars* and *Saturday Night Fever* entertained the masses. The comic strip *Garfield* first appeared, and bottled water became mainstream trendy. Daily living was paper-based, with none of the electronics of today – certainly no cell phones, no laptops, no internet, no email.

In 1977, I was a recent graduate of Southern Illinois University at Carbondale, with a degree in cinema and photography production. My prior four years at Georgia Tech had failed to advance my dreams of becoming an astronaut or earning a degree, so a transition to the visual arts and change of educational scenery turned out to be worthwhile moves. Though secure with a job offer in Chattanooga, Tennessee, to make training films for employees of service industries, I altered my priorities based on the intrigue of foreign travel and learning another language. Exposure to this Peace Corps adventure came about quite by accident and led me to Rabat, Morocco's capital city – a bustling metropolis with urban conveniences left by French colonials.

My story here is, no doubt, one of thousands – a 40-year-old collection of memories, a pedestrian account of survival in a foreign land – though mine is a story no one else can tell. To round out my recollections, I reached out to others in our Volunteer Class of 1977, collecting favorite memories from 20 contributors, mostly English teachers, volunteers and others living all over Morocco. Their remembrances clarify and define what the Peace Corps experience was all about.

I often reminisce on what my life was like four decades ago. Like my colleagues from the Morocco we knew in the late 1970s, I hope this memory never expires.

Here goes.

# The Couscous Chronicles
A PEACE CORPS MEMOIR

# PART ONE

## This Land was Made for You ... and (Hopefully) Me

"I lived in New York City for six months to get ready for this!" Stan hollered through a crush of humanity toward my general direction. Elbows, shoulders and smelly armpits crowded my face, while the scratch of wooly djellabas chafed my arms, bared by short sleeves.

"Whatever happened to standing in a line?" I shouted back at Stan. A mass of men shuffled toward the window, and the two of us were swept up in their tide. Surrounded by loud Arabic chatter, eye contact and hand motions were our best means of communication. I'd thought hanging out with my dorm neighbor Stan and his French fragments would help us at Rabat's main post office.

Handing over a purple bill at the counter, we completed a simple transaction – a dozen two-dirham stamps for letters and 10 stamps for postcards – and extracted ourselves and our purchases from the crowd.

An hour earlier, we had leaned on the assistance of a Peace Corps training staffer to change money at a nearby bank. He left us on our own to buy stamps – we thought we were ready to fly solo. The unnerving, though educational encounter opened our eyes to the accepted behaviors of our newly adopted culture.

Our entry into Moroccan society was fast and furious.

## What Kind of World Were We Entering?

Flash back three weeks:

All of us received instructions to assemble at the Hotel Sonesta in Atlanta's Buckhead neighborhood for three days of orientation and final health clearances. The paperwork made it clear we were all Peace Corps trainees, pending successful completion of a 10-week in-country training program.

Once I learned I was accepted to a Peace Corps program in Morocco, I borrowed the M volume of my neighbor's *Encyclopedia Britannica* to read up on the place. I found more helpful references and maps thumbing through the card catalog at the Dunwoody branch of our public library in suburban Atlanta.

Morocco – quite an interesting place, I discovered; a cornerstone of the Arab world. Maybe we had read a few lines about it in a high school world history or geography class – an elongated country on the forehead of Africa, forming half of the funnel where the Mediterranean Sea sifts through the Strait of Gibraltar to meet the Atlantic Ocean. It's roughly the size of California and was home to some 20 million people in the late 1970s. Its largest city, Casablanca, evokes the romance and mystique of *The Arabian Nights*. And it's a fact: Morocco is not one big desert, as so often depicted in books and movies – though the southern third of the country is a disputed, desolate territory once referred to as Spanish Sahara.

Declaring its independence in 1956, Morocco was no longer a colony of France and officially became the Kingdom of Morocco. French and other European influences were most evident in the larger cities, plus the roads and infrastructure networks that aided development of commercial and agricultural areas. The country is commonly confused with Monaco, the luxury principality across the Mediterranean on the southern coast of France.

The United States has enjoyed a long history of friendship and partnership with Morocco. President John F. Kennedy established the Peace Corps by executive order in March 1961; the agency sent its first group of volunteers to Morocco two years later. From that point, assignments to the Peace Corps Morocco program had been considered among the most popular and comfortable positions available around the world.

Each summer, a new group of volunteers replaced those completing their two years of service. My Class of 1977 numbered 92, a diverse group of mostly young adults: 80 assigned to Teach English as a Foreign Language (TEFL) and my group of 12 assigned to agricultural, urban development and social services programs. Our class was 60 percent male, all white, mostly in their mid-twenties with a few in the thirty to forty-five age group, and included three married couples and one energetic woman over sixty.

Arriving at the hotel and trading glances among us, we all had the resigned look of "We're in the Army now!"

## Cleared for Takeoff

Our initial get-together was well-organized: arrive Sunday, June 26, by 11 a.m., country overview, lunch, program meetings all afternoon, followed by dinner and medical appointments. By 8:30 that evening, time was left for an Open House, one mass meet and greet.

Geographically, our class represented a varied demographic. We had arrived in Atlanta from dozens of states; I was the lone trainee from Georgia.

Many of us were fresh out of college, anxious to see the world. The relatively high unemployment rate at the time attracted those struggling to find a job or an opportunity to collect work experience. I learned later that a few Vietnam veterans were in our class. Others had worked a year or two after college, become bored or frustrated and wanted a change of scenery.

Each carried personal dreams of experiencing a foreign culture. For three days, a palpable excitement surrounded us. We would soon launch ourselves into the unknown, taking along American ideals and our desires to make positive impressions.

Several in-service volunteers joined us in Atlanta. They had completed visits to the United States and were hitching a ride with us back to Morocco. We peppered them with questions about what life might be like in Morocco and collected many helpful suggestions. Jerry from Pittsburgh recommended we pack a handful of Kennedy half dollars, noting the coins would come in handy for soliciting favors or expressing gratitude; Moroccans respected and admired JFK.

A cassette tape recorder and a sleeping bag were the two items most commonly recommended. We had a weight limit of 80 pounds, but I had received an allowance for extra weight to cover my camera equipment and other supplies needed for my assignment. Living in suburban Atlanta, I was able to run home in the evenings and rethink my final packing for living and working two years overseas.

Back at the hotel, program meetings proved informative. Our agricultural group of a dozen trainees discussed the upcoming training process. We learned that 300 hours of French instruction and 20 hours of introductory Arabic awaited us in Rabat. Housing was arranged for the entire group, dormitory style, in a girls' boarding school in the center of town – a campus that was vacant for the summer months.

During a break in our agenda, a woman spoke up from the other end of the conference table. "Is there a Charles Wallace here?"

In the mishmash of bureaucratic paperwork, Peace Corps Washington had provided Becky Mangus from Denver with my father's name to identify her new co-worker. Quite a memorable way to get acquainted! Paul Huntsman from Idaho was there too – the third member of our audiovisual team set to work for the Ministry of Agriculture in Rabat producing training films, slideshows and printed materials for farmers.

Two architects, a few engineers and urban planners, a mechanic and a surveyor joined us at the table. Casual introductions followed, with each person announcing their name and hometown. In many cases (especially with common names) the connection to a city or home state would become our system of distinguishing folks scattered across the country; last names more or less disappeared.

And those medical appointments … line up! Medical personnel arrived from the nearby Centers for Disease Control. Everyone was issued individual International Certificates of Vaccination from the U.S. Public Health Service. Pages of the yellow pocket-sized form unfolded to list vaccinations or revaccinations against smallpox, yellow fever and cholera. The final page was a chart of other immunizations: tetanus, typhoid, the polio vaccine plus inoculations against rabies and hepatitis. Throw in a TB test for good measure. Whatever injections were missed on the first day, a three-hour session on the next day's agenda would cover. Once in Morocco, that certificate would be updated to show revaccinations against hepatitis (every four months) and cholera (every six months) plus completion of the series of three rabies shots. Reactions and side effects to all the injections were explained and widely expected.

On Day Two, we reviewed more Peace Corps rules and regulations covered in the 60-page handbook we had received in the mail. One final plea to back out was made for anyone with second thoughts about accepting the Peace Corps mission and missing two years of life in America. We had a brief, personal interview with a doctor to discuss any pre-existing medical conditions – issues already noted on our applications. The bank of pay phones in the lobby got a workout for collect calls to friends and family.

Day Three started with another three-hour lecture of Peace Corps policies and administrative tasks before we checked out of the hotel: lots of rules to follow when the U.S. government transplants its people to a foreign country. Two hours of free time followed lunch – time to handle last-minute packing, personal phone calls and introductions to one another – before lining up to receive our special-issue passports and plane tickets.

A mountain of luggage, mostly backpacks and duffle bags, covered the sidewalks in front of the hotel. Several parents had hung around while we prepared to leave and were there as we boarded buses heading to the airport. My dad and my older brother Bill came to see me off. Bill worked as the assignment editor in the news department of the CBS affiliate in Atlanta, so he dispatched a camera crew to document our departure and develop a story for the 11 o'clock news.

My mother had settled for a telephone goodbye, I assumed to avoid a tearful scene. Of all family members, my mother was most disturbed by my decision to run off to Morocco. At times, she implied, "Hollywood is the *other* way if you want to go make movies!" It likely didn't help matters that I chose Mother's Day to reveal my decision to accept the Peace Corps invitation. During the call, she reminded me to use my sunblock, work hard and always try to wear clean clothes. She wished me well and expressed her love. I returned the sentiment and did my best to cheer her up, signing off with, "Oh, and, Mom, I didn't forget: Happy Birthday." She ended the call smiling, I'm sure.

## Touchdown

With all the preliminaries completed, we were finally ready to leave the country. Three buses took us to Atlanta's Hartsfield International Airport. A charter flight awaited our group – a Braniff International Airways Boeing 707 jetliner.

We arrived at the terminal reserved for charter flights and patiently waited another two hours on benches while the luggage was loaded – more opportunities to meet fellow trainees. I felt the anticipation and energetic optimism, an excitement that pervaded the room. With cameras at the ready, Paul Huntsman and I caught each other in our viewfinders photographing the class. That well-documented sampling of American society, approved by Washington to handle JFK's mission as ambassadors of peace, was about to be assimilated into the Arab culture.

Finally boarding the plane, we had room to spread out with two people assigned to every row of three seats. As the plane ascended, we knew our adventures were just beginning and were ready to celebrate.

The flight became one big party as the Braniff flight attendants more or less threw the book out. Free beer flowed. Joe, the mechanic from Massachusetts, joined another trainee to perform guitar and harmonica numbers on the intercom. Robert from Delaware was a little late reading the cover story of *Esquire* magazine, "How to Get a Job." Female trainees played flight attendants for one day, helping to serve meals.

We enjoyed ample time for chats with folks with whom we would soon share a new country. Comparing collections of cassette tapes was a popular conversation starter. Our favorite music would play a vital role in our day-to-day survival. Some teachers had plans to use music in their classes too. The Eagles, Fleetwood Mac and Linda Ronstadt topped the charts that summer.

After roaming the center aisle and talking photography with Becky and Paul, I encountered a new face. A woman seated on the aisle abruptly stood and introduced herself.

"Hi, I'm Maura Murray from Moore, Oklahoma."

I tried to recall if I had ever visited the state. I knew Oklahoma was home of the infamous tornado alley. Not much of a conversation starter, I thought.

"How did you end up here?" was a line I often used to launch a friendly chat. Maura, I learned, had just graduated from the University of Oklahoma with a degree in education and French language studies. Any ability in French would be helpful, I thought.

"Did Peace Corps give you a choice of where to go?" I asked.

"I was offered Togo. But the day I called to accept, they said, 'Sorry, Togo is closed due to an assassination attempt on the president. So, you can wait for an undefined time or go to Morocco.' I chose to go to Morocco. I had no particular desire to go there. I just wanted to go to Africa and a French-speaking country," she explained.

Maura, proudly Irish – and Catholic, like many of us – left five brothers and three sisters back home. I assumed she would get plenty of mail. With her cheerful personality and contagious laugh, she and I would become lifelong friends.

At dawn, a two-hour refueling stop in the Azores allowed us to step off the plane and stretch. We witnessed some impressive scenery on that volcanic outcropping in the Atlantic. The airport's single runway nestled in the caldera of an ancient volcano, encircled by jagged cliffs devoid of any vegetation – like the terrain of another planet.

A bunch of us strolled across the airfield, climbed a hill and surveyed the place. Our plane rested on the runway – the only aircraft in sight – while trucks gassed it up for the homestretch.

One final takeoff and landing: we all made it into Rabat without much sleep. Morocco greeted us with overcast skies; it was cooler there than in Atlanta.

Rabat's airport appeared to be out in the middle of nowhere. Established volunteers greeted us, cheering us a hearty "Welcome!" from a second-floor terrace as we walked across the tarmac into the terminal. Once inside, we found encouragement in talking with them and meeting some of the Peace Corps Morocco staff.

Our plane's crew had departed for their hotel, leaving the Moroccan ground crew to figure out how to open the plane and unload our luggage. Emptying the plane of the massive luggage load took time, so we sat in the airport for more than two hours before claiming our two-year supply of personal items.

The terminal featured a large framed portrait of King Hassan II – the same portrait of the country's revered leader that adorned every business and virtually every home in Morocco. I was surprised by the lack of local activity around the airport as we caught our first glimpses of the Moroccan population. Veiled women, men with turbans wearing hooded djellabas – by their clothing alone, we could tell we faced a totally different culture.

### one volunteer remembers ...

When we got to Rabat, I remember sitting in this tiny terminal with no AC for hours waiting for them to figure out how to open the plane to get our luggage. Eventually, they put us on a bus and going into town I looked out the window and saw a guy plowing a rocky field with a handheld plow pulled by a camel and a donkey. I was shocked!

They took us to the Café Français for lunch. I turned green from jet lag, the heat and the awful smell and begged to be taken to the hotel, but our rooms were not ready. Finally at the hotel, I became upset because the toilets flushed differently and the light switches were different. It was all so disorienting! I felt completely out of control and unable to predict the simplest things or take anything for granted ... a case of sensory overload.

Mark Dressman
TEFL Instructor
Kasba Tadla

Three tour buses made a roundabout swing through Rabat as in-service volunteers pointed out historic landmarks. I was surprised to see the capital city featured few tall buildings; most were six stories or fewer. The exception was one giant structure, a government office building under construction in the city's center, that towered to about 15 floors.

I caught a short nap on the way into the city where our group was dispersed among three restaurants and three hotels in the downtown area. By noon, my group sat in the Café Saadi Restaurant, lunching on our first sampling of Moroccan cuisine. Sofa-like banquettes lined the walls facing low tables. A salad, some fresh fruit and a chicken dish satisfied a lot of hungry, curious Americans that day. The meal was topped off by the customary display of serving boiling hot tea in slender glasses stuffed with sugar cubes and leaves of mint. Servers arched the teapot over each glass and drew it up high above the table, not spilling a drop. The challenge remained to pick up that red-hot glass and sip our first taste of a classic Moroccan beverage.

## Now Hear This

Our entire group reassembled at a theater for a brief Peace Corps welcome meeting and more forms to complete. Country Director Everett Woodman introduced us to key staff members, and the U.S. Embassy sent a few representatives to roll out the welcome mat. Several in our group slept through most of the session.

The next day, we heard more detailed presentations regarding our extensive training that would begin the following week and inch us closer to fulfilling Peace Corps Washington's current mantra of meeting the "basic human needs" of our hosts, be it teaching English or providing technical services. We learned to refer to Moroccans in government-speak as Host Country Nationals, or HCNs, and added that to our litany of abbreviations and acronyms born in Washington.

An embassy staffer explained how and why our group would assume a symbolic, quasi-diplomatic role. Back in 1777, Morocco was one of the first foreign lands to recognize the sovereignty of the newly independent United States. As a result, our planeload had been tagged the Bicentennial Group of volunteers who annually arrived to continue that legacy of positive foreign relations. The staffer told us the majority of Moroccans appreciated Americans so we should feel welcomed into their society.

Our Moroccan orientation continued its variety with a brief introduction to the metric system. Forget about pounds, inches and miles – now it was all kilograms, centimeters and kilometers. Curiously, one Peace Corps staffer explained male volunteers typically lost weight while in Morocco, while the women gained weight. I never understood the rationale behind that theory, but it proved to be true.

Further speeches educated us on appropriate conduct in our assigned jobs and in our communities. The culture mandated some interesting new habits, especially in the smaller towns: Women didn't go out alone after dark. And there was a dress code to follow, in line with Muslim etiquette; modesty was paramount. When planning anything or declaring a fact, the country operated on the *Inshallah* Principle, meaning "God willing" or "if God wills it." We would hear that expression often.

"I will arrive on the 2 o'clock bus ... Inshallah."

"My father's birthday is coming up ... Inshallah."

One female speaker made quite an entrance. With the demeanor of a high school guidance counselor, she told us point-blank, "Some of you will find romance in the Peace Corps," and added guidelines on how to manage a serious relationship far from home. Her declaration turned out to be accurate.

Having lived in Morocco for three years, she also expressed her opinion of how women are treated, often as second-class citizens. She cautioned female trainees to be prepared for episodes of misogyny. More truth told.

Embassy officials discussed procedures for leaving Morocco in case of civil unrest or a natural disaster. Those living in the Rabat vicinity would evacuate to the embassy. All others would get to a regional location and wait to be picked up. While they had our attention, officials commanded us not to engage in any political activity while living there.

Another embassy staffer explained how the presence of Americans, especially in smaller towns, might be perceived with suspicions by local populations. One or two single Americans showing up to teach in their schools may generate questions:

"Why are you *really* here? Do you work for the CIA?"

"Why aren't you married?"

Influenced by American movies and TV shows, Moroccans typically perceived all Americans as being wealthy. "Get used to it," we were told and further instructed to explain we were there to serve Morocco and promote a positive impression of Americans. The speaker told us we were not the only strangers in the country. Several European countries and even Japan had volunteer agencies similar to Peace Corps operating in the country at the time.

Personal health and safety were stressed repeatedly. Two Peace Corps Volunteers had died tragically the previous year due to misuse of a butane gas heater.

Dolores Sidi Hida, Health Director for Peace Corps Morocco, was introduced. We came to know her simply as Nurse Dolores, a real character. An American, trained and experienced as a midwife in Morocco, Dolores was married to a Moroccan and spoke Spanish and Arabic. With her white dress, short hair and stocky build, she looked like a missionary. She was ultimately responsible for keeping us all healthy.

I would periodically collect her initials in my International Certificates of Vaccination after required injections in her office. Her presentation introduced some health-minded tips I have used to this day, including thoroughly washing my hands every time I return home – and every chance I get – and always carrying a handkerchief. I doubted the usefulness of a handkerchief; I had never carried one, though I had packed a few – but, over time, I discovered too many uses to count.

Dolores continued with the "No Drugs Allowed" lecture (again) and a preview of what Moroccan jails were like: "Dark, dingy, hot and smelling like a house full of dead animals." Volunteers were banned from owning or driving a car or the popular mopeds we noticed buzzing around town: too dangerous. We were to assume every dog in Morocco carried rabies – so don't think about owning or even petting one – and to be sure to complete our series of three shots.

She was proud to show off a new government-issued Personal Medical Kit that we would receive following training. The molded plastic carrying case held essential items to keep us healthy – a deluxe first aid kit, actually. Dolores was adamant that we return the case and any leftover supplies to her office at the completion of service ... as if we would not be allowed to leave the country if she didn't get her plastic box back. Yeah, right.

Money matters piqued everyone's interests. Once at our sites, we would be paid a monthly living allowance in the local currency and be responsible for securing our own housing. Those assigned to the big cities received a larger allowance since expenses ran higher there. Living in Rabat, I would pick up a check at the Peace Corps office and cash it at a local bank. Those living in small towns were paid by a kind of money order – called a *mandat* – claimed and cashed at their post office. For every month of Peace Corps service, $125 was set aside for us to collect as a readjustment allowance when we returned to the States. Complete two years and receive a check for $3,000, less taxes and deductions. We were encouraged to fill out yet another form to activate a Personal Articles Insurance Policy for an annual deduction of $67, covering valuables like my camera equipment.

That orientation once on the ground in Morocco took on a higher level of importance. If all went according to plan, I would become an official Peace Corps Volunteer (PCV) on September 3. And to make us look official around town, we were issued a wallet-sized identification card that folded in half with one of our extra passport pictures stapled to the inside panel. In French, the card identified me as a volunteer member of the Peace Corps from America and notified anyone to call the Peace Corps office in Rabat in case of emergency. It was signed by Mr. Woodman and had the circular stamp of the embassy. I never had the opportunity to show that card to anybody.

Our first few nights in Morocco would be spent at the Hotel de la Paix; other volunteers filled the nearby Hotel Royale; and the third bus went to the Grand Hotel. Our hotel was quite comfortable and, by later comparison, perhaps the nicest of the three. Our second-floor balcony provided a good vantage point to the sights and sounds of Rabat's busy street below, featuring honking horns and constantly buzzing mopeds.

My roommate was Mark Postnikoff from Independence, Missouri, one of the TEFL teachers. We compared backgrounds, and another lifelong friendship was established. Mark arrived with a degree in history and secondary education from Graceland University in Lamoni, Iowa. After college, he had been a student teacher for six months and worked in a metal shop. TV and magazine ads for the Peace Corps caught his attention; he knew he wanted to travel. Once invited to the program in Morocco, he had read up on the country in *The Statesman's Yearbook*.

## Culture 101

In-service volunteers and staffers from the Peace Corps office guided our initial days in Morocco. Many volunteers – all TEFL teachers – helped with the training program known as the *stage,* using the French pronunciation "stahj." As a kind of goodwill ambassadors for Peace Corps, they fielded our every question and showed us around town.

Following our first meeting, staffer Wally Swanson, who would serve as program coordinator for those working in agriculture, collected a group for a sunset tour of Rabat's nearby medina. He was a husky man, taller than most of the locals, and easy to follow along the stroll from our hotel, down Rabat's version of Main Street: Avenue Mohammed V. Most Moroccan cities or towns of any size featured a main thoroughfare of the same name, honoring King Mohammed V who led the country to independence in 1956.

Wally offered a mini-lesson in Arabic as we walked. *La bes* was the standard greeting for "Hello," and *la* meant "no" – our best response for all the vendors begging to sell us stuff. Wally knew the street kids would be all over us, begging for money, as we made our way through the crowded streets.

"Give those kids a stern look and yell *'Seerf!'* at 'em ... that means 'Get lost, beat it, go away,'" Wally advised us. "If that doesn't work, try *'Seerf haleek!'*... that means 'Get lost, go to hell,' as if you're really serious. That line usually does the trick."

A walled-in quarter of the city, the medina is a feature of many North African cities, noted for its maze of narrow streets, mostly without motorized vehicles. The neighborhood is typically a wild assortment of residential and commercial structures, all jumbled tightly together. Reaching one end of Avenue Mohammed V, we walked through an arched entrance carved into thick stone walls, left the European-inspired metropolis behind us and discovered another world.

We felt like tourists. Make no mistake: we looked like tourists.

No library book or reference article could have prepared us for what we encountered. There was the scene: a colony of commotion, most often portrayed in movies and literature – a combination flea market, restaurant, department store and grocery. We ended up single file, managing our way through noisy crowds of locals toting large straw bags.

Every few steps delivered sensory surprises: the sights – pairs of men held hands as they shopped; the sounds – radios blared Arabic music, and merchants bargained loudly with customers; and the smells – a variety of excrements littered edges of the walkway.

For a stretch, we passed colorful carpets and bolts of fabric, then handmade brass plates and trinkets, followed by gold and silver necklaces, rings and bracelets. Some stalls had barely enough room for the solo merchant, with goods piled up at least 15 feet on three sides. The seller used a pole with a hook to snag shoppers' items beyond his reach.

Next came the food: Beef kabobs sizzled on smoky charcoal fires and came served with assorted delicacies we were challenged to identify. Rows of fresh vegetables fanned out like a rainbow. Cones of spices sold by the gram were displayed on slanted tables – all the colors of a box of crayons – saffron, turmeric, cumin; along with almonds and assorted fruits. Cheeses, butter, eggs ... it was all there.

Swarms of flies suddenly surprised us – welcome to the meat department. We witnessed butchers under strings of bare light bulbs, carving up sides of beef and hanging up the bloody cuts at arm's length in front of us. Mounds of ground beef were stacked on the counters. Chickens were already plucked, gutted and hung by their necks. Not much in the way of refrigeration was evident, so we assumed everything was to be sold right away and if it was well cooked ... well, forget about the flies.

Purchases were wrapped in thick purple paper and sealed with masking tape. In a darkened corner, I noticed a disheveled man – talking to himself and probably intoxicated – urinating against a building. An elderly man sat on the ground by one stall with a burlap bag, selling his single commodity: snails.

Wally saved the best medina attraction for last: a stop for his favorite dessert. Bubbling vats of oil fried *sfenjs,* something like a funnel cake or a doughnut dusted with sugar and served hot in a sheet of newspaper. We became instant fans. A sweet ending to our immersion into Moroccan culture!

Leaving the medina, we crossed busy streets to visit the mausoleum of Mohammed V, the most visited landmark in Rabat. Completed six years before we arrived, it was widely considered an architectural masterpiece. The site's wide hilltop plaza incorporated the Hassan Tower, the red limestone remains of a 12th-century minaret that was never completed, though envisioned centuries ago to be the tallest minaret and largest mosque in the world. Across a floor of polished granite, dozens of stone columns indicated the footprint of the massive mosque that never was.

Guards in full ceremonial dress were stationed at the entrances to the mausoleum. Inside, we walked reverently around a balcony overlooking the ornate tomb situated beneath a conical chandelier of sparkling cut glass. Elaborate mosaics and ceramic tilework covered the walls; the ceiling featured impressive cedar carvings and gold leaf.

Stepping outside, we discovered the surrounding plaza with gardens was a popular gathering place for locals. As the sun set, we enjoyed plenty of photo opportunities before returning to our hotel. The trek was an eye-opener and a helpful indoctrination to Moroccan city life.

## Parlez-Vous?

We were free to roam around town between meetings and Peace Corps orientation. We had been issued walk-around money to acquaint us with the local currency – dirhams, with approximately four dirhams to every U.S. dollar. Bills came in different colors, like Monopoly money; coins had a silver or gold finish.

English was worthless; it simply did not exist. On a rare occasion, a merchant or taxi driver may have known a few words to deal with tourists, but that was about it.

Many in our group of 92 trainees had traveled before, and several knew basic French. A few had minored in French in college or had grown up around family members who spoke the language. Two women had worked as nannies in France for a year, and another had actually visited Morocco before. My strategy was to hang out with one of those part-time French speakers as often as possible. Speaking Arabic was a talent unknown to all of us.

## Moroccan Travel: A Primer

Our training headquarters – that boarding school in Rabat – was not ready for our group to move in. In the meantime, we were all assigned to go on a five-day trip, called a homestay, to the work sites of in-service Peace Corps Volunteers. Small groups of us would travel to each site; our guides were TEFL teachers out for the summer. The objective was to experience actual work and living conditions plus get a taste of travel in Morocco. Those in the TEFL program would get a preview of the countryside, too, helping them later to select their preferences for a place to live and work for the next two years.

Paul Huntsman and I already knew our job assignment would keep us in Rabat, but we had to go someplace. We tagged along with Mark, Roger and Michael to Kasba Tadla, a small agricultural town in central Morocco. Robin, our tall, lanky host, was the only American living there.

We waited in front of the medina at a dusty lot to hire a grand taxi, typically an aging diesel-powered Mercedes or a full-size American sedan converted to diesel. Drivers would wait for a full load of six passengers, which happened to describe our group. We left Rabat at 11 a.m. We were off!

The taxi took us to Casablanca, where we saw some of that huge city and waited to transfer to a bus headed to Kasba Tadla. We boarded a souk bus – the moniker for a dilapidated second-class bus, brightly painted in the country's green and red. Souk buses operated on irregular schedules between small towns and big cities and carried (in addition to passengers) everything from livestock to bicycles and farm equipment. The driver functioned as the ticket seller, the baggage handler and mechanic. He most likely owned the bus as well.

Once packed to capacity, the bus lurched forward to begin our five-hour noisy, bouncy ride in tiny seats. No one else on the bus spoke a word of English, so we freely discussed the Moroccans around us. During one of the frequent stops, a crowd of vendors jumped on to sell hard-boiled eggs, pastries and drinks. At another stop, a comedy team hopped on to entertain in Arabic. People laughed as they joked and played their small instruments. As the bus rolled away from each stop, the vendors and any visitors bailed out the back door of the bus.

The region's landscape reminded me of Kansas: flat, open fields of wheat and grasslands. Spotty areas were rocky and unsuitable for farming or grazing. We caught a glimpse of our first camels.

### one volunteer remembers...

On our way to visit Azrou for our homestay, we stopped in Meknes for lunch. Our host, second-year volunteer Jeanne, suggested we try the local cuisine at a tiny eatery near the grand taxi station. The place had no room on the ground floor, so the cook told us to go upstairs. There, two guys were sitting at a small table with a mountain of loose tobacco that they were mixing with hashish to make kif. They were totally unperturbed by our invasion of their space and continued mixing as if it were nothing special. It was a unique glimpse at Morocco after just a few days in the country. And, no, none of us had a smoke.

Piotr Kostrzewski
*TEFL Instructor*
Khenifra

## Our Homestay Adventure

We arrived in Kasba Tadla around 6 that evening. The town was an assortment of mostly one-story concrete block buildings, situated at the foot of the Middle Atlas Mountains. In the 1940s and 1950s, the town was a French Army garrison.

Our host shared an eight-room house with a Frenchman, also a teacher. We had plenty of space. With Robin being the only American in the town, our arrival was widely noticed by the local folks; the word got around fast!

The next morning, we were up early to shop for breakfast items: eggs, milk, butter, bread and fruit. Roger took a turn as chef in the kitchen and served our crew, assisted by Robin's maid, Zhora. We were introduced to the typical appliances of a Moroccan kitchen. The two-burner stove was fueled by a portable bottle of *Butagas* (propane), connected by a hose and stored in a cabinet beneath the stove. Butagas had many applications, we discovered, and could also be used for fueling space heaters, an oven or a water heater.

Using the bathroom added to our cultural adventures. Opening the door, we thought something was missing.

"Yeah, the decorator used up all his imagination on the rest of the house," Robin deadpanned.

The house featured a Turkish toilet, also called a squat toilet. The fixture, enclosed in its own tiny room, was standard equipment for many homes across Africa and Asia; must have been the origin of the term *water closet*, I thought. Installed flush with the floor, a porcelain platform featured two molded footprints with a hole in the middle. That was it. Men had no issues taking a leak; women required some agility to squat and hit the hole every time. With your business done, pull the chain connected to a tank of water mounted high up on the wall and gravity provided a generous flushing of the platform you were standing on. The trick was to stand back and avoid the sloshing wave. Homes without indoor plumbing kept a bucket filled with water next to the toilet for flushing.

A walk around town brought continued stares. Already, less than a week in the country, I had become accustomed to locals staring at my red hair. Paul insisted on wearing his cowboy hat, generating more curious looks. Strolling the town's streets, we turned a corner and were surprised to see a reminder from home: a Texaco gas station.

Around noon, we piled into a grand taxi heading to El Ksiba, a Berber village 20 kilometers east, closer to the mountains. The Berbers are the indigenous people of North Africa, with their own language, customs and distinctive dress. Upon arrival, we explored our first souk – the weekly open-air market that circulated from town to town, where everything was sold, bartered or traded.

Robin pointed out the various services available. One man got a haircut and beard trimming. Practitioners of various medical procedures clustered in one corner of the souk. An elderly man visited the outdoor dentist. Another man sat calmly, upright in a chair, while leeches clung to the back of his head and neck. "Supposed to relieve headaches, I've heard," was Robin's explanation.

In the midday sun, at least 20 men crowded under a large upright umbrella with a drape that covered their backs down to their waists, shielding passersby. "I think that's the pornography shop there – some sort of peep show; a very popular spot, I'm sure," Robin surmised.

Throughout the tour, Robin threw out more bits of essential Arabic. If we wanted to buy something there with our walk-around money *(floos)*, we could ask "How much?" *(B'shall?)*. Numbers would require a later lesson; merchants were happy to scribble their prices on a scrap of paper for us to consider. Bargaining was expected. Once the price was good *(MOO-ziyen)*, we could complete the purchase and tell the seller "Thanks a lot" *(SHOW-kron)*.

Berbers came and went from the souk on donkeys. A makeshift parking lot for donkeys was fenced in near the souk, another interesting photo op. I wondered how a Berber man could claim his pack animal from such a crowded pen for his trip back into the mountains. Robin later explained that a numbered tag was usually tied around the animal's tail – sort of like the claim check at a parking garage.

We returned to Kasba Tadla by taxi – an old Dodge Polara. Before loading up, we watched a bunch of Berbers cram two sheep into the trunk of their grand taxi. The lively sheep did not seem to mind.

## Finally, Some Home Cookin'

We learned quickly: we would eat a lot of lamb in Morocco. Robin had arranged for us to dine with the family of one of his students that evening. People dined late, typically around 9.

First, we had time to take a bath – the once-a-week Moroccan way. We visited the local public bath, the hammam, a quiet place with origins dating back to the Roman Empire. Moroccans appreciated the importance of purifying one's body before prayers and having time for personal reflection … not to mention the lack of hot water in most homes.

Modesty was the law; so, wearing our swim trunks, we all went into a steaming, hot room. We scrubbed ourselves with a porous volcanic rock that cleaned deeply. Soap and a final rinse followed as we worked with buckets of hot water drawn from a huge tub in the middle of the room. The drying-off procedure was long, and the whole event took over two hours; it was a ritual: preparation, washing, drying – and it all cost 23 cents! That was some economy spa. We were the only ones there at the time, so it was an exclusive experience. Afterward, I felt great!

We made it to dinner by 9. The dimly lit home, only a short walk away, featured tile floors and high ceilings. And there it was again: the king's portrait hung in their living room.

The father worked for the mayor's office and supported seven kids and his wife, earning less than what the Peace Corps paid Robin each month. The family still enjoyed a TV and a refrigerator, both luxury items. We watched our first Moroccan TV: a dance show. The student was proud to show us his stereo.

Only the father and Robin's student joined us for dinner. The rest of the family ate in another room. A vegetable salad was followed by a large bowl of lamb chunks in gravy, with olives and fried potatoes on the side. We ate Moroccan style – with our hands. Right hand only, I constantly reminded myself of the Islamic tradition – a bit of a chore for me, being left-handed. Pieces of bread handled the gravy and olives. It was all delicious, but there was more to come!

Next came the traditional dish of couscous, something like ground cornbread or Cream of Wheat that had the texture of dry grits. To eat it, we were supposed to make a ball of it in our cupped hands and pop it in. We made a mess trying to do that. On top of that large dish were cooked carrots, squash, onions and … more lamb! We were stuffed.

Finally, dessert came: chunks of watermelon, topped off with a shot of hot mint tea in those tiny glasses and enjoyed with the entire family. Quite a meal – a homestyle cultural experience. We thanked our hosts and returned to Robin's place by midnight.

### one volunteer remembers ...

When we were assigned our homestays, I was to visit Azrou, hosted by second-year volunteer Jeanne, a Gauloise-smoking woman who was stationed there. During our visit, she had arranged for a dinner with a local family with whom she was friendly.

As we walked over to the family's house, Jeanne coached us up. She told us not to eat until we were full, but to stop beforehand, because, inevitably, we would be enjoined by the family to eat more: "Kul!" Jeanne instructed us to do this two or three times, and then declare "Shibat" meaning "I'm full." We all tried to come up with a mnemonic to help us with the key phrase – sounded like Tibet.

(As it turned out, the family hosting our dinner had previously been very close to my college roommate, Mr. Williams, who coincidentally had served as a Peace Corps Volunteer in Azrou. As soon as this came to light, I was only addressed as "SaHab Mr. Williams" – Mr. Williams' friend.)

The meal was a classic Moroccan tajine, featuring a huge mound of couscous served on an immense meter-wide platter. One by one, we all followed the protocol, acceding to the urging to eat more until we spoke the magic word and finally put down our spoon by the communal couscous plate. At the family's insistence, I was the penultimate to finish.

Meanwhile, Piotr – the towering Polish-American trainee who was head and shoulders above the rest of us – was still hungry. He continued to wolf spoonful after spoonful into his mouth. All the while, the ladies in the kitchen made brief appearances, peering around a doorway, to see if it was finally time to clean up. Still, Piotr ate. Everyone else had stopped eating... they were just waiting for Piotr to utter the magic word. When he finally started to feel that he might be full and was not hearing more "Kuls" from the family, he put his spoon down and proclaimed "Shibat!" The plate was whisked away immediately.

Steve Long<br>
*TEFL Instructor*<br>
*Midelt*

# Happy Independence Day

The Fourth of July in Morocco was different. Monday was the day of the week for Kasba Tadla's traveling souk. We took a look-see and discovered much the same thing as in the Berber village the previous day.

After lunch, we traveled by grand taxi to Beni Mellal and on to the town of Fkih ben Salah. We saw more of the agricultural region that had been developed over the past 30 years, aided by extensive irrigation. Our grand taxi was a dark red souped-up 1952 Ford. After loading it with six people and all our luggage, the driver tried to push it to get the thing started. We finally arrived at Fkih around 5 p.m. Other Peace Corps groups visiting nearby came, too, for a July Fourth celebration. Another massive lamb meal was produced along with potatoes, noodles, homemade bread and Moroccan wine.

The French brought vineyards to Morocco. During the colonial era (before 1956), Morocco was considered an important exporter of wine. Local wines were quite good, plentiful; and the best vintages were under $2 a bottle. Beer was more expensive and never cold, so we drank liters of Coca-Cola. Ice in drinks was a rarity outside the large cities. We had already learned about the popularity of mint tea.

Nearly 30 Peace Corps in-service volunteers and trainees gathered for the party at the home of second-year volunteer Melanie. It was interesting to hear about the neighboring cities others had visited on their homestays.

I caught up with Mark Dressman from my group. Gauging his Peace Corps experience so far, *everything* was new to Mark. Until he got on a plane to meet us in Atlanta, he had never flown before or lived away from home. He was from northern Kentucky, where he attended a small Catholic liberal arts college, majoring in English and psychology with a minor in secondary education. Like many others, he'd had difficulty finding a teaching job after college. Some limited opportunities did not interest him – he knew the world was a bigger and more interesting place and wanted a change of scenery. He noticed a Peace Corps poster on campus one day.

"The JFK-Catholic thing kicked in for me," he told me. He mailed a postcard requesting an application.

"I struggled to find eight references and fill out the lengthy paperwork," he recalled. Two months later, a recruiter in Atlanta called him. "He said there was a position open for an English teacher in Morocco. I knew where Morocco was on a map and I knew it was an Arab country, but that was about it. I remember thinking quickly to myself what I'd need to survive: I had to have running water and electricity and asked if those existed in Morocco. The answer was 'Yes,' and so I said, 'Yes,' too. I didn't know I'd have another choice, so I took what was offered me."

I asked him, "And what did your family think of your decision?"

"My father was all for it, but my mother was very upset and wanted me to take one of my offers at a nearby university. None of my friends believed I'd do it and, until the very end, they expected me to back out. But I was determined. I shocked my family and all my friends by getting on that plane to Atlanta," he declared, chuckling over his "Watch me … I'll show you" satisfaction.

After the party, most of us spent the night on the rooftop terrace of Melanie's house. We had plenty of room, and it soon cooled off. The moon was almost full, and lots of stars were out; it was like camping. Shooting stars supplied our fireworks.

The next day, we were up early to catch taxis back to Rabat at 6 a.m. All the travelers filled up five taxis, creating our own convoy. One taxi experienced recurring mechanical problems; overheating required several roadside stops. But Joe, the mechanic in our group, kept that clunker rolling.

During one stop for repairs, we wandered around the surrounding landscape, shuffling our shoes across the dusty turf. We wondered how anybody could raise a crop in such lumpy, gritty soil. Scattered plants and grasses barely survived, providing minimal grazing fodder for the half dozen horses and mules we noticed. There was not a fence in sight. To keep the animals from wandering off, their front legs were bound together just above the hooves. It appeared a practical solution to the absence of fencing. The animals could graze with short hops between clumps of grass.

Paul surveyed the roadside scene, leaning against a solitary utility pole and chewing on a long blade of grass. With his cowboy hat, western-style shirt and casual gaze across the wide-open spaces, he reminded me of the Marlboro Man. The Cole Porter tune "Don't Fence Me In" played in my head.

We covered a different route into Rabat, noticing some new terrain: rolling grasslands with herds of sheep and, later, rugged hills. The landscape reminded me of New Mexico or Arizona. We saw about a dozen camels on that trip; the larger caravans were much farther south.

By noon, we were delivered to the school in Rabat where we would have our language and cultural training. Hearing stories from people returning from all over Morocco was entertaining. Some had traveled up to 13 hours to reach their homestay locations.

## Home Sweet Dorm

Our group of 92 trainees settled into the boarding school complex. Lycée (lee-SAY) Princesse Lalla Neuzha contained a three-story dormitory, cafeteria, classrooms, even laundry service. The living quarters were on one side of a busy street with the classrooms on the other – a campus three blocks south of the main post office and center of town.

Accommodations featuring bunk beds weren't too luxurious, but I decided I could survive there for the 10-week session. Women on the second floor, men on the third floor, with one large shared bathroom with showers per floor. Each trainee had a full bunk bed: sleep on the lower bunk and use the upper bunk for books and items needed during the day. Chuck Dammers, one of the engineers, and Larry Berube, the surveyor, and I arranged our three bunks in a U-shape facing the center aisle. Fellow trainees used similar configurations down the length of the floor, creating habitat clusters. Large windows along the ceiling flooded the place with daylight. My buddies Stan and Mark Dressman were our neighbors next door.

Each trainee was assigned a wall-mounted locker large enough to store their haul from home; everyone had brought a padlock to secure it. We had been forewarned more than once to keep an eye on our belongings; Moroccans cherished American goods, and anything left unattended could be considered free for the taking.

The food was surprisingly good: plenty of fresh vegetables and fruit, meat and tons of bread. Breakfast included a basic offering of coffee and freshly squeezed orange juice, yogurt, croissants and other pastries, plus assorted fruits. Lunch became our main meal of the day, featuring meats (lamb, chicken, chopped steak), bowls of rice and vegetables, salad, more bread and fruit. The evening meal was a lighter version of lunch. Sugar beets – one of the country's most abundant crops – were featured generously at both lunch and dinner.

## Back to School

Our daily routine kept us active: breakfast at 7 a.m., classes from 8 until noon, then lunch. A short rest period (free time) ahead of afternoon classes from 2 to 5. Dinner around 7 p.m. and cultural presentations about Morocco in the evening. My group would also receive technical orientation – a look into how our jobs would work within the Moroccan government's structure. Our technical group of 12 trainees – the engineers and architects, the mechanic and surveyor, plus our audiovisual team – concentrated on learning French, the language of most professional/technical people in the larger cities. All others (80 TEFL teachers) worked on learning Darija, the variant of Arabic spoken in mainstream Morocco.

I was surprised at how much we covered during my first French class. We took care of basic greetings, days of the week, numbers and much more. With only three people in a class, we were dwarfed in the classrooms that were outfitted for 30 students. I was joined by Joe, the mechanic, and Tom, one of the architects. Throughout the day, the teachers rotated to different classrooms, so we were never bored. Each teacher specialized in a fast-learning technique.

Peace Corps provided our group with five excellent teachers – three women and two men, all Moroccan – who were well-educated and spoke multiple languages. Fatima (fa-TEEM-a) directed both our curriculum and the other teachers. A slender, short Moroccan beauty with long black hair tinted with henna, she was personable and funny. Fadela (fa-DEE-la) was the youngest and shiest teacher. And Aziza, who spoke five languages, came from an upper-class family in Tangier (tawn-JAY in French). She was well-traveled with a European look – a short hairstyle and typical dress of floral-print sundresses, slacks and other Western fashions. Always smiling and full of questions about life in America, she became a favorite with everyone in our group.

Since the two men were both named Abdou, we labeled them Abdou One and Abdou Two outside of class. Abdou One was the oldest faculty member. Balding, with his full beard and calm demeanor, he had the distinguished look of a learned scholar – the classic professor. Abdou Two was another story: about our age, he was quite in love with himself and often a real smart-ass in class. If you could overlook his ego, he was a good French instructor.

The lycée's campus was built to accommodate 300 girls, so it provided us plenty of room to spread out. Buildings on both sides of that busy street surrounded central courtyards. On the dorm side, the space was a convenient meeting place for outdoor gatherings. During breaks, trainees could find a shady spot to read mail from home, make entries in their journals or write letters. On the classroom side, the courtyard was a dusty playground, with a few swing sets and two rusty basketball goals at either end of a concrete surface. When class was in session, we rarely interacted with the TEFL trainees; they used an adjacent wing of the three-story building.

Lunchtime was shared by everyone and was a chance to compare notes on how learning a foreign language was going. My buddy Stan from Raleigh, North Carolina, (stereotypically Southern in his speech) was having his share of problems tackling the difficult Arabic. His first day in class, he was commended on his excellent pronunciation. Stan admitted later he made it through the exercise coughing, still suffering the effects of a cold.

## Mail Call

A daily highlight after lunch was the delivery of our mail from the Peace Corps office. We had been instructed to use the local office address for Peace Corps Morocco during the training period until we received our assignments and established long-term addresses. The mail was stacked on a long table in alphabetical order by last name, and we made quite a scramble when it arrived. Sure enough, some trainees were more popular than others when hearing from home.

My first letter arrived July 7. With a touch of expected homesickness, I read about reactions to my departure. My mother explained how my father returned from seeing us depart, then went in the bathroom and quietly cried. And I had made the 11 o'clock news. She also reported that the day after I left, my college diploma from SIU arrived in the mail.

Correspondence became more interesting and regular after that. For only 22 cents, family and friends could fill up a prepaid blue sheet of paper called an aerogramme, fold it up, lick the flaps and seal it (with no enclosures) and drop it in the mail, sending it to Morocco by airmail. A little tricky to open with the glued flaps, the aerogramme became a popular communication tool.

## Twilight: Education & Culture

Cultural presentations filled our evenings. During our first week, the teachers staged a comical skit, "How Moroccans See Americans." They acted out some of the classic faux pas tourists make: constantly taking pictures, wearing shorts and eating left-handed. A later skit covered how to best bargain with a craftsman in the medina.

Two Moroccan instructors for the TEFL teachers demonstrated the customary handshake. We had noticed the local people (mostly the men) would greet each other, shake hands, then briefly touch their hearts. The instructors explained the gesture conveyed the message "Meeting you is dear to me." In the interest of fitting in, we were encouraged to adopt the habit, especially when meeting Moroccans for the first time.

As a related follow-up, the instructors elaborated on the standard greeting La bes. Expressed as a question when meeting someone, "La bes?" asked a person, "Are you fine/OK?" Used as a response, "La bes" meant "Yes, I'm fine/OK," often followed by *Al Hamdullah,* meaning "Praise God" or "Praise Be to God."

But then, things got tricky. Friends and family who possibly had not seen each other in some time might create a long string of La bes questions and responses, asking in paired dialogues:

"Is your family OK?"
"Is your mother OK?"
"Is your father OK?"
"Is your brother and/or sister OK?"
"Is your son (name) OK?"
"Is your daughter (name) OK?"

"It's like an extended 'Hi, how are you and yours doing?'" one instructor explained. One more cultural insight for us to absorb and process.

Another presentation included a lengthy geography lesson. A slideshow explained the diversity of Morocco's terrain and corresponding climates. The general rule was moderate weather closer to the coast with more weather extremes inland.

We were reminded that the town of Agadir was our southern travel boundary. Skiing in Morocco? It was possible in the Atlas Mountains during winter months at several locations east of Marrakesh. Crossing the mountains heading farther south reached the edge of the Sahara. Those travel highlights gave the TEFL teachers some insights about where in the country they might like to eventually live and work.

Some of the language teachers and school staffers staged a mock Moroccan wedding one night. Our head French instructor, Fatima, dressed in a flowing hooded gown and played the bride. With heavy jewelry and ceremonial makeup, she resembled Cleopatra. As the music played, she was paraded around the courtyard for all to honor, seated in a large round shallow bucket and hoisted on to the shoulders of the groom's male attendants. Pascal, one of the TEFL coordinators from the office, acted as the groom, dressed in the traditional white hooded overgarment. He greeted members of his wedding party and joined Fatima, seated on an elevated platform. The ceremony was elaborate, a colorful display of Moroccan finery, and went on for hours, ending with excited dancing.

On another evening, we watched the film *In the Name of Allah*, a one-hour black-and-white documentary narrated by James Mason. It was informative and traced the typical lifestyle of a Muslim. A week later, we viewed *The Green March,* a documentary chronicling the 1975 mass occupation of the Spanish Sahara territory by 350,000 protesting Moroccans.

## Celebration & Evaluation

We carpooled after class one afternoon to the U.S. Embassy to meet Ambassador Robert Anderson and his staff. We got a basic tour of the building and an introduction to what went on there. A squad of U.S. Marines provided security. Ambassador Anderson was tall, and many trainees thought he was a John Wayne look-alike ... sort of talked like him too. What I remember most was the cold Budweiser beer and chocolate chip cookies served as we gathered in the embassy's safe room – a fortified central courtyard with a retractable roof for housing the staff in case of an emergency (think invasion, riot or civil uprising).

In his remarks, Ambassador Anderson clarified America's diplomatic status in Morocco and categorized our Peace Corps service as "foreign aid" to the country's government. He welcomed us to Morocco on behalf of President Jimmy Carter and said he looked forward to seeing us all again at the conclusion of the stage when we would become full-fledged volunteers.

The time came to evaluate our progress at the end of three weeks of classes. So, on a Friday afternoon, we had our first of four oral interviews, each lasting about 45 minutes and covering several points of grammar. We also had to talk for three minutes about ourselves, listen to the instructor speak, then summarize what we had heard. It was all very comprehensive. I was the last to take the test and was impressed with my score: 122 out of 136 points. Some of the others had studied French in college; I took two years of Spanish. But I had been doing my homework. I was determined to get the most from the semi-private lessons.

Finishing the test was a relief. To celebrate, the Peace Corps staff arranged a *mishwee,* or Moroccan-style lamb barbeque, in the courtyard of the lycée. They bought 10 lambs (20 halves) and added vegetables and bread. The party brought together more than a hundred people – trainees, staff and Peace Corps officials. Later, a local band arrived for Moroccan music and dancing on the large patio.

## Meeting a Mentor

The day arrived to meet our new boss at the Ministry of Agriculture. We also met Phil Hanson, Program & Planning Officer in the Peace Corps office. He was thirty-one, athletic (an avid tennis player) and tanned, with a full head of blond hair. Though he hailed from Mason City, Iowa, Phil had the look of a well-dressed California surfer. He had graduated from the University of Arizona with a degree in international relations, then served as a volunteer in the Ivory Coast for two years. He aspired to work in the Foreign Service one day. Phil would become our go-to man for any questions or issues involving our living situations or work assignments.

Becky, Paul and I dressed up for the meeting – a coat-and-tie occasion for Paul and me. Phil picked us up in an office car, and we took a long, hot ride to the suburbs of Rabat. Turning off the main road, we entered a complex of aging two-story government buildings.

Fortunately, Phil handled the French; mine was still in bits and pieces. Our new boss (actually a supervisor), Mr. Jebbor, shook our hands and appeared surprised – perhaps overwhelmed – to see three American rookies ... his eyes shifted rapidly among us. Moroccan workers had left for the day, but we had a chance to see the working conditions and equipment. It was all a fairly adequate setup.

"Come on over for a drink," Phil invited us after our brief meet and greet. Wally Swanson joined us, bringing the other agricultural trainees to Phil's beautiful home in an upscale neighborhood. The wine flowed, plus vodka-tonics (with ice). Enjoying an evening away from the stage, our group relaxed in the sunset breezes in Phil's driveway.

To start our evening, Phil made a toast: "Welcome to the front lines of freedom!"

He encouraged us to make the most of our unique experience, implying we were not in Morocco "to change the world" but rather to contribute our skills and enhance the country's impressions of Americans.

"And you might have a lot of fun along the way," he added.

True, we were free to do whatever we wanted beyond the requirements of our work assignments. Get the job done and stay out of trouble, then we could travel, meet all kinds of people and live beyond our wildest dreams (within reason). Food for thought.

We met Phil's lovely Moroccan wife, Anissa, who worked at the U.S. Embassy. She whipped up a Moroccan dish, a traditional tajine, and we ate and drank ... and drank some more.

Relaxing indoors on soft sofas and upholstered armchairs after the meal, we paged through American magazines, while Phil proudly demonstrated his elaborate stereo system and his fascination with the music of singer-songwriter Barry White. The evening was like being in the neighbor's living room back home. We didn't get back to the lycée until after midnight.

## Pay Day

It seemed like every time we turned around Peace Corps handed us money. Pay days varied between Fridays and Mondays, depending on class schedules and holidays. After lunches, we would initial a roster sheet confirming we received little white envelopes: eight dirhams ($2) per diem, 39 dirhams (about $10) to cover our weekend meals when the lycée's cafeteria was closed, plus one of three travel allowances for 60 dirhams (about $15) to cover weekend trips.

All TEFL teachers were encouraged to explore the country on weekends, visit more in-service volunteers and collect their preferences for school assignments. Near the end of training, they would be asked to list three choices for their new home. Work locations for our technical group were mostly predetermined in the larger cities.

## The Weekend Break

Our first free weekend finally came. Many trainees caught up on lost sleep. I partnered with Larry Berube, the surveyor from New Hampshire, for a beach excursion. One of the instructors suggested we head north, not far out of Rabat. Three women joined us – Louise, Jane and Sally.

Louise hailed from Connecticut, where she had worked as a newspaper reporter for two years. She fit the mold of many trainees who had finished college and worked in a not-too-exciting job before joining the Peace Corps for some adventure.

Jane was a world-traveling adventurer. After college, she had spent time in Africa, climbing both Mount Kenya and Mount Kilimanjaro two years before coming to Morocco. We compared climbs to the summit of Mount Kilimanjaro, a trip I had made a year ahead of her. Her climb of the more challenging Mount Kenya impressed me.

And Sally? She was from a small town outside Rochester, New York. Larry and Sally had been spending a lot of time together. The same could be said of three or four other couples forming serious relationships.

The five of us went to the grand taxi lot in the center of town ... I had yet to figure out how or why the vehicles were considered *grand*. We had to wait until a sixth passenger – some sixteen-year-old kid – hopped in our beat-up diesel Ford. We headed toward Kenitra to the north but hopped out early, 19 kilometers out of Rabat, onto a road that led us to La Plage National, the national beach. Three dirhams each (about 75 cents) was our bargain fare.

We had to walk about a mile to the beach. There, on a high bluff, stood one plush luxury hotel and nothing else. The beach and coast remained otherwise undeveloped. The tremendous pounding surf was some sight, with waves breaking six or eight times before reaching the beach – some eight feet tall! I had never seen anything like it.

We arrived before 11 and there were few people around. We dined on a huge patio overlooking the beach. Our waiter was decked out in a white tux and black bow tie, and Jane's French was good enough to communicate our orders. Prices were higher than in the city, but we could swing it. What a sight: the five of us sitting at a fancy hotel with our omelets and fresh orange juice – and Uncle Sam paying for it all!

After eating, we hit the water. It was cold but refreshing. The waves were monstrous compared to the surf I knew from the shores of Georgia and Florida. We had been warned of tremendous undertow in Morocco's surf. It was true. I never went in over chest high, but the undertow there could take my feet out from under me. After a rest on the beach, four of us took a long walk – at least one and a half miles down the mostly deserted beach. Larry & Sally jogged ahead, while Louise and I walked. It was a sunny day, and I almost emptied my small bottle of sunscreen.

Back on the hotel patio, we splurged for cheeseburgers and fries with more orange juice and split a 2-liter bottle of Sidi Harazem, the water we were now very familiar with.

By 5 p.m. it was time to return to Rabat, hitchhiking – no taxi stands there. Several carloads were leaving the beach area. We split up for a better chance of a ride; none of those small cars (mostly Fiat 124s and 128s) could hold all five of us. Barely 100 yards out on the road, we all had a ride! I felt lucky on my first hitchhiking attempt.

Jane, Louise and I hopped in a dilapidated Saab sedan driven by a Frenchman. The trip was an experience! With all of us in it, his poor car couldn't go over 45 kilometers an hour (about 35 miles per hour) ... that was slow in Morocco. Everything passed us on the highway – even cycles. It was a leisurely ride, and we amused our driver with our attempts at speaking French.

He made one stop at a roadside market to buy some greens and a watermelon, then pulled over at a Moroccan festival called Fantasia. We later learned the event was part of the celebration of King Hassan's birthday, July 9. There, on what looked like a football field, Arabian horsemen – in groups of 10 or more abreast – rode in charging formations while waving guns, only to suddenly stop in a cloud of dust and fire their guns in unison. Some good action photos resulted there. I caught the mystified reactions of two horsemen, looking over a Polaroid photo of themselves handed to them by a tourist on the sidelines. The 60-second excitement of seeing their image appear instantly in their hands confounded them both.

Finally, we rolled into Rabat. That nice guy took us right to the door of the lycée. Despite our language barriers, we had enjoyed an educational ride.

After shaking out the sand and taking a two-hour nap, Larry and I headed for a pizza place. There, we traded stories of how we ended up eating pizza in Africa.

Larry had a varied background. He had spent six years of his childhood in an orphanage run by the Sisters of Charity nuns in Manchester, New Hampshire. Half of his day was in French, the other half in English, so he became bilingual at an early age. Right out of high school, he enlisted in the Army, serving in the 25th Infantry Division in Vietnam during 1966. He learned surveying while in the Army. Once his three-year hitch was completed, he returned to New England and used the GI Bill to earn a two-year associate degree in Architectural Engineering. He returned to New Hampshire, working seasonal construction jobs for several years. Between jobs, he noticed an ad in the local paper for a surveyor and drove over to the Howard Johnson's in a nearby town for an interview, only to discover the job advertised was a volunteer position in the Peace Corps. He was offered Lesotho (English-speaking) and Morocco. Thinking his bygone French would come in handy, he chose Morocco.

"Honestly, I was kind of surprised they accepted me," Larry admitted. "During those meetings in Atlanta, I asked the lady in charge if any others had applied for the spot. She responded, 'No, you were the only one!'"

Back at the stage, a small party was underway in the courtyard, and we all enjoyed sharing some of the low-priced, full-bodied Moroccan red wine. The nighttime breezes from the ocean supplied welcome relief from a long day in the sun. A highlight of my evening was the chance to chat with two women I had met briefly at our communal lunches. I was curious to know more about both of them.

Liz was the senior trainee of our class, in her early sixties. Mother of three, she followed in the footsteps of President Carter's mother, Miss Lillian, who at sixty-eight had been a Peace Corps Volunteer in India a decade earlier. Always smiling and with a story to tell, Liz was popular with all trainees, especially the women, and socialized with our much younger crowd at every opportunity. She loved to talk about her three grandchildren too.

"My husband had a boat built and wanted to sail around the world for two years," she told me. "I was not particularly interested in that project, so I told him of my idea to teach English in Morocco. So, here I am. A few months down the line, we're making plans to meet when he docks in Casablanca. I'm looking forward to that very much."

And Tinker Goggans? Her name alone made me curious.

"My legal name is Margie Leigh. My brother was three when I was born and gave me the nickname Tinkerbell after having been taken to see *Peter Pan*. Since then, I've been Tinker to my family and friends," she explained.

Tinker majored in English and French at Grinnell College in Iowa and then studied at the Sorbonne for a year while working as a nanny in Paris. The strong North African influence there – with cafés and music – piqued her interest in learning Arabic. A chance encounter with a Moroccan made an impression.

"Toward the end of my stay, I took a train to the south of France. It was packed with soldiers, so we were crammed into overloaded compartments for the long ride. We were all hungry and ill-prepared for the trip, but a Moroccan man in my compartment, traveling alone, had brought a bottomless bag of food from which he extracted roast chickens, bread and fruit. He had brought food for a large group because he didn't plan to eat unless he could offer food to everyone traveling with him. This was my first glimpse at Moroccan hospitality, and it was intriguing. I suppose his generosity played a part in my decision to choose Morocco."

After returning from France, Tinker moved to Austin, Texas, and worked as a waitress while getting her secondary teaching certificate from the University of Texas. Peace Corps recruiters visited the campus, and she had the itch to go abroad again to teach – especially to a francophone country. The prospect of learning Arabic added to the appeal of North Africa.

"At first, the recruiter offered me a position as a motorcycle courier in the Central African Republic, if you can believe that!" she told me. "He even said, 'We'll teach you how to repair the bike in case you break down in the bush.' I told the guy, 'No thanks!' When teaching in Morocco became available a few weeks later, I was in."

I could tell she was happy with her decision. It was always a pleasure meeting people from such a wide range of backgrounds, all interested in exploring a foreign culture.

Too many wine bottles were empty. The party broke up around midnight, and everyone trudged up the stairs. Another Saturday night in my bunk. It was official: I missed water skiing on Lake Lanier, my Wheaties and baked potatoes.

## Classes for the Masses

As the weeks flew by, I felt I was picking up the basics of French. We advanced to increasing our vocabulary and adding grammar knowledge. Each day, we received an additional hour of technical language training to help us in our specific jobs. Cross-cultural exercises continued at least three evenings a week.

During a break in the schedule one afternoon, Wally came by the stage and escorted a bunch of us to Studio Bensalah, a tiny excuse for a portrait studio near the main post office. We were learning from our cross-cultural sessions that we needed more identification photos to attach to official documents once we became part of the local population. These added to the six extra passport photos we had provided with our applications.

The studio was a cramped two-room operation. We lined up outside, awaiting our turn to stand against a black backdrop inside the studio and face a single blinding flash. For less than $5, we collected a dozen headshots after waiting outside for about 20 minutes. As for quality, the overly contrasty black-and-white prints – about the size of a jumbo postage stamp – would suffice.

## Bad News, Good News

Combining our group of 90-plus energetic Americans – a unique cross-section of the U.S. population – and landing them in a foreign country was bound to result in some unfortunate events ... all among the TEFL teachers. After two weeks in the country, one woman – about forty-five – abruptly packed up and left. Two others decided that learning Arabic was not for them and returned home.

Some medical issues also cropped up: one volunteer with a positive TB test earned a free ticket home. My friend Randy had his pre-service dental work fall apart, so he left. One of the married guys tore some ligaments in his ankle while playing basketball and had to hop around in a cast on crutches. My buddy Dennis from New Jersey considered leaving. He was one of the first to get diarrhea and had it for two weeks. He lost a lot of weight and confessed to me that if he continued at his present rate, he would weigh 73 pounds by the end of training.

Fortunately, our tight-knit group of 12 – the technical folks learning French – remained intact. Field trips were added to the lesson plans. One afternoon, we all walked to a café in the city's center, conversing only in French. While sipping mint tea and enjoying fresh pastries, we spotted a group of older American tourists there (from New Jersey, we later learned), draped with their cameras. The men wore shorts and the women, sleeveless dresses – two wardrobe no-nos. And I thought we stuck out in a crowd!

## Meeting a Few Good Men

Across town, the detachment of eight U.S. Marines who guarded the embassy in Rabat shared a roomy residence. Their place reminded me of a fraternity house on the Georgia Tech campus. Twice a month on Friday evenings, they held an open house … call it an all-American party – American beer, American music and food, plus a whole new set of friendly American faces. Embassy staffers and teachers from the Rabat American School (for dependents of government and civilian contract personnel) filled out the crowd.

Upon entering the house, we signed in and received a punch card to tally our personal bar bill to pay on the way out. Those gatherings were a great diversion from the rigorous training schedule, a chance to relax. And they ended late – wrapping up around 2 a.m. We usually walked back to the lycée (about a mile) through the empty main streets of Rabat, bathed in the orange glow of streetlamps.

Staff Sergeant Landry and his Marine buddy Frank later sent a message to the Peace Corps office, challenging trainees to a friendly game of softball one Sunday afternoon. The Marines would supply American beer and the equipment. We would play at the American School.

Talking it up through the stage all week, we collected enough players to field a team. That Sunday, we showed up – most of us not having played in a while. Becky and Jane joined our team, along with a bunch of TEFL teachers. The Marines took it seriously; they arrived all decked out in uniforms. We set a few rules: over the short fence was a double, and we would play nine innings with 10 players (adding a short fielder). Then we got down to business. I played catcher mostly, then second base during some later innings.

Our starting pitcher was TEFL trainee Mike Kendellen. Mike had a liberal arts degree from the University of Wisconsin at Milwaukee. He came to Morocco nine months after leaving Venezuela where he was a Peace Corps Volunteer running youth sports programs, among other projects. I would later meet others in our group who were also doing a "second tour" with Peace Corps. Mike was quite a baseball player, despite losing the use of his right arm to polio when he was three. After Mike threw his left-handed fastball for a strike, he would grab his glove from under his arm and catch my return throw.

Mike was an excellent pitcher. After fighting off a late Marine charge in the eighth inning, we won 9-7. We couldn't believe it! The Marines took it pretty well, though they stung from the loss; I didn't think they could believe it, either. Everybody played their hardest. Unfortunately, I flied out every time at bat, so I didn't contribute to the final score. We made plans to play again two weeks later.

That second game was a different story. Since our first contest, the Marines found a few better men. After the Leathernecks' shocking loss, they showed up with three new hotshot players who helped them to a 17-12 victory. We were down 12-2 at one point. It was all a lot of fun; a Sunday afternoon with cold American beer could not be denied.

## Around Town

One Saturday afternoon, caught up on letter-writing, I took my first solo stroll in Rabat. I usually tagged along with someone with a better handle on French or even a little Arabic knowledge. That time, I confidently relied on my growing skills.

Walking along the streets, I felt part of the populous and tried my best to blend in, though I dressed and looked quite different than everyone around me. Getting around town with others from the stage, we often attracted stares, as if we were lost tourists. It was enjoyable going solo; I've always appreciated time to myself – time for my own space. I walked to a restaurant near the medina and ordered my lunch in French ... and actually got what I ordered.

On the way back, I stopped in a few medina shops and conversed in my basic French about items I'd had trouble finding. I bought toothpaste – they had Colgate – and two pens with no problems. I was encouraged. Saturday afternoons in Rabat, the traffic was light, which enabled me to see a lot at a leisurely pace.

Before heading back to the lycée, I bought the latest edition of *The International Herald Tribune* – an English newspaper printed in Paris – and read about the New York City blackout and the week's sports scores.

Back at the dorm, it was late afternoon. The buildings shaded most of the courtyard – the perfect place to relax and savor the light breezes through the palm trees. It was also a place to meet other trainees. I threw out my typical conversation starter to hook a new face. "How did you end up here?"

TEFL trainee John Schroeder had earned a degree in history from the University of Oregon. He was intrigued by the Middle East after seeing the movie *Lawrence of Arabia* and studying Greek and Roman history in college. Graduating in 1972, he joined the Peace Corps and was part of the first group of volunteers sent to the Sultanate of Oman on the Arabian Peninsula. When his two years there ended, he stayed in Oman another year and a half working for a magazine and a printing company.

"I returned to the States and, for four months, I was unable to find a job," John told me. "On top of that, I was suffering from what I called 'return culture shock.' I went into a phone booth in Eugene and called the local Peace Corps office to tell them, 'You've got to get me out of here!'"

Over the phone, he was offered South Korea or Morocco. Smiling, he told me, "The choice was easy."

## In Search of Seafood

We had heard from in-service volunteers about Asilah, a small seaside town due north of Rabat and 40 kilometers south of Tangier. Asilah was known for its seafood, and we were ready for something better than the bland fried fish we were served occasionally at the lycée.

Stan, Rich Eckert (a TEFL trainee) and I got to the train station early one Saturday morning to buy our tickets. We traveled light, taking bottled water and some fresh bread and cheese to eat along the way. We boarded the train and were riding the rails by 9:30; trains were modern and inexpensive. With our second-class tickets, we found three seats together in a compartment for eight. It took about four hours to get to Asilah. The train station there was a mile from the center of town. As we walked into town along the beach, we noticed the Spanish influence more prevalent in northern Morocco. Most of the buildings were white rather than the clay brown featured in Rabat.

By 6, we had found a hotel and taken a brief walk through town. The amount of English spoken there surprised us; even kids on the street spoke some English. We had picked a smaller town, hoping to practice our languages – Stan and Rich were learning Arabic.

We entered the town's medina and found more stark white buildings. Our destination was a clothing shop where they hand-embroidered the trim on djellabas, the full-length hooded shirts that looked like nightshirts. After an exchange of greetings, the owner invited us through a curtain of beads into a private back room where he could show off his finest work for the "rich" Americans. The room was well-lit. Bolts of colorful fabrics lined two walls and piles of carpets and tapestries spanned another. With incense burning, the scene was set for one special Arabian night ... all that was missing was a genie coming out of a bottle, I thought. We took a seat on a knee-high stack of plush carpets.

After the owner showed us his best merchandise, we must have tried on a dozen garments among us and survived an hour-and-a-half bargaining session. Rich and I bought ones of different styles, and Stan still wanted to look around. Mine was off-white, made of a soft cotton-like material. I really wanted one with a pocket and that one had it – most did not. Perfect: a pocket and collar trimmed in white; it would make a great lounge-around-the-house item ... my Arab disguise, I thought to myself. I certainly wouldn't wear it outside. I ended up paying around $15 for it.

By 8 p.m. we were starving, so we headed for a seafood restaurant overlooking the small harbor where boats came in at night. We thought it might be expensive but enjoyed a full meal for less than $4 – salad, dessert and a main course of squid and swordfish, plus great wine. That was some meal! It took us two hours to eat. Service was Moroccan style: slow. Not much happened on a big Saturday night in Asilah, so we walked on the beach and made our way back to the hotel.

We slept late Sunday and had a small breakfast featuring pastries at a café. I tried ordering orange juice, and the server could only manage a giant bottle of Fanta orange soda. Close enough.

I wanted to get some pictures with the morning light, so we wandered back into the compact medina for a long walk through the winding, narrow streets lined with blazing all-white buildings. Blue doors, red doors, green doors – each provided stark contrast between the white walls and the brilliant blue sky.

After checking out of the hotel, we walked to the train station to buy our return tickets to Rabat. The train wouldn't leave until 4 p.m., so we hit the beach for the afternoon.

We boarded the southbound train by 5; it was running late out of Tangier. That train was packed! All the weekenders from Tangier were heading back to Rabat or Casablanca. We stood for a while and, later, shared a pair of fold-out seats in the aisle. Luckily, the stops were short, and we seemed to be going faster than on our trip the day before. We were back in Rabat by 9, tired but encouraged by lessons learned about traveling in Morocco ... it was easy.

Back at the lycée, Sunday nights all seemed the same – the place became one big study hall. No music played. Everybody studied languages, and the English teachers prepared for their practice teaching classes. Beginning the following day, groups of local students would be brought in to simulate classroom environments.

What must have functioned as a teacher's lounge on the ground floor of the lycée was furnished with padded chairs and low sofas – a quieter place to study when the dorm areas were noisy. We could also watch a TV in one corner of the large room, catching old episodes of *The Muppet Show* and *Marcus Welby, M.D.* dubbed in French.

Now, after a month, the lycée seemed more like home ... we often forgot we were in Africa.

### one volunteer remembers...

I became fast friends with David (who went by the nickname Red) during the training stage. Red was an excellent athlete, particularly good at basketball. I was a wrestler in high school, not a basketball player, but I was fit enough to race up and down the dusty court on the lycée's playground. We were going through a pair of Moroccan-made tennis shoes every ten days or so.

We befriended one of the super vols who had spent three years in-country, a tall, bespectacled, wispily ginger-bearded fellow, named Bill. He invited Red and me to tag along with him on a trip to visit the family of the showesh*, the doorman at the lycée.

By bus, we headed out into the middle of nowhere on the eastern side of the Middle Atlas. The bus came to a stop. I clearly recall climbing off the bus and looking around to see absolutely nothing. Then we spied a man plowing a lonely patch of rough ground with a camel and a donkey. He called out and across the way we saw his wife waving at us to come into their one-room earthen hut. She lit a fire in the corner on the dirt floor under a hole in the ceiling that served as the flue.

After the sun had set, our host came into the hut with a limp form in his arms – he had slaughtered a goat in our honor. Over the next three days, we lived on the goat and his wife's cornbread.

One morning, we decided to take a hike up the hill by their house to survey the totality of the emptiness where they lived. About three-quarters of the way up, we met a young, flute-playing shepherd boy. Not long after, we saw a wild dog, barking its head off, running up the hill straight at us. The boy picked up a rock, and with deadly accuracy, hurled the rock in a direct hit on the dog. The dog howled, recoiled and took up the attack again. Three times the cycle continued – attack, hurled rock, howl and resumed attack. Finally, the stones were too much for the animal, and it limped away. "Good dog," said our protector.

That night, we sat around the smoky fire in their hut. Bill recounted the day to the couple and the wife's brother who had come to see who the visiting strangers were. Our host informed us that he was from Ait (his Berber tribe) and that his wife and brother were from a neighboring tribe. They asked Bill what tribe we were from. Without missing a beat, Bill replied that we were from Ait MenaDHar, the eyeglass tribe (as we all wore glasses), much to the enjoyment of our hosts.

Steve Long<br>
TEFL Instructor<br>
Midelt

*TEFL volunteers reported these guys were helpful, respected institutions at every lycée. They sat at the door all day and did things like sort mail and keep track of who was and wasn't on the premises. Due to the incompatibility of the alphabets, there's room for variations in spelling: chauwech, shauwesh, shoush. – RW*

## Another Year Older

Nearly every week, somebody in our class had a birthday. My twenty-fifth arrived August 1. I had only mentioned it to a few people weeks before, but by that day, most everybody knew about it. News traveled fast at the stage.

I received a handmade birthday card, signed by a bunch of people.

"Just think, today your insurance rates dropped 25 percent!" TEFL trainee Howard – an accounting major in college – reminded me.

All trainees sang a hearty "Happy Birthday" at dinner. Afterward, seven of us headed for Rabat's Restaurant Italia – home of the best ice cream – for a celebratory banana split.

While we were out, a few of the women had decorated our small living area in the dorm with a "Happy Birthday, Richard!" banner they had made that afternoon. By the time we got back from banana splits, Dennis arrived with an authentic birthday cake. He probably walked miles – and I know he spent hours – trying to find one in Rabat. Pastry shops were all over, but something that even slightly resembled a birthday cake was hard to come by. Ten of us sat around and ate it all. It was a great evening and a memorable birthday!

## Finally, A Day Off

Everybody was excited about a four-day weekend that popped up unexpectedly, beginning when classes ended at noon on Friday. Lining up for a quick lunch, we also received our weekend travel allowance. Many of us were going to Tangier by various means.

I preferred not to go in a large group, so I traveled with civil engineer Chuck Dammers – my bunk buddy and fellow French student. We were moving on a ragtag souk bus by 4:30. Terry and Cheryl had tried to thumb it all the way to Tangier (250 kilometers), but they decided to hop on our bus after walking the first three kilometers to the edge of the city. Our little American delegation of four joined a bus full of Moroccans and a few French folks.

We arrived in Tangier around 10. The place was packed with tourists, and a hotel room was impossible to find. By 2 a.m. we were desperately thinking of going to Tetuoan, 65 kilometers east, to find a room. Describing our dilemma to an all-night snack bar manager, he offered us his basement dining room for the night. We gladly accepted rows of padded chairs in between tables to catch a few winks.

For some reason, the basement floor was wet. We all tried to sleep. By 7 a.m. we were awakened by the sound of running water and an inch of water all over. Turned out, an open faucet in the bathroom was flooding the basement! We had no idea the faucet was open when we arrived because water was off at the time; water was being rationed in the city, so it went on and off at weird hours of the day.

The owner arrived. He wasn't angry, and we left … he didn't even want to take money for his inconvenience. We headed for a quick breakfast and then searched for a hotel to dump our luggage. With some luck, we got into a nice place right in the center of town. We could really enjoy the town once we had a place to stay.

Dozens of trainees had traveled to Tangier that weekend. Around 10 we met Becky and others near the bus station and took a group tour through the city's medina and the fortified casbah. Tourists everywhere! Pictures were hard to get because of the crowds and the constant pestering of street kids – one of whom experienced an interesting encounter with Becky.

"This kid was hassling me for money … just would not stop bugging me as I walked down the street," she told me. "Out of nowhere, he suddenly stopped, did a summersault in the street, stuck his hand out and demanded money. I handed him 50 centimes (half a dirham). Then I turned the tables on him. I showed him how it was done, doing my own summersault right before his eyes, then demanded my money back. With a defeated look, he handed the coins back and ran away – I guess before any of his friends realized what had just happened. Took care of that!"

We met another bunch of trainees for a Moroccan dinner that evening, then took a long stroll around town with Terry and Cheryl. The city was lit up and decorated and not as jammed with people as the night before. A couple of the Arabic teachers from our stage recognized Terry and Cheryl and invited us all for a drink at a nearby café. Since most Muslims didn't drink alcohol, a drink meant a Coke or the ubiquitous mint tea.

Back at the hotel just before midnight, we sat on our little balcony and did what *Fodor's,* the travel guidebook, suggested we do in Tangier: "sit and watch the world go by."

Sunday morning began with another tour of the medina. Only Chuck and I went, mainly to take some photographs. Everybody tried to sell us something and, when we refused, would berate us with their crude attempts at English, yelling as we walked away, "What's wrong with you? Are you Jewish?"

## Time for Tea in Tangier

After stumbling over crowds of tourists for two days, I was ready to relax. We took it easy most of the afternoon, watched more of the world go by and got ready for a 4 o'clock tea party hosted by Aziza – our French teacher who lived there with her family. Aziza taught Peace Corps trainees at our lycée every summer in Rabat. She had finished her teaching assignment with us and was preparing to start another teaching job in Tetuoan.

Her house was easy to find. She had given us directions with respect to the luxury Hotel Chellah, situated on the Avenue du Prince Heritier. Six others were coming from the beach but didn't arrive until an hour later.

Looking at Aziza's nondescript house from the street, no one would guess an established, upper-class family lived there. Inside, her family's home was beautifully decorated. The kitchen occupied most of the first floor. We made our way inside the front door and immediately ascended a marble staircase to the main salon, a spacious room lined with big cushions. Plush wool carpets covered the floor, and the room had three floor-to-ceiling windows and a small balcony off of it. Colorful ceramic tile and glass chandeliers completed the decor. Massive mirrors hung from the walls, and a china cabinet filled with ornate dinnerware and serving pieces stood at one end of the room.

Aziza lived with her parents and several of her 10 brothers and sisters. Gradually, most of them arrived with their spouses – some brought children. For an hour, it was just Chuck and I, Aziza and two of her brothers. We talked mostly about our first impressions of Tangier. Her brothers worked together in a lucrative import-export business – mostly textiles and shoes. I asked one brother what he did, exactly.

"Many things ... if I said I did only one thing, I would be lying to you," was his somewhat mysterious reply.

OK, I thought to myself ... maybe we should talk about soccer.

As more people arrived, we enhanced our understanding of Moroccan social life. Aziza's father was a *haj* – a person of social significance for having completed a pilgrimage to Mecca. He made an initial brief appearance and wanted us to speak some French so he could judge what kind of teacher his daughter was. He kidded around with us ... reminded me of my grandfather. Most all the family members spoke English. The brothers had all traveled to and done business in America. The entire family was well-educated. A younger brother was about to leave for Italy the next day, hoping to enter medical school there; he was in and out of the room the whole evening.

Aziza revealed that "tea at 4" meant dinner too. Having attended two lamb mishwees in Rabat, we had an idea what that entailed and prepared for a leisurely evening of tea and Coke. Finally, the other six Peace Corps people showed up, and we settled in for quite a party. More relatives and their friends kept arriving, and by 7 p.m. we probably had 30 hungry people there. Still, there was plenty of room to circulate.

After snacks of cookies and pastries, they brought around a silver dispenser of rose water – a fragrant solution to sprinkle all over ourselves. It was like getting baptized all over again. Next came a portable washbasin with a soap dish – also silver – for washing our hands. Then we were ready to eat. What seemed like an endless parade of food started, and we ate for almost two hours. Lamb served over couscous was the main course. Mint tea and more pastries followed.

Chuck and I were staying in Tangier that night, but the other trainees had to catch a late-night bus back to Rabat. Two of Aziza's brothers gave them rides to the bus station. A few relatives and friends said their goodbyes too.

Bits of food remained, and we conversed more with the father – a fascinating person – who had rejoined us. His name was too long to pronounce, much less remember. He spoke fairly good English – but preferred French – and also spoke Spanish and Italian. He had made his fortune in phosphates, Morocco's leading export used in fertilizers. He challenged Chuck and I with more questions about his daughter's teaching ability and our experiences in Rabat since arriving. He was interested in our Peace Corps work assignments, too, and was somewhat familiar with the agency – known as *Corps de la Paix* in French.

Talking to family members about their backgrounds and occupations was most enlightening. We formulated some impressions of Moroccan upper-class living. Just like in the United States, a social ladder of the haves and have-nots existed in Morocco.

A little past midnight, Chuck and I returned to our hotel. We slept well that night and caught a bus to Rabat the next morning with some improved memories of Tangier. We learned that only the summer months were busy there, so I looked forward to seeing more of the city and surrounding area if I ever got back up north.

Back in Rabat, Chuck and I headed to lunch at the lycée while we reflected on the fact that, the day before, we had attended an eight-hour tea party!

## More French, Kitchen Skills & Training

French class intensified. We tackled the near future tense and, on a Friday, encountered our second oral interviews. I was making steady progress. I found out later I did *très bien* – very good – on it and graduated to Level Two (using a State Department language proficiency rating system of 1 to 5, 5 indicating fluency).

Some of us began writing sample letters in French and getting them reviewed by an instructor. The exercise helped me visualize what we were saying. A few of the TEFL trainees expressed an interest in learning to write in Arabic, but that presented significant challenges. An in-service volunteer admitted she had been working on learning to write her name in Arabic for the past year. Some complex concepts were involved, she explained. For starters, everything in Arabic was read right to left.

Later in the week, six of us walked to the home of a volunteer for a cooking lesson. Our objective was to prepare (and enjoy) a basic tajine, the one-pot mainstay of Moroccan cuisine. We carried two of the straw baskets everybody shopped with around town. They were filled with the necessary ingredients and loaves of bread from a market near the medina. Two other baskets contained cheese and a half dozen bottles of wine, which clanked together as we scaled three flights of stairs to the apartment.

Second-year volunteers Mary Ann and Jack introduced us to the workings of a Moroccan kitchen. The basic stove had two burners, fueled by a tank of Butagas beneath the counter. The shallow sink was adequate for washing the peppers and carrots that went into the chicken tajine along with olives, onion and assorted spices.

Once everything was assembled in a round clay pot topped with a cone-shaped lid, our tajine would simmer on the stove for the next hour. We used that time to enjoy the cheese and wine and collect more valuable cooking tips, such as how to make tomato sauce from scratch. We should start by peeling tomatoes … imported canned goods were expensive. A sharp knife was essential, and the needed skill would take practice to avoid wasting half the tomato.

Handling eggs required more words of caution: always break eggs into a cup or bowl instead of directly to any dish being prepared. Eggs were typically sold from a pile right off the counter, without refrigeration. Most volunteers had experienced breaking into a rotten one – the green slime contained a foul odor that lingered for hours.

We also discussed the recipes for soups, breads and variations of the standard tajine that were collected in the Peace Corps cookbooks we had each received at the stage.

Our meal was a success and cleanup a snap. We realized that, once on our own after training, cooking would become an acquired skill and an essential activity of daily life.

A few days each week, Becky, Paul and I visited our ministry office to see how things worked there and to meet everybody. John, the Peace Corps Volunteer cinematographer from Philadelphia, was beginning his second year. He showed us around the three-room office and introduced us to some of our future Host Country National (Moroccan) co-workers.

We met the man in charge of production, Marc, a Belgian contract worker who spoke excellent English. Our supervisor, Mr. Jebbor, informed us that, in October, we would move to a brand-new, more spacious office, currently under construction in the town's center.

Back at the lycée, French class continued to go well. Only three weeks remained, and I finally found time to get a haircut. My red hair was unusual enough without extra length. One of the English teachers had cut hair while in the Army, so for a bottle of wine that cost less than $2, I got a nice haircut. Moroccans still stared, though.

Everybody was anxious about the final weeks of training. Our technical group received some basic Arabic instruction. Learning the numbers one through ten, essential greetings and other common phrases could help us sound amiable and polite or impress a merchant when we were bargaining for the best price. So much of the technical language used in our jobs, though, was based on the French equivalent. We discovered the Arabic word for *cinema* was ... cinema.

While visiting the stage after lunch one day, Nurse Dolores lined us up for the second of three required rabies shots. According to her, we had crossed the medical health threshold. After eight weeks in country, we should have acclimated to the weather, the water and the food.

Certainly, I had no problems with the food. I still weighed 155 pounds ... no change. Several trainees had battled diarrhea and lost weight. My biggest challenge was the cool weather. Lack of exercise was no one's concern – we walked everywhere!

## Another Dose of Culture: Ramadan

We entered the lunar month of Ramadan, the period of all-day fasting for Muslims. Our teachers and other volunteers warned us that Moroccans, in general, would be irritable throughout the month. Each day in Rabat, a massive cannon at the Royal Palace officially sounded the beginning and the end of the daily fast. One morning, I heard it at 4:30. It sounded like a distant bomb blast, immediately followed by the wailing of the *muezzin* (the prayer priest), calling Muslims to early prayer. The whole event was over in less than two minutes.

Most businesses switched to Ramadan hours. I was just getting used to the Moroccan summer hours: 8 a.m. to noon and 4 to 7 p.m. New business hours were an abbreviated 9 a.m. to 2 p.m. in most places.

# The "King" Was Dead

Our French instructor Abdou Two often opened class with a lame joke or some smart-aleck comment. To start one Wednesday class, he hurried in and announced with a smirk, "Did you hear? Elvis is dead!"

We thought he was joking. He swore it to be the truth. That afternoon, we made a beeline for the newsstand next to the post office to buy *The International Herald Tribune*. Sure enough, the headline confirmed his report. As the news spread throughout the stage, trainees recalled their favorite Elvis memories.

After dinner, I noticed Patty Balch – the only Mississippi trainee – from Tupelo (Elvis' hometown) was upset. I had met her briefly on the plane ride. Since she was an English teacher learning Arabic, our paths rarely crossed.

Patty had fond memories of actually meeting Elvis when she was a third grader at Rankin Elementary School. Elvis had gone home to visit around the Christmas holidays. He stopped by the school one Thursday in time for their weekly assembly. Mrs. Murphree, the third-grade teacher, selected Patty and two others to play Christmas carols on the piano for a sing-along with Elvis. Patty nervously managed a rendition of "Noel."

"I got through it," she admitted. "My piano skills in third grade were pretty basic. I guess it was my three minutes of fame."

Both being Southerners, we made a point to become better acquainted over the next few days. Another lifelong friendship was hatched.

Patty had just graduated from Vanderbilt in May with a degree in physics, a minor in English, plus some pre-med courses. Peace Corps commercials on TV had piqued her interest when she was young: guys in rice fields and girls teaching, with the tagline, "The toughest job you'll ever love." Her sorority sisters encouraged her to join before going to medical school and being saddled with debt.

During the application process, Patty was offered a program in South Korea. "Too far away," she responded, and that was all she heard from her recruiter.

Weeks passed before an early morning phone call to her sorority house woke her up. "I was half asleep. I thought the man said Monaco." She laughed.

"I told him, 'Sure, I'll take Monaco; sign me up!' I just assumed the tiny municipality known for luxury living on the French Riviera had its share of poor people wanting to learn English." Once Morocco was clarified, she was happy to accept an invitation.

Trying to speak Arabic with her Southern accent proved challenging. Traveling around the country on weekends, though, allowed Patty to engage with the people she met.

"I'd tell people, 'I'm from Mississippi,' and they would just stare at me and ask, 'Is that really a state?' Or, I'd get cynical remarks like, 'Was it invented by the CIA?' and 'Can you cook fried chicken for us?'"

## And Your New Home Is ...

The wait was over. Right after lunch one Thursday, a typewritten roster in alphabetical order was posted – *TEFL Site Placements for 1977–78*. Now, the English teachers knew their work sites for the next two years. Peace Corps Morocco had the country covered with TEFL trainees from A to Z, literally: Arnold to Zarbo.

Following the TEFL placements was a recap of where our Ag group would be working, along with the sites for the urban development and social services trainees. For me, that sheet became a handy directory of who lived where and evidence of all the people I had not yet met. Many of the people I knew best would live in the vicinities of Rabat and north central Morocco, and I looked forward to visiting them and their towns.

Most teachers were satisfied with their assignments, though some of the placements seemed unusual. My friend Maura from Oklahoma was assigned to Lycée Mohammadia in Ksar el Kebir, a small town of about 20,000 people in the Spanish-speaking part of northern Morocco ... curious because she had listed on her application that her college background included French language studies. Go figure.

John Schroeder from Oregon – the Peace Corps veteran by way of Oman – would live his *Lawrence of Arabia* dream in Ouarzazate, near the edge of the Sahara.

Mark Dressman – my buddy from our homestay group that ventured to Kasba Tadla – made that town his top choice and got it.

Several TEFL teachers had selected their homestay locations for their new homes. Stan, my dorm neighbor from North Carolina, was happy to be returning to Boujad. Others, by default, were assigned to tiny villages like El Menzel and Sidi Bennour – places they had never heard of.

Mike Kendellen, our dynamite pitcher, was to report to a school in Khenifra, an agricultural town in central Morocco. He would have company.

Polish-born Piotr Kostrzewski lived in Tunisia as a teenager before he and his family immigrated to America. His father took TEFL classes their last year in Tunisia – classes taught by Peace Corps Volunteers. Piotr went on to earn a degree in biochemistry from Pace University. He knew he wanted to return to North Africa – not as a visitor, but possibly as a volunteer. In his mid-twenties, he also wanted a total change from life in New York City where he'd worked five years as an editor.

Joining the Peace Corps presented an attractive option. Piotr's degree generated several offers related to science or health, but neither the countries nor the job descriptions interested him. He felt unqualified for an offer to teach math. With his background as an editor, he thought he could teach English. Months went by, then his recruiter called with the TEFL offer to Morocco.

"It was an immediate 'Yes!'," he told me. At 6 feet, 7 inches tall, Piotr towered over everyone at the stage. He was likable, with an easy-going personality.

Mike and Piotr would join Candy, a volunteer in her second year, teaching at Lycée Abou el Kassim Azzayani.

## Home Shopping

No classes were held the following Monday because the TEFL teachers were processing their work assignments and visiting their new cities and towns. The quote of the week came from Darrell, an English teacher who visited his new work location near Marrakesh: "I blinked and almost missed my town!"

All volunteers were responsible for arranging their own housing. My engineer friend Chuck returned from Fes where he signed a lease on a brand-new five-bedroom house; he would share it with four TEFL teachers. The fancy place even had a garage, though none of us could own a car.

I wanted to start looking again for an apartment. The place I had originally lined up in the center of town – being vacated by a departing volunteer – had shot up in monthly rent with the change in tenant. That was a standard practice in Rabat. It was already high, so the boost priced it beyond my means. I was confident I would find something else, though.

My French was improving, and I could read parts of the newspapers. After lunch one day, I reviewed the classified ads and made my first phone calls in Morocco. It was an experience! The people on the other end were fast talkers; only one spoke some English. I asked our French instructor Abdou One to help me get set up with a couple of real estate agencies.

Paul, Becky and I had independently been looking for places to live. The three of us sat down one evening to discuss the subject. Paul announced he had arranged to share a place with an older volunteer who was transferring to a new position in Rabat.

Finding a place a single Peace Corps Volunteer could afford was tough. With the days slipping away before training ended, Becky and I decided to pool our resources and look for a place together.

How was this going to work? Living together? After weeks of French classes, field trips and celebrations, I had gotten to know Becky fairly well.

She loved Colorado but wanted to travel and experience other places. She had graduated from Colorado State with a degree in technical journalism. After working one year with the county extension service in the audiovisual department, Becky moved to the Denver Public Library as a videotape technician.

One afternoon, a friend asked her, "Will you go with me to the Peace Corps office?" Becky had not seriously thought of volunteering. During conversations at the office, the recruiter turned to Becky and asked, "And what do you do?" It was nearly closing time as Becky explained her background and desire to see the world. The recruiter mentioned the spot for an audiovisual specialist in Morocco that would close to candidates that day. Becky became instantly interested. A quick call to Washington held the spot open, and Becky sent in her application – using a new high-tech device at her library, called a fax machine. She was accepted the next day.

So ... there we were, planning to cohabitate. Me – the Catholic Eagle Scout from Georgia – living with a woman from Colorado? What would my family think of this arrangement? Where would we start house hunting?

Nurse Dolores came to our rescue. Her Moroccan husband had a friend who operated a real estate agency. On a Saturday morning, Dolores picked us up in a Peace Corps staff car. We found his office in the *Quartier de l'Ocean* (Ocean District) – a Spanish-Moroccan neighborhood near the lycée and bordered by the ocean and the medina. Dolores explained the cultural dilemma of two single Americans living together. She advised us to assume the roles of husband and wife to bypass any resistance from the agent ... and for the sake of the neighbors. OK, I thought. I was willing to try.

Having Dolores at our side while the agent explained leases, deposits and when monthly rents were due and how they should be paid was a lifesaver. The agent was joined by his two sisters. They made the discussion even more lively, sliding between Spanish and Arabic ... occasionally, a bit of French flew past us novice newlyweds. Dolores joined us to look over the possibilities with the agent.

From the beginning, Becky and I had our disagreements. Looking at seven apartments, we played our parts with plenty of "Yes, dear." and "What do you think, dear?" We narrowed the choices down to two: Becky wanted the ground-floor place that featured a small garden out front, and I preferred an upper-floor apartment with a view.

We thanked Dolores for bringing us that far along in the process. We left her and the agent and retreated to Café Jour et Nuit for a late lunch and a two-hour discussion that ended in my favor. The two-bedroom apartment on the fourth floor of a brand-new building was in a great location and would be within easy walking distance to work once the office moved in October, as planned. The building was so new, service lines for water and electricity had not yet been connected. Its selling feature was the fantastic view of the city and ocean from the wraparound balcony.

Pooling our resources, Becky and I decided we could swing the monthly rent of 1,000 dirhams (about $250). Our monthly living allowance would be 1,300 dirhams each. We signed a lease for Apartment 11 at 39 Rue Abidjan, on the corner of Avenue de la Résistance – our new home.

One evening, the Ag group met us for a tour and brought housewarming gifts: a small potted pine tree, six glasses and decorative floor mats. Sitting in a circle on the polished concrete floor of the living room, we christened the apartment with a few bottles of wine by candlelight.

## More Memorable Evenings Together

As the training stage wound down, Country Director Everett Woodman invited everyone to his house for an elaborate cocktail party. I found out later it was an annual end-of-training event.

His residence could make anybody think twice about government Foreign Service. Beautifully landscaped with fruit trees and a row of tall palms across the front, his home was located in the Beverly Hills section of Rabat.

Mr. Woodman announced he would be leaving Morocco soon and we would have a new country director, Paul J. Hare, the following month. Only thirty-nine, Paul had entered the Foreign Service in 1960. He had already collected extensive international experience with posts in Kuwait, Vietnam, Tunisia and Australia, plus State Department positions in Washington, D.C.

All of us hoped the new director could match Mr. Woodman's parties. His punch had some kick to it. We devoured stacks of Pringles and Fig Newtons – along with more American beer – before heading back to the lycée for dinner.

Three evenings later, Wally Swanson organized an all-American meal for the six new Ag program volunteers. A few French teachers and Peace Corps staff rounded out his guest list.

When we arrived, we noticed more than a dozen huge steaks on the charcoal grill. Baked potatoes were in the oven, and a large salad made its entrance. The beef was premium stuff, and I had almost forgotten what a baked potato tasted like. We were in culinary heaven, savoring every bite.

"You're gonna enjoy living in Rabat," Wally told me – as if eating like that would be the norm. He smiled broadly through his beard. "Volunteers are always passing through here. One thing's for sure: you'll never get lonely!"

The final days of the stage were counting down – we would officially become Peace Corps Volunteers in less than a week. Looking back over the training period, it all seemed to go by so fast. We had done and learned so much: daily French classes, weekend trips to different places, celebrations marking various crossroads – all time well spent. Like many others, though, I was eager to get to work.

I took time to reflect and recall how I ended up there.

## The Accidental Interview

Flash back to October 1976:

I was busy editing my thesis film to complete my degree in cinema and photography production at Southern Illinois University at Carbondale. My 16-millimeter documentary, *Climb to Kibo,* recapped my 1974 climb to the summit of Mount Kilimanjaro in Tanzania.

Landing a job upon graduation in December was my primary concern. During occasional visits to the Placement Center on campus, I picked up job-hunting and resumé tips but not much in the way of job postings for film editors. A poster announcing the arrival of a Peace Corps recruiter from St. Louis caught my attention ... could be a unique opportunity to see the world, I thought. But I assumed the Peace Corps had no positions for photographers or filmmakers.

What the hell, I decided, I'll talk to the guy and chalk up the meeting as a practice interview those career counselors had suggested. I signed up for an appointment.

I enjoyed meeting Bert Rava. Around thirty, with a full head of curly black hair and glasses, Bert showcased the unique experience of joining the Peace Corps. He worked from his checklist of questions to survey my background and gauge my potential interest in volunteering.

He was happy to hear I met some basic requirements: American citizen, in good health and never convicted of a felony. His pitch centered around the agency's mantra, "The Peace Corps is for optimistic, adventurous, concerned men and women who want to make things better for some of the less fortunate peoples of the world." He read that line from his copy of the *Peace Corps Handbook* that he cradled in his hands and referred to often.

Bert had no specific programs in mind that gelled with my resumé. He offered other fields – like health education and youth activities – and promoted the extensive in-country training volunteers received before starting an assignment. Answering all his questions, I enjoyed a pleasant conversation. We shook hands, and I headed back to my place ... thinking it was a worthwhile tune-up interview with someone I would never see again.

I left the interview with some brochures and a lengthy application in case I decided to pursue the Peace Corps after graduation. At best, I considered it a remote possibility. I finished the semester and returned to Atlanta.

Over the Christmas holidays, I collected the eight required references and completed and submitted the application ... part of my backup plans. Every few weeks, Bert called to see if I might be interested in volunteering to help with a sanitation project in Botswana or a reforestation program in Thailand. I had to pass, I told him.

March rolled around, and things weren't shaping up on the job-hunting front. I received a call from Bert concerning the position of cinematographer for the Ministry of Agriculture in the Kingdom of Morocco. My initial interest was intense. Bert disclosed that, at the time, only two Peace Corps people in the entire world worked in photo-related assignments. That was one primo spot, but before I knew it, two other candidates were being considered for the slot. He did everything he could to put my name at the front of the line, but it was not possible.

The others being considered – Paul Huntsman and Becky Mangus – both ended up in Morocco: Paul as the cinematographer and Becky in a newly created position of audiovisual specialist. Bert recalled the words "good drawing ability" on my application under the heading Other Skills. Peace Corps wanted to know everything, so I had put it down. Those three words ultimately brought me to Morocco.

Bert explained in a series of long, involved phone conversations that the position of Commercial/Graphic Artist was available in the same ministry office with the film production unit. They wanted somebody with a film background who could also do animation. Titles and graphics for films were part of the job, along with designing posters and printed materials. Not bad, I thought, but not a cinematographer's position.

My decision to accept the invitation was, in many ways, a gamble. I was betting Paul might have a change of heart and I could assume his position. The timing was right too. If I wanted a Peace Corps position, it had to be then – not a year or two later. I hoped a few things would work out in my favor. I contacted Bert and told him we had a deal. Sign me up.

Soon, my mailbox filled with form letters, memos and various packets of information about what was ahead. Right away, I became familiar with the U.S. government's obsession with paper.

The first notice I received, confirming I was going to Morocco, was a yellow carbon copy of a handwritten Route Slip – ACTION Form PC-279 – that simply had my first name scribbled in the top TO slot and the following terse message under REMARKS: "We have invited you to the Morocco Ag program and have accepted you. If you have any questions, call Frank West." No signature, just Frank's toll-free number and extension. Well, I thought, not very official-looking, but it would do.

A week later, a Dear Applicant form letter arrived, confirming my invitation to a Peace Corps training program – contingent on me passing final legal and medical clearances – and asking for my reply of acceptance as soon as possible. I mailed my letter of acceptance the next day.

By the end of March, I was receiving more form letters from other ACTION officials, congratulating me and thanking me for volunteering. I received two information packets describing living and working in a Third World country.

One packet included a two-page ACTION document titled *Trainee Assignment Criteria* that spelled out the objectives and duties of my position and overall goal: "… promoting new and improved agricultural practices for farmers." Working hours, holidays and vacation time were also defined. An overview of living in Rabat was included, plus what to expect in terms of the food, travel around the country, even the weather.

I also received instructions on how to get fingerprinted locally and a stack of medical forms – a comprehensive physical – that our family doctor needed to complete. Since I lived in the Atlanta area, I could stop by the Centers for Disease Control headquarters and start my required vaccinations. Every week, it seemed, was a project to complete.

Another form letter arrived from Country Director Everett M. Woodman in Rabat. He repeated a common theme of earlier letters. Morocco "… is a country of contrasts and contradictions, a place most Volunteers find fascinating, frustrating, challenging, discouraging, exciting and demanding – all at the same time." He sounded downright philosophical, noting that Peace Corps service "… requires recognition of one's own strengths and weaknesses and readiness to apply one's full capacity to learn and grow in the unfamiliar value system of another branch of the family of man." I had to think about that a while.

Finally, about three weeks before I left the States, I received a personal letter from Phil Hanson, the Program & Planning Officer in the Rabat office. Phil outlined what the work environment would be like and regretted that the volunteer I would be replacing had just departed so I would not have any overlap with him on the job.

Packing, closing my bank account, calling friends and relatives … the final days before departure were hectic. Time to sign more forms and papers. I was eligible to have my student loan payments suspended. Peace Corps signed me up for a $10,000 life insurance policy issued by The Travelers Insurance Company; I needed to designate my beneficiary … just in case.

## Swearing to Volunteer

Past the tedious forms and mountains of paper, I also made it through orientation, a trip across the ocean and 10 weeks of intense training. Saturday, September 3 had finally arrived.

We all gathered at 10 a.m. in the dusty courtyard to take the Peace Corps oath, administered by Ambassador Anderson. The ambassador acknowledged us again as the Bicentennial Group of Peace Corps Volunteers, while people all over the country celebrated "200 years of friendship with the United States." He proudly recognized our group as "Americans who would begin another 200 years of a successful alliance with Morocco." In so many words, I guessed, we were being told "Don't screw it up!"

A dozen Moroccan officials I had not seen before joined the ambassador, all our instructors and the Peace Corps Morocco office staff. Raising my right hand, I repeated his words:

"I, Richard Wallace, do solemnly swear that I will support and defend the Constitution of the United States against all enemies, foreign and domestic; that I will bear true faith and allegiance to the same; that I take this obligation freely, without any mental reservation or evasion; and that I will well and faithfully discharge my duties in the Peace Corps, so help me God."

"Congratulations!" Ambassador Anderson announced after the brief ceremony.

It was official: we were all full-fledged Peace Corps Volunteers – no longer lowly trainees.

Scattered cheers, a few hugs and many good-luck handshakes joined a chorus of Goodbyes as our assembly disbanded. Our next project was vacating the lycée that had been our first home in Morocco.

Starting Monday, I would begin work for the Ministry of Agriculture. I received my *Visa de Retour*, an important document we were required to carry whenever we left the country; it allowed us back in. I was also issued my *Carte d'Identite*, my green card – a key piece of identification with my photo (from Studio Bensalah) that labeled me a foreigner approved to work in Morocco for the next year. Seemed odd to be starting my job on Labor Day – maybe that was a good omen.

# Part Two
Into September
... and Beyond!

## Moving Day

The process of moving out of the lycée matched the commotion of our arrival in June. Packing up all our belongings was complicated by everyone's excitement for reaching new homes and starting work. The large patio near the lycée's entrance resembled the sidewalks at the Hotel Sonesta in Atlanta – stacks of duffle bags, straw bags, odd boxes and suitcases piled high.

In our third-floor dorm area, a crew of Moroccans we had not seen before began cleaning. We focused on emptying our lockers and collecting the last round of laundry, just delivered to our bunks. For me, everything I owned fit except my bulky hiking boots.

I made a few trips carrying things to the first floor. Just before leaving, John from Oregon (heading far south to Ourazazate) noticed my concern for more packing space and compared our respective situations.

"What are you worried about?" John challenged me. "You have to go barely a kilometer, and I have to think about crossing the High Atlas Mountains." I was the fortunate one that moving day.

Hoping to catch the 11 a.m. bus to Khenifra, Mike and Piotr rushed by me with a quick wave on their way out. They were the first volunteers to leave the stage.

I made a final descent with my sleeping bag and last-minute laundry when I noticed I had forgotten my hiking boots. I sprinted back upstairs to find the bottom of my open locker completely empty; my boots had vanished. I searched everywhere – under bunks, even in bathroom stalls – any place my boots may have been stashed. Asking the cleaning staff if they had seen any boots floating around, I was met with a bunch of "Sorry, fella" shrugs.

The victim of my first Moroccan theft, I knew the loss wasn't the end of the world; however, the boots had personal value. I wore them to the summit of Mount Kilimanjaro. I had fitted them with Vibram soles for that climb, too. My only clue who took them: some guy who wore a size 10. Lesson learned.

In the meantime, taxis – compact blue Fiats – crowded the entrance, as TEFL teachers departed for bus and train stations. Becky had diplomatically talked Ahmed from the Peace Corps staff into giving us a lift to our apartment in the office van he drove. The transfer to our new place was uneventful. It was certainly a relief to be free of the lycée's dorm lifestyle.

With our last load carried up four flights of stairs and dumped in the living room, I recalled our made-up marriage to rent the place and kidded Becky at our front door, "Do I need to carry you over the threshold, dear?"

She replied with a chuckle, "I don't think so!"

With training completed, we were on our own. It was a different feeling – no more planned meals to simply show up and get in line for, no more scheduled routine of classes or activities every day. Talk about freedom!

## Starting Over: The House

In addition to our 1,300-dirham monthly living allowance, Peace Corps gave each of us an extra 1,500 dirhams (about $375) as a settling-in allowance. Our two-bedroom place resembled a penthouse. Visiting volunteers expressed amazement that we had conveniences like an electric hot water heater and a sit-down toilet in the bathroom. I had to admit – it was not the mud hut and thatched roof often associated with Peace Corps assignments.

We bought a stove for 150 dirhams, a dining room set for 175, my bed for 200, plus some bamboo and wicker furniture for another 250. We did a lot of furnishing with our 3,000 dirhams. The place was starting to look like a home. Luckily, we were the tallest apartment building around, so curtains weren't necessary. All our windows came equipped with roll-down wooden shutters in case of dust storms.

For the first five days, though, we needed water. Fortunately, the family next door generously supplied us with water in any container we provided. The husband taught history at the local university and had just moved in with his wife and two small children. I never figured out how they had water and we did not.

We hired a maid, Latifa. Correction: we inherited a maid – a middle-aged lady known to other Americans and volunteers in town. That was how things worked ... we talked up our needs at the Peace Corps office or over dinner with other volunteers and, through a network of contacts, we would find a solution. With a qualified referral, we were confident Latifa would do a good job for us. As a bonus, she spoke some English.

Peace Corps encouraged all volunteers to hire Host Country National maids as a show of goodwill in the community and to possibly help us improve our language skills. Latifa came by on Tuesdays and Fridays; we paid her the going rate of 12 dirhams (about $3) per day.

Preparing meals was another hurdle. We had the handy cookbook, showing us how to get the best nutritional value using the abundant – and always fresh – fruits and vegetables. We inherited kitchen utensils and cookware, plus a table, from a departing Peace Corps married couple. Becky was an accomplished cook, and we soon settled into a routine: I shopped, she cooked. We had agreed to each put 300 dirhams a month into a jar stashed in a kitchen cabinet for buying food and paying Latifa.

In our neighborhood, we had a large bakery and several butcher shops with fresh meat dangling in the windows. With monthly savings, we hoped to acquire a small refrigerator too ... a luxury item.

Every neighborhood featured several *hanoots,* small convenience stores that carried a bit of everything – imagine a tiny Walmart with goods stacked to the ceiling. If more than five people entered to shop at once, the store was officially crowded.

We had our choice of three hanoots on our street. Our preference came down to which proprietor we wanted to deal with on a daily basis for fresh bread, butter, eggs and household supplies. Becky and I made a project out of the selection, calling our effort *Looking for Mr. Goodbar,* after the Diane Keaton-Richard Gere movie about to release in the United States. Our search took about a week and required a few visits to each location to gauge service, prices and inventory, as well as the personality behind the counter. Turned out, our pick was the closest of the three, just steps beyond our building's entrance.

Instead of trying to pronounce his name, we referred to our choice at home as Mr. Goodbar. He was a skinny man with curly black hair and a pencil-thin moustache, always dressed in what looked like a long white lab coat. If he didn't have what we needed, he could get it for us. With our deposit, Mr. Goodbar even supplied us with the bottles of Butagas to fuel our stove and gladly delivered them to our apartment ... or directed a local kid to haul it up our stairway and leave with the empty bottle.

## Residential Hassles

I quickly encountered the challenges of getting a new home operational. We hit one snag after another, mostly because our brand-new building had no previous utility records. That wasn't our only complication. With the crazy business hours during Ramadan, most places only operated 9 a.m. to 2 p.m. I also rapidly exhausted my newly acquired French vocabulary while dealing with various Moroccans – the utility company, our landlord, our real estate agent and others.

We still needed electricity and water. Whenever I asked, I heard a term pronounced "somdee." I thought it was the French word for Saturday *(Samedi)*. For two days, I thought people were telling me "go to Saturday." Finally, my real estate agent led me to the main office of the nationalized utility company. We stood in the street, and he pointed to the giant letters on the building where everyone had been directing me: SMD. That settled that.

I found further humor when, after nine days, we finally got electricity. Only three lights in the whole place worked, and one switch by our front door turned on lights in two rooms. Though I hadn't had a spare minute to alert our landlord to the goofy wiring, an electrician appeared. I was very glad to see him! He walked in clutching all the tools he needed: his trusty wire cutters, two screwdrivers and a circuit tester. With sketchy French, I told him which lights worked *(les lumières qui marchent)* and which ones didn't. By then, it was 4:30 p.m. He snipped away at some wires, checked the main electrical box and then headed for the individual switches and fixtures in each room. Turned out, that was where the trouble was.

It fascinated me to observe the change in a person's temperament as late afternoon hunger set in. We had devised the saying "It must be near harira time!" to describe a person who was grumpy or emotionless and lethargic. By late afternoon, all Muslims could think about were their bowls of harira, the spicy "Ramadan soup."

By 5 p.m. – with his soup just two hours away – our electrician continued to work what I considered to be electronic miracles by getting all our lights to function. He worked with live wires as if they were spaghetti. Not once did he get shocked, though he did fall off a stool. He clearly had electrical smarts but lacked coordination.

His success with the lights impressed me – no more cooking and writing letters by candlelight. As he finished, I threw out one of our old French standards, *"Vous êtes intelligent"* (You are smart). He only managed a blank stare.

> **one volunteer remembers...**
>
> Early in my stay, I was on the bus home from Rabat. It was around 4 p.m., and we had just stopped in Ezhilliga, between Romani and Oued Zem. There had been a souk in Ezhilliga, and the bus was packed with farmers and goats (on top). It was also about 100 degrees on the bus and, of course, no windows were open because you didn't want to let the djinns* in. I had never been so miserable in my life, physically. But looking around me, I didn't see another Western face or sign of "modernity" anywhere (except we were on a bus). I remember thinking to myself, "I don't know if I can take much more," but then at the same time saying to myself, "I can't do anything about it ... and wasn't it fascinating?" It was a turning point for me. I decided from that point that, as uncomfortable as I was, I was sticking Peace Corps out, no matter what. The experience was just too amazing to let go of.
>
> 
> Mark Dressman<br>
> TEFL Instructor<br>
> Kasba Tadla
> 
>
> *A djinn is a spirit (a 'genie," from the same word). They come with flowing things, like the wind and water. Our maid, Meriem, used to lecture me regularly not to put hot water down the drain because it would piss off the djinns. - MD

# A New Job Begins

I evaluated my first week at work. My co-workers were cooperative, and I believed I could contribute to the ministry's services.

Months before I arrived, the Ministry of Agriculture decided it would like to produce animated films along with its regular productions. So, they bought new equipment without considering if anybody around the office knew how to use it. The equipment was all French or German but similar in operation to equipment I had used at SIU.

Peace Corps requested my help to get the animation operation rolling. I looked forward to the challenge and thought, "How do you make growing seeds into a good cartoon?" I planned to learn how, while my co-workers thought I was the expert.

My first assignment was ambitious but interesting: animate the life cycle of a gypsy moth – or *bililou* in French. That bug infested cork trees in northern Morocco. To get started, I viewed an hour's worth of film of those moths doing everything. They led a very active life. On a previous trip to Tangier, I rode through the middle of Morocco's largest cork forest and found it funny to see those large trees wrapped in what would one day become bottle corks and bulletin boards.

## Already a Day Off

Ramadan ended on a Thursday, marking the beginning of a national holiday period that stretched through the weekend. I was ready to go someplace. I couldn't believe it: I had only worked eight days and already earned a four-day weekend ... what timing!

Becky's mother had snagged a special travel club airfare and decided to visit us. She had been on a European tour and wanted to see Morocco before returning to Denver. Her energetic, bubbly personality matched the vibrant summertime colors she wore. She was entertaining, open-minded and full of motherly questions about our Moroccan life. I enjoyed meeting her. Our living situation posed no problems for her. Like Becky, she was a genuine go-with-the-flow woman.

During her first evening in Rabat, we introduced Becky's mother to the local flavors at El Bahia Restaurant. She was about the same age as Brahim, the waiter we were getting to know there. He flirted with her as he meticulously explained the menu in his limited English. We enjoyed harira, salad and beef brochettes with fresh bread, topped off with the requisite glass of mint tea.

Becky mapped out an ambitious four-day Moroccan tour that would set some distance records, if completed. The holiday weekend clogged all public transportation, and our packed itinerary did not allow for waiting on buses. We had to get back by Sunday night to be at work Monday morning. At the suggestion of Phil Hanson, we rented a car. Becky had an international driver's license that earned us a fairly new Renault R4L with front-wheel drive and a strange four-speed stick shift protruding from the dashboard.

We crammed everything in and set off bright and early. Traffic was surprisingly light. Riding in a car was a switch from bouncing around in buses. We headed inland toward Meknes, passing small farms and driving through Khimmeset, a small town where two friends were stationed.

I was surprised what a large, modern city Meknes was. Beyond the city, the terrain became less agricultural with more irrigation; olive groves covered many of the terraced hills.

Entering Fes, we looked for the new home of our engineer friend Chuck. We found him later in town, and he insisted on a quick tour of the phenomenal Fes medina. That massive medina (the old city) rested on lumpy hills. Chuck led us to the impressive arched entrance of the University of Al-Karaouine, founded in 859 and considered the world's oldest university; Christians were not allowed to enter. Climbing layers of steps, we overlooked the town's famous tanneries where hides were dyed in a rainbow of colors for making leather goods sold all over the country. We spent the night in Chuck's new house, a roomy five-bedroom place he shared with four other volunteers. Chuck's residence was considered one of the top Peace Corps properties, although there was not one stick of furniture inside. His bamboo furnishings shipped by train from Rabat hadn't arrived yet. Fortunately, we all had sleeping bags. It had been a long day.

We were up by 7 the next day and off to Midelt by way of Ifrane, home of Morocco's best pastry shop that was closed for the holiday. We drove through the Middle Atlas Mountains, rising above rolling, somewhat barren hills that morphed into thick pine forests – reminiscent of Oregon or North Carolina. I was surprised to see such large trees. Traffic remained extremely light – we would see another car every 15 minutes or so. The roads had been excellent; no center line, though – and drivers loved to pass on a hill.

Farther south and out of the mountains, the road flattened into a desert-like plain. The mountains had marked the difference. On the Rabat coastal side were rich, fertile lands; over the mountains were the leftovers – flat, rocky land made only for what it was: desert. Once in a while, a village popped up around a spring or a gas station.

Around noon, we rolled into Midelt, a town of 20,000 people at the base of the mighty High Atlas Mountains – similar to a Colorado town backed up to the Rockies. The city was about 5,000 feet above sea level and was known as one of the coldest spots in Africa; winters were unreal. It took some doing, but we located our Peace Corps friends. In a town that size, a few queries about the Americans in one or two hanoots (popular points of information exchange) typically produced directions. Luckily, they were home at their two-bedroom house. They had an indoor well – a luxury in Midelt; most wells were outside.

Mark, my hotel roommate during our arrival meetings in Rabat, had received Midelt as his TEFL assignment. So far, he appeared to like it.

The school where he would teach was new, and the cost of living was unbelievably low – he paid about 2 cents for a pound of perfect tomatoes. Mark shared the house with another TEFL teacher, Marjie, one of Becky's favorite friends from training. They had bought virtually everything they needed for the house (even an electric iron) and still had a lot of dirhams leftover.

I decided to hop off the whirlwind tour to stay in Midelt one night, then head back to Rabat. Marjie took my seat in the car, joining Becky and her mother. They left right away for more of southern Morocco, back across the mountains to Marrakesh, then north to Rabat. I was relieved to slow down.

The first thing I did was borrow a jacket from Mark. It was already chilly. We walked all over the town and met some of his future students. We also bought some of those bargain tomatoes and made a pot of the best cream of tomato soup, using a Peace Corps cookbook recipe. That soup hit the spot on our frosty night in Midelt.

Another volunteer from our class, Steve Long, joined us for dinner with two of his students and some fresh bread. It was an opportunity to hear Mark and Steve conduct a friendly conversation in Arabic with the two teenage boys. We had an educational discussion of Midelt life in three languages: French, Arabic and bits of English.

Steve came to Morocco after graduating from Colorado College in Colorado Springs with a degree in English literature and foreign languages.

"I was slated to go to Afghanistan, but then a revolution broke out and the program was cancelled," he told me. "My recruiter called me with an offer to go to either South Korea or Saint Lucia in the Caribbean. A few days later, I received a call offering an immediate position in Morocco. At first, I hesitated because my college roommate had been a volunteer in Azrou, and I didn't want to replicate his experience. Then I thought … wait, this is Morocco with its fascinating culture and history. I was in."

Our Saturday morning surprise was the year's first snow on the highest points of neighboring mountains. What a sight! The mountains – and Midelt – would be covered all winter.

Mark joined me on my return to Rabat since he had business to take care of at the Peace Corps office. The souk bus to Azrou was supposed to depart at 10:30. Finally, at 1 p.m. our bus arrived. About the same size as Midelt, Azrou was a hilly and scenic town, sunk into the foothills of the Middle Atlas Mountains.

Patty Balch, the volunteer from Tupelo, Mississippi, had been assigned there. Mark knew where Patty lived with Jean, the second-year volunteer in town. Patty was happy to see familiar faces. She had been lucky – no search for a place to live was necessary; she moved right in with Jean to a home that had been a quasi-headquarters for Peace Corps Volunteers for many years. An old French house with a small garage and the standard rooftop terrace, it featured a wood-fired water heater with a tub and a bidet in the bathroom. Visiting volunteers signed up to take a hot bath. The bidet became a popular dispenser for sangria during social gatherings.

Patty and Jean's maid, Fatima, was considered a living legend among Peace Corps folks, working for them year after year. Jean spoke excellent Arabic; Fatima was never interested in learning English, apparently.

Mark wanted to visit the artisans' workshop in town. It was full of locally produced stone, metal and wood art objects, plus elaborate carpets and woven tapestries. Later, the two of us ate all we could at a little restaurant in the center of town, and the bill was only 6 dirhams! Life in the small towns was like that. With winter approaching, I decided I preferred the higher prices in Rabat to a well in a frigid kitchen.

Sunday, we hopped an uneventful bus ride to Meknes, then caught a late train to Rabat. Back home in 12 hours from Azrou – that was good for Moroccan travel. Becky and her mother had returned safely with Arabian travel tales of their own.

## Yours, Mine ... & Theirs

In the early weeks, our new apartment became something of a Peace Corps warehouse. Friends left books, typewriters, Personal Medical Kits and other bulky items while they traveled to their towns to secure housing. At one point, we had over 30 pieces of wicker and bamboo furniture in our apartment – and that was before we started furnishing the place.

Many volunteers routinely passed through Rabat to handle business at the main office, address medical issues or pick up teaching supplies. Our apartment became a popular stop as well.

One evening, a dozen volunteers ended up at our place for dinner – all TEFL teachers from our training stage who had just returned from their work sites after arranging housing. They didn't begin work until later in the month. Beverly, a volunteer known for her cooking skills, whipped up the best beef stroganoff. Everybody chipped in, and we exchanged stories about living situations in various parts of Morocco.

Volunteers visiting from tiny towns in the middle of nowhere observed all we had – electric hot water heater in the bathroom with a sit-down toilet, tiled walls, our view – and would ask, "When are the dishwasher and color TV being delivered?"

I knew we were without many of the inconveniences of small-town Moroccan living. Some places only had water available four or five hours a day. We had it 24 hours a day, seven days a week. Living there was definitely worth scaling four flights of stairs a few times a day ... sort of like mandatory exercise, I rationalized. We planned to enjoy our comfortable living situation.

But the comfort would come at a price, I theorized. The Peace Corps world revolved around Rabat, so it seemed our instant crowd of visitors might become a trend. Time would tell.

Whenever we had company for dinner, American music played in the background. Becky had brought a portable stereo cassette player with an AM/FM radio, suitable for our complete home entertainment center. She had also packed a varied selection of the latest pop tunes, including the group America and Dan Fogelberg. She even brought a tape of Christmas music.

After-dinner conversations covered a wide range of topics – mostly the difficulties and misadventures of finding suitable housing, buying and preparing meals and interacting with Moroccans.

One advantage to entertaining TEFL volunteers was adding to our limited Arabic vocabulary, since the teachers had more practical experience with the language than Becky and I did. I was most interested in reviewing the numbers one through 10 and days of the week to handle basic transactions with Mr. Goodbar.

A pair of Arabic expressions would come in handy, according to Margaret, a TEFL teacher stationed in El Menzel. If a difference of opinion existed between two people, one could shrug it off and end the conversation with *Bizotta,* with a meaning along the lines of "I'm not impressed" or "You've got to be kidding." Another catchy comeback – *She-bess maKane* – implied "It doesn't matter" or "So what?"

Marie from New York shared a humorous account of how a simple slip in pronunciation could interrupt casual conversation attempts.

"The day after I moved in, I went to my nearest hanoot to buy some olives," Marie told us, trying not to laugh. "'I want to buy your olives there,' I told the man, pointing to the pile of olives in the corner of his stand. The man's eyes widened, shocked at what he heard from this American female attempting to speak his language. 'No, I don't have those to sell,' he responded, trying to be polite. I said, 'Sure you do; I can see you have them,' pointing to the pile in the corner. The man insisted they were not for sale. Turned out, a misplaced consonant in my pronunciation made my word for olives sound like Arabic slang for testicles! Before I knew it, the whole town knew about my mix-up from another customer who overheard us."

As the evening wound down, most of our dinner guests returned to their hotels. A handful had arrived with sleeping bags, indicating they would be happy to recline on any flat surface available at our place. That's when I knew our address would become known among volunteers as *Hôtel l'Ocean* – the Ocean Hotel.

> **one volunteer remembers...**
>
> Fatna, our maid, came into the house that Red and I shared in Midelt. She was carrying a bag from the pharmacy. In my halting, baby Derija, I said, "I know where you have been."
> She replied, "Where?"
> "You went to the pharmacy."
> "That's right, Steve," she said.
> "And I know what you bought," I continued with pride.
> "What did I buy, Steve?"
> "You bought *tinat.*"
> Tinat means cunts; I meant to say *kinat*, meaning pills.
> She doubled over with laughter and said, "Those are from Allah, Steve, not from the pharmacy."
>
> Steve Long
> TEFL Instructor
> Midelt

## Words on the Street

On their own and away from the supervision at the stage, volunteers tended to return to former pastimes and diversions. Those digressions included bending the rules. In addition to its reputation for its fascinating history and culture, Morocco was also the hash capital of North Africa. Hashish and marijuana were the two most popular combustible products hawked on the street. Also widely available was kif – pot mixed with black tobacco.

Volunteers looking for recreational relief from extremes in weather, personal stress levels and everyday life found occasional solace with discreet uses of pot. They didn't have to look far, either. Dealers of all ages, selling an assortment of products for getting high, regularly hassled foreigners walking down any street in the country.

"Won sm'stuff?" was the standard pitch, whispered to us from behind as we walked or waited to cross a busy street – anywhere, day or night. Most would accept our assertive "La" as the end of the conversation, while some became belligerent.

One TEFL teacher became incensed during an encounter with a street dealer. Hearing "Won sm'stuff?" whispered behind him one too many times, he abruptly turned around and went toe to toe with the guy, enunciating dramatically while shouting in his face, "It's 'Do You Want Some Stuff?' If you want to ask us something in English, get it right!" The dealer could only respond with a stare of surprise and confusion before staggering away.

## Back to Work

As September days were crossed off the calendar, our first full days on the non-Ramadan schedule began. We worked 8:30 to noon and 2:30 to 6. We ate around 8 p.m., and it was typically 10 or later before I could write letters home or read a newspaper. The day sure went by fast. On Fridays we got an extra-long lunch – 11:30 to 3 – allowing Muslims time for midday prayers at their mosques.

The office had been crowded with visitors who collaborated with us on our film about the gypsy moth; I was producing four animated sequences for it. The work was frustrating at first: starting a graphic and discovering I did not have the pens, tracing paper or acetate sheets I needed. Once I figured out the procedures for ordering supplies, my project progressed.

Setting up the animation work was tedious and took longer than expected due to regular interruptions from Jamal, the Moroccan graphic artist I was to work with closely. For some reason, he never had any work to do – he always hung on the edge of my table, watching every move I made. Jamal, about twenty-two and a chain-smoker, had bugged me like hell for a couple of weeks before I came up with the idea to trade some English for a little French vocabulary each day. I was relieved to discover a reasonable compromise of what to do with some of his idle time, while I remained stacked with work.

Paul stayed busy working with John, getting familiar with the equipment and production schedules. John was happy to have some English-speaking company. Staffing a newly created position, Becky started from scratch – arranging her workspace, meeting our Moroccan co-workers and learning how things operate in a foreign government's office.

We found variety in the characters with whom we worked. Mohammed was one of the more personable workers in our department, always with a story to tell about his latest travels. About forty-five, he was the Moroccan equivalent of a county extension agent. He traveled around the agricultural provinces with his trusty projector and showed the films we made: how to plant, how to fertilize, how to drive a tractor – some "epic dramas" from the ministry's film library.

For us three rookies in the office, the language was a daily hurdle during our first month on the job. Our Moroccan co-workers could manage conversations in French, but Arabic was popular too.

Once we got past basic introductions, we gravitated to one or two workers we could easily chat with and ask our questions. Mr. Jebbor, our supervisor, occupied his office down a long hallway. We might have seen him once or twice a week. Marc, our Belgian production chief, provided some background on the boss.

"Jebbor can speak fairly good English," he told us. "Watch. When he wants to make a point with us or becomes irritated, he will switch to English."

Production schedules and daily activities required frequent mentions of King Hassan II and his son – the two most revered people in the country. Marc and John cautioned us one afternoon: our conversations mentioning the king and the crown prince by their names might suggest to our HCN co-workers that we had less-than-glorious impressions of the royal pair. Hearing their names in our English dialogues could lead to suspicions that we did not support their leadership efforts. (A 1970s reality check: talking about the King at all in public was problematic.) For the sake of avoiding any misunderstandings, Marc and John created the in-house rule to refer to King Hassan II as Frank Sinatra and his son as Frank Sinatra Jr.

One perk of our government jobs was the work bus that motored through our neighborhood. Every morning, just three blocks away, we caught the bus to our office door. It even brought us back for lunch. Available to all government employees, it didn't stop as often as the public buses; plus, it was free. City buses would have cost each of us 40 dirhams a month and were always crowded.

### one volunteer remembers...

A few days after arriving in Beni Mellal, I went to investigate the school where I would be teaching. To my surprise, it was three long kilometers up a steep and winding road to the school, which was surrounded by almond groves and uninhabited hills. Lycée Moha ou Hammou (the name of a Berber military leader) had been an agricultural school and still served as a boarding school for Berber farmers' kids, all boys, many older than me (twenty-two at the time) since they had taken time off from school to help their parents.

My first real day of school, exhaustedly climbing the road with a mass of students, as all the other teachers whizzed by me in their cars, I heard nonstop jeers (or what sounded to be) in Arabic.

Very upset, I wrote home, and a short while later I received an oversized white lab coat in the mail from my scientist father, who thought this would stop them from messing with me. This time, as I walked up the hill in my huge white getup, I heard voices around me (in French, to make sure I would understand), saying, "Who is she? A doctor, an astronaut, a scientist, a ghost ..." Now I could barely stop laughing as this continued the whole way up the hill.

Eventually, I made friends with a young Moroccan teacher who gave me rides on his motorcycle every morning. It remained a tough year – many students didn't see the use of learning English. But some of them welcomed my gifts of paperbacks in English and amazed me with their fluency and understanding of American women writers writing about worlds so far from their own.

Terry Lajtha
*TEFL Instructor*
*Beni Mella*

## Challenging Days, New Friends

Those first weeks – with the transfer from secure training to survival in the real Morocco – had been challenging at times. I was settling into the Moroccan way of life. Work moved along slowly, and it sank in that I was going to be there for a while. Bottom line: it was like having any other job. Peace Corps only acted as the personnel service to Morocco. All my job-related support materials came from the Ministry of Agriculture. Peace Corps kept me healthy and wealthy, more or less. Each day moved along a little smoother than the previous one. The language was no longer a major obstacle; my French grew by a few words each day.

John helped us get settled into our apartment and oriented to living in Rabat. He shared a house across town where Becky and I enjoyed evening and weekend visits, collecting household tips and preparing meals together. He also introduced us to a small circle of local friends.

Mandy and Rory were a British couple with contract teaching jobs in Rabat. They hung out at John's house so frequently, they were almost part of the Peace Corps family. A few years older than us, they were often the life of the party. Driss (pronounced *Dreese*) was another friend we acquired through John. A Moroccan in his late twenties, Driss worked in the legal field, either as a lawyer or a paralegal studying to become a lawyer. We never figured out his exact status, although he spoke excellent English. His claim to fame was that two years earlier he was among the 350,000 participants in the Green March – the mass protest of Moroccans to reclaim the Spanish Sahara territory to the south.

Driss lived near our apartment, and Becky and I welcomed him and his girlfriend, Sofi, over for dinner one evening. The next week, Driss invited us to his home for tea after work. The invitation to tea meant dinner, too, and we were treated to more excellent Moroccan dishes. Two other Moroccan couples joined us, and we all enjoyed a pleasant evening of cross-cultural conversations.

After dinner, we viewed our first TV in weeks – a French-dubbed version of *The Bionic Woman,* called *Super Jamie.* Television was nationalized in Morocco, so there was only one channel. Some 16 stations around the country broadcast the lone schedule of programs.

Following *Super Jamie,* we watched a Moroccan newscast. It opened with a flashy world map and zippy Moroccan music. We assumed the Moroccan Walter Cronkite was named either Ali or Mohammed – he came on with the top stories. We noticed very little use of slides, film or tape. All the commercials ran together at one time during each hour, so the anchorman had no breaks. It was quite a switch from the 6 o'clock *NewsScene* back in Atlanta. The broadcast lasted 25 minutes and came on at 8:45 ... or did it?

While watching TV that night, Becky and I asked six people with watches (at the same moment) what time they had. We got answers covering a range of 20 minutes. My long-held theory was proven: nobody in that country knew the correct time. Occasionally, we got a beep on the hour from the radio and could use that as a rough guide. It became difficult to be on time for anything when we didn't know what time it was. Fortunately – except for train schedules – punctuality was rarely important in Morocco. A perpetual 20-minute window (plus or minus) existed for events.

### one volunteer remembers...

Upon reaching our assignments, the TEFL volunteers were eagerly awaiting the start of classes. Alas, we were quick to discover that no one knew when classes would actually begin. There was an official date to be sure, but the only ones who controlled when classes would actually begin were the students. The delay to the school year could be interminable as students threatened and carried out strikes over the shortage of books, dormitory conditions, curriculum, etc. Sitting around could get quite boring. I was posted to Ouarzazate, over the mountains to the south of Marrakesh; and my girlfriend at the time (and current wife), Debbie, was residing in Beni Mellal, 241 miles away. Our only means of communication was by mail – very efficient and timely, taking a good two to three days between our towns. To break up the boredom, I decided to take the trip to Beni and informed Debbie by mail that I was on my way.

The first leg by bus was a fairly harrowing voyage to Marrakesh that I eventually got used to. Buses had a schedule but really never left until all the seats were sold. Did I mention one learned patience in Morocco? I always wanted to sit by a window that I could open and control, even though at 6 feet 3 inches an aisle seat would have been more comfortable. Moroccans never wanted the windows open no matter how high the temperature. Withstanding the glares of the disapproving passengers was well worth it! There were many switchbacks and precipices to reconnoiter going over the Atlas Mountains, and the drivers were rather skilled, although you could see the wreckage of trucks and cars that had gone over the edge. The buses always stopped at the summit of the pass at Taddart Oufella for a rest stop. It was a narrow, one road village nestled between steep cliffs on either side. When getting off the bus, the aroma of brochette stands was welcome relief from the odors that filled the bus.

While walking around to stretch my legs, I noticed another bus going in the opposite direction back to Ouarzazate. On a whim and premonition, I thought I'd walk along the side of that bus, and lo and behold, there was Debbie sitting by a window. I remember shouting in a high-pitched voice, "Debbie!" She was rather stunned to see me standing outside looking in. I ran back to my bus, grabbed my bag and jumped on her bus. We then discovered we had both written letters announcing our impending arrivals, which of course hadn't arrived soon enough! Debbie then introduced me to a kindly farmer from a village near Ouarzazate who had admonished some younger men that had been hassling her on the bus. We had a nice conversation, and he invited us to his home. After a few days in Ouarzazate, we decided to visit him and were treated to the wonderful and generous hospitality Moroccans are known for.

John Schroeder
*TEFL Instructor*
*Ouarzazate*

## Finally: Our Living Room

Becky and I were determined to finally acquire furniture for our living room. We had heard of a place on the edge of town that custom-made banquettes, the Moroccan-style sofa. Residents typically bought a pair of banquettes for facing walls and put a small table between them. Large pillow-type cushions were placed along the back of each banquette. The way a banquette sat on a wooden frame – low to the floor – reminded me of a futon.

Taking a taxi on a Saturday afternoon and following directions provided by our landlord, we located an open-air market that resembled a giant garage sale, spread across a wide, dusty field. Everything for the home was there, sold from makeshift stalls.

We met Abdou One, our French instructor from training, while surveying the first row of merchants. He was in the neighborhood visiting a friend. We explained our shopping objective, and he eagerly offered to help. He knew a man at the massive market who could do a good job for us.

Abdou insisted I hold hands with him as we strolled through the maze of merchants. I realized there was no chance of running into anyone I knew and thought, "OK, what the hell ... when in Rome!" It was a memorable cultural experience, to say the least. Becky followed behind us in customary Moroccan fashion.

After a brief walk holding hands with my former French teacher, we met the man who could make what we wanted. Abdou introduced us to Ali, the shop owner, then left us to complete the order on our own. Ali only spoke Arabic, so we got a local teenager to translate everything into French for us. I had a rough sketch of what we were shopping for and, in that situation, a picture really was worth a thousand words!

Ali told our helper how much fabric (in meters) our size of banquettes would require. The kid then led us around to several fabric merchants, and we picked out the material we wanted. It was 4:30 p.m. by the time we returned with all the fabric for the pair of banquettes (each 2 meters long) and six cushions – three for each banquette. Certainly, we thought, Ali would need at least a week to do all the work, considering what we already knew about the Moroccan work pace.

He said, "Come back 6 p.m. Sunday!" We couldn't believe it. So, we settled on the total cost and some service charges and left saying, "See you tomorrow."

We went back the next day at 6 to find everything ready to go: two banquettes packed solid with heavy straw weighing just under 50 kilos each (or about 110 pounds apiece) and six cushions with zippers for easy removal for cleaning. He had done all that work on a little treadle machine in one day, and we were impressed with his craftsmanship. He sold us the supporting wooden frames as well.

Our final project that day was to get it all up four flights of stairs. We had some help from the guy who hauled it home for us. It was worth every dirham we paid him.

At last, our living room was taking shape. The banquettes gave us much-needed seating for all the visitors. They doubled as convenient guest beds too.

**one volunteer remembers ...**

My buddy Mike told me this story of his settling in:

He went to buy a woven mat for his flat; his maid offered to accompany him to make sure he paid a fair price. Wanting to assert his independence, he refused her offer and went to market. There he found a mat, negotiated a price, paid and put the rolled-up mat over his shoulder for the walk home.

Along the way, people began to ask – in the friendly, nosy manner of Moroccans – how much he had paid. He said 100, to which people responded, '*Bazeff*' (a lot, too much).

To the next inquiry, Mike responded 80 and got the response, '*Bazeff*.' To another, he reported 60 ... '*Bazeff*' was the constant response.

By the time he got home, his maid was waiting. She asked him how much, and he answered 20. '*Bazeff*,' she said.

Steve Long
TEFL Instructor
Midelt

## A Health Scare

Maybe it was something in the water. Some weird Moroccan virus kept me overheated far too long. Our deluxe first aid kit included a thermometer, and I recorded more than two days of a fever above 103 degrees. I sweated profusely. Maybe it was the flu.

I got myself to the Peace Corps office and insisted on seeing a doctor. Nurse Dolores had kept me on the basic rest and aspirin formula. With my prolonged fever, I earned my first trip to Kenitra, north of Rabat, and the U.S. Naval Air Station for a few lab tests. I had missed three days at work so far, but it looked like I would survive. Due to my lack of an appetite, I had lost about 10 pounds; none of my pants would stay up.

The drive to Kenitra, with Nurse Dolores at the wheel of a Peace Corps staff car, put me one-on-one with her. She was interested in hearing how living with Becky was going. Her prying, personal questions about our living arrangement caught me off guard. I reminded her the place did, in fact, have two bedrooms. I explained to Dolores how we had convinced Moroccans in our neighborhood that Becky and I were married, but that the locals could not figure out why we didn't have at least four or five kids running around. We were having a lot of fun playing hubby and honey when we went shopping.

I could tell Dolores was looking for any tidbit of the latest gossip I may have picked up through Peace Corps channels. Gossip was rampant throughout the country. Many conversations with volunteers passing through our place started with "Did you hear?" or "Have you heard about so-and-so?" Dolores even tried to disguise a question about the sexual orientation of certain trainees – Were they gay? – as some kind of medical inquiry. Really, Dolores? Fortunately, our conversation ended abruptly as we approached the guard station at the Naval base, and Dolores had to show her identification.

The doctor was an older naval officer. He gave me a thorough examination, making notes of my fever and sore throat. He injected a steroid treatment for fast-acting relief and handed me a bottle of antibiotics. The trip to Kenitra solved my medical ailment. By that afternoon, I was on the road to a complete recovery and made a pledge to myself to stay that way.

Liberated from the doctor, I had time to visit the base cafeteria for authentic American food. I grabbed a BLT on fresh Wonder Bread and a quart of cold milk … real Foremost milk – none of that watery goat's milk or whatever it was Moroccan dairies produced (pasteurized but not homogenized) and sold in tiny pyramid-shaped cartons.

Being out of the office for three days cost us the deadline for our film project. It couldn't have been avoided. Besides, I had discovered deadlines never really meant much at our office.

I was so excited about being back on the road to good health, I ran out and bought something I always wanted in our apartment: a toilet seat. The builder put everything in except a seat on the commode, and our landlord wasn't concerned about it – so I went out and bought one myself. Sure made a difference.

## Far from a Perfect World

Our doorbell rang. On the last day of the month, the building superintendent collected 20 dirhams ($5) from each tenant. His duties included collecting our garbage and keeping the stairs clean. He reported he finally got the stairwell lights working. Handing him a purple 20, I told him we appreciated his efforts and explained how coming home at night with a load of groceries was much safer. On each floor, we could hit a button and the lights would come on, then turn off automatically two minutes later.

Over the following few days, our appreciation for our living conditions grew. Volunteers from our class – all of them English teachers – began wandering back to Rabat with horrible stories of no available housing; hostile, anti-American townspeople; and periods of severe dysentery and depression. Becky and I tried our best to cheer up some of them, but several were packing their bags and pulling out.

Of course, many others settled quickly into new homes and started their jobs. We were fortunate to be able to leave the training center and walk right over to our new apartment. Others only had hotels to look forward to once they got to their towns with all their belongings.

### one volunteer remembers...

After our intensive Moroccan Arabic language and TEFL training program in Rabat, we were finally given the names of the schools and the sites we had been assigned to. As September approached and training concluded, we were all getting anxious to move to our various sites, find places to live and start our new jobs as teachers of English.

I learned I had been placed in Beni Mellal, a bustling provincial capital in an agricultural area about halfway between Fes and Marrakesh. I then looked on the list of volunteers to see who else might have been placed there and was delighted to find the name of Terry Lajtha, another female volunteer I knew. We excitedly discussed what might lay in store for us there, and she agreed to join me on what would become our joint adventure!

Arriving by bus, we made straight for a modest local hotel that another volunteer had recommended. He had once passed through Beni Mellal, just spending the night there before catching a bus out early the next morning. He said it was right by the bus station, was small and inexpensive with the toilet down the hall, but a public *douche* (shower) was conveniently located nearby.

We needed to stay someplace cheap, since it could take weeks to locate an affordable rental in a conservative town with little inventory and where most housing was built for large families. Housing was typically unfurnished; once we found a place, we would also need to shop for all our basic household items. Although Peace Corps gave us a settling-in allowance, it would have to stretch a long way, thus we were glad to know of this inexpensive place to stay.

Each day, we'd go back and forth from our hotel, visit the douche, pass by the busy bus station and then slog through meetings with realtors over mint tea, walk around the city looking at large, expensive villas they thought foreigners wanted and then check out various hanoots for possible future purchases. We often saw groups of young high school-age males eyeing us. Or, we'd see teenage girls with their families looking at us curiously. We wondered if some of these kids might eventually be our students and hoped we were projecting an appropriate image. As grassroots representatives of America, we wanted to be seen as a very different type of foreigner, so we dressed modestly, spoke politely in the Moroccan Arabic we'd just studied and quietly went about our business hoping to make a good first impression in this town that would be our home for the next two years.

In the evenings after eating a simple meal, we'd return to crash in our hot, tiny hotel room to read or write letters home. After we'd turned out the lights, we were surprised to suddenly hear loud music and laughter coming from other rooms. We wondered if there was some Berber holiday we were not aware of, or perhaps this hotel was a popular spot for Beni Mellal's honeymooners. Eventually, we fell asleep, but, after a couple more nights of this and running into giggling, satin clad women wearing a lot of makeup coming in and out of the toilet, we figured it out – you guessed it – Beni Mellal's new American teachers were staying at the local brothel! So much for first impressions!

Debbie Beck<br>
TEFL Instructor<br>
Beni Mellal

## October Finally Arrived

Amazing what turning a page on the calendar could do for a person's psyche.

I had survived the challenges of the first month on the job and daily life in a big, foreign city. Minor frustrations at the office (lack of needed materials) made me wonder at times how I would make it through two years. I discovered most volunteers in my class were feeling likewise and dealing with their own first-month hurdles; I found some solace in those reports. I was not alone.

My personal appraisal after that first month was "I can do this." Fixing up our apartment, cooking meals – each activity was its own project; but we learned quickly. Moments of discouragement passed. I kept telling myself: check my emotions and get with the program. Morocco was outside the front door … deal with it.

Work for the ministry chugged along. Periods of encouragement existed. I had almost completed my four animated sequences for the gypsy moth film, and Mr. Jebbor seemed impressed with my neatness and work speed.

A few of my HCN co-workers appeared disturbed by my steady completion of assignments and aimed their bothered stares in my direction. I was certain, too, that Becky, Paul and I were daily subjects of their conversations, disguised in Arabic. That was a temporary bother to me, but I learned to overlook it – a relief. We had a definite difference in our concepts of a work ethic, and I chalked it up to another cross-cultural factor worth my understanding.

## The Home Connection

Most volunteers stationed in Rabat retained the Peace Corps office as their mailing address. Although each volunteer in the country had a mail slot on a large wall just inside the office's front door, many TEFL teachers received mail at their schools. Some in very small towns picked up theirs at local post offices.

For all volunteers, communications from home delivered vital doses of support. From the beginning, my personal strategy was to write letters in hopes of receiving letters in return. At both ends, we had to assume everything mentioned in any letter took place about two weeks before. The shift in time between then and now adjusted our thought processes into another dimension. Everything we read about was basically history – immune to our input, reaction or comment.

During the early weeks, I bought a pair of identical wall maps of Morocco and mailed one of them home to help family members reference the places around the country I was traveling to and writing about.

My mother was a voracious writer, able to pack more words on a single-sheet aerogramme than any other correspondent. For most of those early months in Morocco, my mother included in every letter a list of obscure questions for me to answer. She wanted to know how often we did our laundry, the number of windows in our apartment and if we had carpeting on the floors, among other unusual inquiries – motherly concerns, I was sure.

My dad scribbled his thoughtful notes in handwriting that resembled hieroglyphics, which were always a challenge to read, but I greatly appreciated his effort. I imagined he wrote them during evenings on the road; he was a sales rep for a manufacturer of folding cartons. My older brother and two sisters sent infrequent but welcome surprises to my mailbox.

After putting off the revelation for more than a month, I finally dropped the bombshell news about Becky being my roommate and collected varied reactions. Mom sort of understood (generating more questions), and my brother simply admitted "We kinda suspected that!" Dad wanted more details and became somewhat philosophical, writing "I hope the situation works out for the long haul, and you can remember it as a good and pleasant experience …"

I often considered my dad and other World War II soldiers who left the States and were gone for years at a time. Regular correspondence became an important support mechanism while overseas. Experiencing a much smaller dose of absence, I could better imagine what they must have felt as the months passed.

## The "Peace Corps Way"

Becky and I developed an end-of-the-day routine, taking turns hopping off our work bus at the stop nearest the office, collecting mail (and the latest gossip), walking home and picking up fresh bread and other grocery items needed for our evening meal.

Late one Thursday, Becky arrived at our apartment with a surprise. Like we inherited a maid and many local friends, we inherited a roommate. Kathy, a third-year volunteer – from Colorado, like Becky – came to Morocco as a TEFL teacher, stationed in Marrakesh. She relocated to Rabat to assist the TEFL program director at the office. Kathy would make periodic evaluation trips all over the country, visiting the English teachers. She needed a place to hang out through the following March, and Becky thought she could join us. What could I say? I was outnumbered. Becky and I both recognized she would help with our expenses.

Kathy proved to be a pleasant addition to the household. With any crowd at our place, she was always the tallest female. She was a few years older than Becky and me – thin with long, black hair lightly tinted with henna. I could tell she had been in the country a while; her Arabic was perfect. She was funny and intelligent and could whip up an amazing pot of spaghetti in no time. Kathy also became a convenient conduit of information about happenings at the Peace Corps office.

She was often gone. When she was around, she was most helpful preparing meals and chiming in with our stream of overnight guests.

"It's the Peace Corps way," she kept telling me, explaining that any volunteer's door was always open to another volunteer away from home. I would give that motto some serious thought, but wondered if that could become Richard's way.

## That Next Payday

Congressional approval of the next Peace Corps budget had been delayed, which blocked money from coming over. Peace Corps Morocco would be unable to pay our living allowances if things didn't shape up by the middle of the month. A terrible predicament, I thought: my new toilet seat and I might be left to wander the streets of Rabat in search of a new home.

Becky and I had blown a wad of dirhams furnishing the place, so we were already looking for that next check. We kept our fingers crossed that Washington politics would come to our rescue and the budget battle would be resolved.

After dinner one night, a bunch of volunteers stopped by our place with some wine and sfenjs. We spent the evening talking about the congressional filibuster, our latest challenges and frustrations and our ongoing issues with maids.

Tales of volunteers' problems earning acceptance in their newly adopted towns concerned us. We heard about Larry's girlfriend, Sally. She had rocks thrown at her while she jogged in her small town. Another female volunteer left her house alone near sunset to visit a neighbor and returned to find the word *whore* spray-painted in Arabic across her front door. Those early months were proving extremely stressful for many volunteers, especially the women.

Several in the group mentioned the brutal treatment their clothing suffered at the hands of their maids. Washing clothes by hand in a tub of hot, soapy water and using a stiff brush to scrub everything was a true test of durability. A few volunteers had also experienced stolen garments from their communal rooftop clotheslines.

We had fired Latifa earlier that week because she wouldn't do all the laundry and was a sloppy cleaner. I was glad to get rid of her.

The maid who cleaned the Peace Corps office was referred to us. Raquia was about forty, married and French-speaking. She would come Tuesdays and Fridays. Raquia did an excellent job – even with the laundry. We asked her to prepare lunch for us once in a while, a common request of maids, but she was not the greatest in that department. We paid her 25 dirhams a week for two full mornings of work, right at $6. That was a top rate in Morocco; maids in Rabat made more. In a small town, the same amount might get a maid five days a week who also cooked a daily meal.

Guests would sometimes leave items behind. I held up some underwear left by a recent overnight guest and asked for suggestions on finding the owner. Michelle looked it over and evaluated, "Well, the crotch and elastic are still intact ... obviously, it doesn't belong to anyone with a Moroccan maid!"

We all laughed at our predicament: lowly Peace Corps Volunteers, talking about problems with our maids!

## Another Week, Another Dirham

One unusual day, wind blew constantly in Rabat, stirring around a lot of dust. At the office, I couldn't get much done due to another shortage of materials. I needed more ink cartridges for my pens, and Paul needed more film editing supplies. Returning from our lunch break, I found my drawing board covered in a thin layer of Moroccan crud; we typically left the large windows of our second-floor office wide open. Later that day, it started raining steadily.

The rain ended by the weekend. Our ocean view had never been better – or more blue – than that clear October Sunday. It had become cooler, especially at night. Many of us missed the colorful fall foliage back home. At least it felt like a change of seasons.

The next work week got off to a late start as I aimed for completion of my four animated sequences. Wednesday afternoon, Mr. Jebbor revealed a floor plan of the new office space. Paul and John were disappointed it would not be as roomy as expected; my space would be OK, though.

Thursday, two volunteers from down south arrived to settle some job problems. Rich Eckert (my buddy from the trip to Asilah during training) and Dick from Baltimore were stationed in small towns where the going had been rough in their classrooms. Each was the only volunteer in his town and the only English-speaking resident. They stayed at our place and admitted they were happy to be around anybody who spoke English.

I was glad to see them because they were football fans, and we could talk about the latest college and NFL standings. We poured over the stack of sports clippings I had received with a recent letter from home.

Dick was most worried about his proficiency at teaching English. Kathy and the TEFL coordinator provided him some new classroom methods to try. Dick shared the funniest stories about calling roll in his classes. He said he would start with Mohammed, and a dozen hands would shoot up. He explained he could get the first part right – Mohammed, Ali or Omar – but those second names presented a challenge. The students laughed at his attempts. Another teacher at his school in the same situation, a Frenchman, told his class, "If you ever expect to speak English, you'd better first get used to people mispronouncing your name!"

We went to the American Embassy for lunch at their tiny snack bar. We could get a real cheeseburger with everything on it, on a real Wonder Bread hamburger bun, with a cold Coke or a Budweiser beer – all at super low prices. Rich and Dick savored the all-American meal before returning to their towns.

As a result of recent elections, Morocco was forming its 14th government since its independence, and the newspapers were full of the details. A new Minister of Agriculture was sworn in, too, but we had not yet met him.

Friday, Rabat was rearranged (literally) for a speech by the king before the new parliament. Getting back to work that afternoon proved a real challenge; everybody was out to see the king go from the Royal Palace to the parliament building, barely a quarter mile. Traffic was jammed all over town.

At the office, I enjoyed some satisfaction to end the week and celebrated an accomplishment. I had completed my animation project for the gypsy moth film – earning my 325 dirhams, I figured.

Maura and her roommate Jackie arrived from Ksar el Kebir, and I produced my Moroccan specialty, right out of the Peace Corps cookbook – *kefta* tajine with tomatoes and eggs. It turned out better every time I prepared it. Kefta was Arabic for ground beef. The dish was basically meatballs spiced with cumin and simmered in a tomato sauce with garlic, coriander, minced parsley and onion, with eggs carefully placed on top and slowly cooked while inside the covered tajine pot. Lifting the lid made quite a presentation at the table. The meal required yet another practical lesson in peeling tomatoes. My cooking was gradually improving.

## The Cousin with a Football

I wanted to see more of the countryside and visit some friends. With all the stories (and Arabic) passing through our place, I decided a weekend getaway could be worthwhile. Before they left our apartment, Maura and Jackie pleaded with me to visit them in Ksar el Kebir, an easy bus jaunt to the north.

"You gotta come see us," Maura insisted. "We can show you our school and what life is like for *real* volunteers."

Ksar was a small town, so my appearance would be noticed. Maura and Jackie had prepped the neighbors, their maid and others for my arrival by informing them that "one of their cousins" would be visiting.

When I asked the women if I could bring anything from the big city, they only asked for the football. A Peace Corps staffer who recently departed Morocco left us his football, and it had been the hottest topic of conversation to hit Rabat since the Green March. Virtually nobody around our neighborhood knew what it was. We said football; they thought soccer. We had been having fun with it in recent weeks tossing passes from our fourth-floor kitchen window to volunteers arriving at our building after shouting or whistling to get our attention.

One Saturday, I packed a few things – including the football – and set off on the 8 a.m. souk bus heading north on a route that included a stop in Ksar el Kebir. Always a cultural experience, the bouncing bus was packed with the usual assortment of Moroccan characters. Despite all the loud chatter and music, a few passengers managed to sleep. After a half dozen stops, I arrived in Ksar el Kebir around noon. Maura and Jackie were at the bus stop to welcome their cousin with hugs.

The main road through Ksar was paved, along with a few streets. Maura and Jackie rented a house on a dirt road, a residence recently vacated by some departing Belgian teachers. As in other small towns I had visited, I noticed houses were one continuous chain of buildings melted together. Iron grates covered most ground-floor windows.

Stepping inside to drop off my sleeping bag, the football and other items in a spare room, I could tell the women were well on their way to making the place a comfortable home. Like Robin's house in Kasba Tadla, theirs was dimly lit, with tiled floors and high ceilings.

We returned to the streets, enjoyed some brochettes and tea at a café, then visited their lycée where they both taught. Along the way, we exchanged greetings in Arabic with neighbors and a few teenagers, presumably their students. I attracted a number of curious stares at the red-headed American cousin who'd come to town. When the locals heard Maura and Jackie speaking Arabic, they would ask if I also knew their language. I could only offer *schweeya* (a little) and let my cousin answer any questions, or I might inquire if they spoke French.

Maura wanted me to meet someone. We turned a corner and knocked on the door of Didier Moity, a young Frenchman teaching science at their school. Didier had been recovering from a rather severe case of hepatitis. Maura had assumed the role of medical assistant to nurse him back to health, and they were becoming close friends in the process. In addition to being one handsome Frenchman, smart and congenial, Didier had another notable feature – he owned a car. His English was pretty good too.

"He was out of school for a few days, and I wondered if he was OK," Maura explained. "He was battling a very bad case of the virus ... when I first saw him, he was the same yellow color as our walls!"

Fortunately, Didier was no longer contagious but well on the road to making a full recovery while continuing to rest. He enjoyed seeing friendly faces.

After a while, Maura and Jackie departed to buy fresh bread and supplies for dinner. They also planned to meet a female teacher friend for their weekly visit to the local hammam. I continued my visit with Didier, fascinated by how he ended up in Ksar el Kebir, of all places.

"Military service is compulsory for all men in France," he explained. "You either spend 12 months in barracks or you could apply for a civil service 18-month mission, in line with your education, called a 'cooperation.' Those missions are in Third World countries, most often a former French colony. Being a recent graduate in electronic engineering, I was originally assigned to the air traffic control center at the Tunis airport. A nice and interesting position, I thought at the time. Then, apparently, somebody with connections took that assignment from me, and I was left with the choice to either go to the army for 12 months or teach physics and chemistry in a remote location of Morocco. Thank God for the Tunisian airline passengers, I did not go to Tunis ... and lucky for me – I was off to Ksar el Kebir with my Renault 5."

I could tell his car, a 1972 Renault 5L, was his prized possession; he cared for it meticulously.

"The engine is the same as in the famous 4L model ... you see those in all the old French movies. But the 5L model has some parts made of plastic," he told me. "A month ago, my car broke down on the way to school. I needed a specific part, a camshaft pulley, that was impossible to get anywhere in Morocco. I decided to contact my parents in France to help me out. My mother came up with the plan to bake the part into a big cake and ship it to me as a gift package, hoping it would get through the customs office. To guarantee delivery to me and only me, she baked the cake, topping it with a superb dry pork sausage – no Moroccan would touch that!"

Islamic law forbade Muslims from consuming or even touching anything from a pig.

"I got the part and made the repair," he said, as both of us laughed.

We chatted for another two hours, comparing our impressions of living and working in Morocco. We agreed a hefty dose of patience was required – a vital ingredient for any foreigner's existence.

"You can take me for a ride sometime," I offered as I departed his house, suggesting that he drive down to Rabat with Maura and Jackie sometime and visit our apartment.

I could tell he was attracted to Maura, the all-American girl from Oklahoma. They had obviously been spending a lot of time together; he genuinely appreciated her caring for him during his illness.

By walking back to the main paved road, I got my bearings and found the house where my day had started. Maura and Jackie were busy preparing a chicken tajine with fresh vegetables. I uncorked a bottle of wine, and we all enjoyed the meal with fresh bread.

We spent the evening enjoying two more bottles and comparing notes about the challenges of our first weeks working in Morocco. I recounted Dick's stories about calling the roll, and Maura could relate.

"Same here ... I think half of my students are named Mohammed!" she told me, laughing. "I threw a kid out of one class, thinking he was being a smart-ass, because he told me his name was Ali Baba (a character from the folk tale *Ali Baba and the Forty Thieves*). I shot back, 'And I'm the Queen of England!' Turned out, his name really was Ali Baba."

Maura shared, "We've already had inspections by the staff at the lycée, to see if our students are learning anything ... and then we got graded. During one inspection, I asked a student to deliver a complete sentence. He recited, 'One sunny afternoon, I lay in the park and watched the stars go by.' I'm not kidding!

"I've already tried using music in my class to teach English vocabulary," Maura continued, singing her favorite sample while trying not to laugh:

'Old Mohammed had a farm, E-I-E-I-O.
And on his farm he had a cow, E-I-E-I-O.'

"The younger students really enjoyed making the animal sounds," she explained. "And then I got adventurous with another class, thinking my older students could handle some advanced words. I started the exercise with:

'Zip-A-Dee-Doo-Dah, Zip-A-Dee-Ay,
My, oh my, what a wonderful day ...'

"All of a sudden – like a fire alarm went off – these two girls in my class jumped up and raced out of the classroom. Some boys started laughing; others just sat there with shocked looks on their faces. I stopped the exercise, told everyone to calm down and asked what was wrong. One of my best students seated in the front row came up and whispered in my direction that 'zip' is an Arabic slang term for penis!

"Believe me, we haven't practiced that song again," Maura admitted, laughing harder.

"I can relate to the 'zip' accident," I told her. "During some down time at our ministry office, I was addressing a letter to a relative in Memphis and discovered I was missing the zip code. I hollered over to Becky at her workstation, 'I need a zip code for Memphis. Do you think there is a Zip Code Directory at the Peace Corps office?' Suddenly, I had attracted the attention of every Moroccan in the office, their eyes widening in shock at what they had just heard. The female secretary ran out of the room – I guess to report my unintentional slip. Becky then replied, 'If the office doesn't have a directory, I'm sure you could find any zip code over at the embassy.' We heard scattered protests to our conversation in Arabic. Before I knew it, Jamal, the other graphic artist, was tugging on my arm, wagging his finger at me, trying not to laugh and saying, *'Non, non, non, tu ne peux pas dire ça!'* (No, you can't say that!) 'What's wrong? What did I say?' I asked him. Jamal proceeded to explain to me in his streetwise French what 'zip' means to Muslims. We shared a good laugh. The office settled down, and we got back to work."

"Did Didier tell you about some of his adventures in the classroom?" Maura asked.

"Not really," I said. "He talked a lot about repairing his car and how much he appreciated your help getting him back on his feet."

"Well, so-called 'Professor Moity' has had his days to remember over at the lycée teaching physics and chemistry, I can tell you," Maura declared, feigning his notoriety and intelligence. "One day, we had to evacuate the lycée when they noticed a strange green smoke pouring out of the windows of his chemistry lab. It was scary. After that disaster, whenever he was doing chemistry lessons, the students never sat in the first three rows of his classroom."

We shared more stories before retiring to our sleeping bags for the night. I savored the quiet of the small town. Absent were the horns and traffic noise of Rabat.

The Islamic call to morning prayer woke us. Hot chocolate, some fruit and yogurt got our Sunday morning started.

Jackie stayed in her pajamas to work on her lesson plans for the upcoming week. She was one of many TEFL teachers who brought a portable typewriter to Morocco for typing tests. A mimeograph machine at the lycée was available for making copies – when it was working. Basic supplies, including paper, were at a premium; I heard too many stories of shortages making TEFL jobs more difficult.

Finally, before I left on the noon bus, the football made its appearance. I stepped out in front of Maura and Jackie's house and tossed it around with a few neighborhood kids. I threw a lot of incomplete passes that day in the dusty street. The kids were curious about its shape and the laces. A pair of Moroccans about my age, who spoke some French, joined us and tried to put a few soccer moves on the football, bouncing it on their knees before attempting to drop-kick it out of the dirt. Two merchants from the nearby hanoot stepped outside to watch us.

When our impromptu workout was over, I was sure the gang had stories to tell about the strange ball they played with that day. One of my objectives for making the trip had been to mix with the locals. It proved to be one of those cross-cultural experiences they talked about so much during training. Luckily, I had never learned the French or Arabic word for pigskin.

I collected my things, said my goodbyes and waited for the noon bus. As usual, it was an hour late and already packed with a wild assortment of the culture. Besides passengers of all ages, shapes and sizes, I joined a menagerie of chickens, two goats and one lamb as I claimed my seat in the rear of the bus.

For most of the ride, I dodged the soupy exhaust from a nauseated passenger behind me who had eaten one brochette too many. Fortunately, I had an extra hanky.

## A Trick to Have Treats

I had the travel routine down pat, so two weeks later I left on the last Saturday of October for Beni Mellal, a small agricultural town in the heart of central Morocco. The region was fast becoming my favorite part of the country – rolling hills mixed with flat plains and eventually a nice view of the Middle Atlas Mountains. I had previously visited the area on my homestay trip in July.

The occasion was a big Halloween party hosted by my friend Joe, the mechanic, and his roommate Lou, a TEFL teacher. Joe, part of our Ag group, maintained farm equipment and vehicles at a regional motor pool based in Beni Mellal.

Back home in Massachusetts, Joe worked at a country club fixing golf carts and the greenskeepers' machinery. During lunch in the break room one day, a TV commercial for the Peace Corps had caught his attention. Eager for some adventure and a chance to travel, Joe applied, figuring he could see some of the world and work on engines anywhere he was sent. The slot in Beni Mellal was perfect for him. Joe was the class clown of our group, always smiling through his full beard and ready to help anyone who needed a favor.

Most every Peace Corps Volunteer in the country knew of the party Joe and Lou were hosting. Work schedules, though, permitted only those within easy traveling distance to reach the town. Maura and Jackie had arrived in Rabat from Ksar el Kebir the night before to travel the rest of the trip with me on the direct five-hour bus ride.

Leaving on the 11:30 souk bus, we traveled southeast through scattered farmlands, rugged hill country and flat, rocky open areas. It amazed me how Moroccans still managed to farm in such rocky terrain. They would clear all the rocks from an area, make a border around the plot with the rocks and start plowing. In several locations on that trip we saw a camel and a mule teamed together, pulling a plow. The odd pairing kept plows level on sloping hillsides.

Bumpy roads led us to our one rest stop at Rommani – known to volunteers as a "brochette stop" where a small roadside café sold miniature beef brochettes right off a charcoal grill. We could also experience a Turkish toilet if we really had to go.

Back on the bus, we bounded along through the small agricultural towns of Oued Zem, Boujad and Kasba Tadla before reaching Beni Mellal around 5. We searched for Joe's house; another volunteer who lived there had drawn a crude map for me. Everything on the map was in relation to a Mobil gas station at a traffic light on the main road to Marrakesh. I assumed a town of Beni's modest size would have only one such station. Not so; we found four – all on that road. Our only option was to stay on the main road, ask people around each station if they knew of any Americans living nearby and hope for the best. As we approached the fourth and final possibility, we ran into a group of visiting volunteers who were out to buy food for the party. The house was not far away.

As it turned out, Joe and Lou's house was clear at the other end of town from the bus station. Our light luggage load was getting heavier, and we were thankful to find the place before dark.

Typical of smaller Moroccan neighborhoods, a colorful window grate or decorative door might be the only clue you were at the right address. We were directed to locate a sky-blue door. Jackie had learned from a student that a blue door symbolized the sky and heaven, reminding residents to lead a spiritual life. We knew we'd found the party when we heard excited English banter behind that door.

Entering the house, we met the crowd's cheerful greetings. It was one large reunion. Since many had to travel early the next day, Joe and Lou had started the party early. The kitchen stayed full of people helping to prepare a meal for 35. The large tub of sangria was a popular gathering spot as well. My buddy Mark from Midelt stayed busy uncorking wine bottles in the kitchen. He also lent a hand making the giant pot of chicken and rice.

For living there barely two months, Joe and Lou had their place appearing well-furnished and lived-in with travel posters and woven fabrics on the walls. Joe had even maximized the utility of his Personal Medical Kit, slicing the plastic clamshell case in half and perforating each side to fabricate convenient speaker cabinets for his stereo system, complete with volume controls.

Joe cranked up his cassette of Fleetwood Mac's *Rumours* album, released just before we left the States. While the music played, conversations flowed about how jobs were going, housing arrangements, availability of food and other details. I was reminded once again how civilized life in Rabat really was. Some volunteers were in towns of 3,000 people with no paved streets, few telephones and a tiny shack for a post office. They felt lucky to have electricity and water in their homes. The cost of living in such places was dirt cheap.

I couldn't believe the variety of costumes. Joe looked like a beach bum with his floppy hat, sunglasses, sweatpants and Gonzaga University sweatshirt. Lou kept it simple, wearing his long underwear with a wide brown belt. Stan, my North Carolina friend living in Boujad, arrived as Humphrey Bogart in a trench coat with fedora; Connie dressed as the Statue of Liberty, complete with torch. Melanie was a nun, and Robin arrived in tuxedo and fez (that round red Shriner's hat) and called himself the king. Maura and Jackie donned traditional garb for Moroccan women, including veils. Tinker wore a more formal gown, like those worn for a wedding. Sandy dressed as a gypsy woman. Larry wore a Lone Ranger mask. Steve and Red from Midelt decided to go counter-culture, wearing dresses despite their full beards.

Since I wanted to take plenty of pictures, I dressed up as a typical American tourist – wearing shorts, white knee socks with sandals and a knit shirt, plus my traveling hat and sunglasses. Draped with all my camera equipment, too, others quickly realized the part I portrayed.

When it came time to declare the costume winner, Connie's Statue of Liberty getup took the prize.

During the wee hours of the morning, sleeping bodies in various states of undress were strewn all over the place. Sunday morning arrived too early, and we struggled to get ourselves to the bus station for the 8 a.m. ride back to Rabat. Few people were out so early. East of town, the Middle Atlas Mountains jutted skyward as the sun peeked above them.

The return bus ride took almost six hours due to more frequent and longer stops. Back in Rabat by 2:30, we all needed to recover from a big weekend. I couldn't believe we had seen and done so much in a little over 24 hours! The chance to see so many friends from training had been worth the effort.

### one volunteer remembers...

I have one specific memory about the Inspector from the Ministry of Education, a British English enthusiast who was not pleased with my teaching performance following a Halloween party in Beni Mellal. I was not prepared, and it showed. At some point in our conversation after class, the Inspector asked me, "Are you pissed?" I thought he meant angry. I said no, but I was irritated at that point because earlier, he had written the word *temperature* on the board and lectured me on its proper Oxford pronunciation (tem-per-a-TOOR, as opposed to my American TEM-pra-chur).

> Later, I realized he had meant drunk (I wasn't, but I think my shirt smelled like beer from the party). Our post-teaching conference ended with him chasing me around the desk, shouting, "You're pissed! Confess! Confess!" It's probably the worst memory of my experience in the Peace Corps. Another inspector came by a few weeks later, and I got a passable review that allowed me to stay another year.
>
> Mark Dressman
> TEFL Instructor
> Kasba Tadla

## On to November

November introduced such a cool dampness to the air that, whenever we walked out the door, we felt like it was about to rain. Laundry took days to dry in such weather. Since Raquia had been sick the last two times she was scheduled for our place, Becky and I spent a cozy evening in the bathroom doing our laundry by hand – a real experience ... I was amazed how much dirt came out.

Our clothing was really taking a beating. The new tennis shoes I had bought right before leaving the States were just about gone from all the walking. We had Tide (known in French as *Teed*) and something like Clorox called Javel, but things wore out faster.

Visiting the Peace Corps office two or three times a week to collect our mail, we learned about updates to the roster of volunteers around the country. Randy – the guy who had to leave training because his dental work fell apart – was back and assigned as an English teacher in Meknes. Dick from Boston had solved his tough teaching problems down south when he received news of his mother's failing health and his sister asked him to return home. I hated to see him go.

The first of our Ag group terminated too. Our lone refrigeration expert – Ron, the Ice Box Man, we had tagged him – couldn't handle the language. His French was terrible. He realized it wasn't working out and decided to leave.

Work at the office had become a make-do activity – as in make do with the limited materials we had. A new lineup of projects arrived. I would work next on a segment for a film about irrigation, followed by a fertilizer distribution project involving a film and some slides. Always something going on at our office – if the materials were available to make it happen. My French continued to improve bit by bit.

## Trouble Brewing?

November 6 marked a big national holiday celebrating two years since the Green March, which had primarily been a mass showing of national pride and determination. Diplomatic fighting over the disputed territory (labeled on maps today as Western Sahara) had continued ever since the big event.

More clues appeared to indicate something was rotten in Morocco. A pair of Moroccans in our office – who had been fairly reliable news sources in the past – hinted that a newly appointed bureaucrat hated programs like Peace Corps (Japan, Belgium and other countries had similar programs) and that the politician would work for their dismissal from Morocco. His stance suggested we took jobs away from skilled Moroccans. News of that situation was a combination of rumors and conjecture and failed to concern us.

Then another surprise. Citing recent tensions on the Algerian border and a planned show of force targeting the reclaimed Spanish Sahara, the government commandeered all fuel used for the cars that took us on photo assignments for exclusive military use instead. They even went so far as to take the gas away from the regional agricultural offices that loaned heavy equipment to farmers. For Morocco, that was a drastic measure, I thought. The next four to six months would be interesting.

## Issues on the Homefront

After volunteers completed the annual Cost of Living Survey, rumors spread that we would receive raises around January or February. That would certainly help with expenses. As it was, we seemed to be down to our last dirham every month.

Life in the big city wasn't cheap. To help the food budget, we discovered a merchant in the medina who sold frozen beef and poultry imported from Argentina – good products at cheaper prices. The whole chickens came cleaned and without the heads, feet and feathers you got – and paid for – at other places.

Meanwhile, life in the penthouse had become a little heated. The time came for Becky and me to have some frank discussions about our personal preferences and living situation, including shared finances and all the visitors. Our first conversation started in the bathroom while we were both using the mirror and continued as we sat on the edge of the bathtub.

I could tell that both working and living together was creating friction between us. Many little things began building up, and Becky appeared concerned. Realizing it was time to have another chat, I hinted it was time for a bathroom talk. That's what we started calling our discussions. Sounded bizarre, but if I got her into the bathroom for a talk, I hoped things would return to normal around the apartment. They could only improve.

The next morning, I thought things were going great while shopping for food together. Once back home, though, things got quiet again. I was learning a lot about living with a woman.

I needed a diversion from domestic concerns, so I went to the track with Terry and Shelly who were in town. Horse racing in Morocco was an experience. Horses ran around the track clockwise; no odds were posted until all the betting was in; and you had no idea of the horses' previous records. It was all a lot of guesswork. I lost a quick 10 dirhams on five two-dirham wagers. A light rain all day made conditions even worse. Rabat's track featured a covered grandstand, though.

Chatting with Terry between races, I learned how she ended up in Morocco.

"I heard about the Peace Corps from my housemates during college at Brown," Terry told me. "One had done two tours in Ethiopia in the late '60s, and the other had been in Chad in the early '70s. I studied literature, linguistics and film, where I learned about the Senegalese director Ousmane Sembène. I became fascinated with Senegal and asked to be posted there. The Peace Corps recruiter called me back and asked, 'How about Morocco?' Around the time I left the States, another housemate of mine was posted to Ghana. And two of my classmates also accepted positions – one went to Nepal and another to Gabon. Who knows why! So far, I'm enjoying teaching in Beni Mellal."

## A Special Invitation

I went into work one Saturday morning to finish a project. Officially, the office operated a half day on Saturdays – typically 8:30 to noon. Our Moroccan bosses understood Americans did not normally work on Saturdays, so our appearance was considered optional. I got away by noon.

Driss, our Moroccan lawyer friend, had asked Becky and me over for lunch. A huge lamb and squash tajine awaited us, and we ate all we could. The occasion was to meet his mother and his three sisters – Lina, Rania and Hadifa – who were visiting from Fes. The family provided an interesting one-way conversation – we couldn't understand a word they said or do much with the little bits of Arabic we did know. Driss translated for us. Seated next to his mother, Driss addressed Becky and I with an announcement: coming up in two weeks, we were cordially invited to share the feast of Aid el-Kbir with his family in Fes. We recognized the honor of joining the family for the Moroccan equivalent of Christmas and gladly accepted the invitation.

Later, Driss, Becky and I strolled through Rabat's medina. Driss knew where to shop; he showed us many places I didn't know existed. We didn't buy anything but, more importantly, we learned where to buy. Turned out, Rabat wasn't the best place to buy handmade items since few artisans actually worked there. Fes and Marrakesh were the major centers of handiwork.

## A Picnic Indoors

The upcoming week at the office would be a short one. November 18 marked Morocco's Independence Day, so that was one day off. The day before, we had the morning off so everybody could see the king in a parade through the center of Rabat. Becky and I arrived at the parade route around 10 to wait for a two-second glimpse of the king standing up and waving in the back of a white Cadillac convertible. A few military units marched by, and some fighter jets flew overhead; that was it – not much of a parade, actually.

Many of the English teachers had the entire week off, so some from the rural areas showed up in Rabat for a taste of civilization. Since we had the whole day off, some visiting volunteers joined us for our own Independence Day picnic at our place. We played a five-hour game of Monopoly and two games of Scrabble, loaned from the Peace Corps office library. We enjoyed relaxing in our living room, exchanging stories of our travels and our jobs and processing the latest gossip that permeated the Peace Corps ranks.

Financial issues remained a popular topic. Most of us had dutifully turned in our Cost of Living Survey well ahead of the deadline. Brady from Chicago had a copy of the Peace Corps newsletter, *Axbar Sharia* – meaning Monthly News – and read us the update from Phil Hanson:

"Results of the annual Cost of Living Survey will be tabulated and recommendations submitted to Director Hare on December 9. These results will be transmitted to Peace Corps Washington who must approve an increase if there is to be one. Washington says money is tight. Assuming they approve, a raise might be coming by March 1, 1978. Sorry, this is not a private company with a slush fund that can grant increases immediately. We are part of the U.S. government ... things move slowly due to budget planning and modification."

The newsletter also repeated precautions about heating our living quarters since winter weather was moving in, especially to the inland areas. If they didn't have a wood-burning stove, many volunteers bought heaters fueled by Butagas that required essential ventilation. Others crawled into their sleeping bags by 7 p.m. to keep warm. Fortunately, Rabat weather remained bearable.

I noticed Brenda near the window, sewing a button on one of her shirts, listening to the discussions and not being very talkative. I sat down beside her to check on her handiwork.

"My grandmother taught me to sew when I was in high school. I made a lot of my own clothes. I even made my dress for the prom. I like knitting too. Sewing and knitting fills the time in the evenings when our house is quiet," she told me. "I can knit anywhere. I'll be knitting something while waiting for a bus or at school if my students decide not to come to class ... that happens once in a while, you know."

I was intrigued by the thick white thread she was using. Turned out, she was using dental floss.

"Have you ever tried to break this stuff?" she asked. "It's great when I have to repair something and I want it to last ... another volunteer told me about it. You need the right needle, though."

Other visitors sifted through sports news and assorted clippings I had received in a letter from home. Recent issues of *Time* magazine were also in the pile. The Peace Corps office had just received a large crate of the last three or four issues for free distribution to volunteers – most likely unsold copies recovered from newsstands across Europe. These international editions were thinner than the copies sold on American newsstands, but they became our regular links to what was happening in the world. Every three or four weeks, we would spend two days catching up on a month's worth of news.

More free stuff was stashed at the office for volunteers to pick up when they passed through town. TEFL teachers could retrieve a copy of the Sears, Roebuck & Company Catalog. Pictures in the catalog provided helpful visual aids for teaching English. If teachers wanted to lug the thick volume home, they could slice them up for a variety of lessons.

Resourcefulness became an acquired skill among the TEFL teachers, I learned. All afternoon, the teachers threw out ideas for keeping their students interested in learning. A little creativity went a long way. Patrick used the last tube of Aquafresh toothpaste he had brought from home to introduce the three colors in every squeeze: red, white and aqua blue. His students were amazed to see it come out. When Sherry had only eight students show up one day, she took them to a nearby market and taught them the names for various vegetables and animals.

As we watched the sunset from our rooftop terrace, our picnic wound down. The teachers eventually wandered back to their hotels and left us with no overnight guests for a change.

## A Festive Time

The following week contained two more holidays on Tuesday and Wednesday. Anticipation built for the Muslim feast of Aid el-Kbir. Before traveling to Fes, Becky and I had spent most of the day making date-nut bread. That project involved my first trip to the *ferran,* the neighborhood public oven.

Carrying the prepared pans three blocks down the street, I caught a whiff of fresh bread baking, and that led me through a slender doorway. An orange glow radiating from the oven's opening lit the dark interior. I appreciated the warm refuge from the damp, chilly confines of our apartment.

A trio of Moroccan women – their black and gray veils released to one side since they were not in public view – were waiting for their goods to bake. Flour left from a morning of kneading their loaves dusted the bottom seams of their black and dark brown djellabas. The ferran served as the epicenter for all the latest neighborhood gossip. I decided my appearance – a *Nazrani* (Moroccan term for a Christian) with red hair, carrying my three little pans of date-nut bread mix – surely provided the women something new to discuss.

Like my presence in the cozy space, my sparkling silver, uncharred pans stood out in the crowd. I tried to occupy my time in front of the oven for the required 45 minutes, but the women's constant Arabic chatter and obvious remarks regarding me made the wait impossible. I sat it out at home.

When I returned, the operator immediately pulled my pans from the cooling rack and gave them to me. After paying a small fee, I walked away from the women and their remarks of surprise that our bread had turned out OK. Wrapped in foil for travel, our three loaves of date-nut bread would provide a delicacy Driss' family in Fes had never tried.

The office atmosphere on Monday resembled our Christmas Eve. With the prospect of two days off work, not much substantive work was accomplished. We had been scheduled for my first big day on location as a camera assistant to film a land distribution ceremony in nearby Khimisett, but a light rain had started the night before and canceled our plans.

That rain brought the Moroccan winter and heavy fog with it too. If it had been any other holiday, I would have given away my seat on that bus to Fes. But it was Aid el-Kbir, and our friend Driss had invited us to share the biggest holiday of the year with his family. He had gone to Fes the previous Thursday to purchase the traditional sacrificial sheep and make other preparations. At twenty-four Driss was considered the head of the family; his father had passed away four years earlier. He had a younger brother, Mohammed (every family had at least one of those), his three sisters, plus his mother. Add up all his cousins and other relatives, and his family was large – typical of Moroccan clans.

Travel during that festive period posed a challenge. We had purchased our bus tickets the previous Wednesday and even then found the earlier Monday night bus sold out. That trip was on a Compagnie de Transport Morocaine (CTM) bus, Morocco's nationalized bus system. Like Greyhound, that company ran regular schedules posted at the central terminal – complete with a waiting area and porters to load luggage – and offered advance ticket purchases for reserved seats. The ride was a definite upgrade from a souk bus.

Arriving in Fes with a light rain and 40-degree temperatures, Driss met us at the bus station and drove us to his family's house. We had a late-night snack of soup and dates before turning in. Entering the bathroom to brush my teeth, I received a surprise greeting from a full-grown sheep tied to the bidet! A few handfuls of straw were scattered on the concrete floor, either a snack for the wooly guy or material to absorb some of his excrement. Unfortunately for him, his hours were numbered ... he was due for execution just after 10 the next morning.

We slept late and rose to coffee and cakes – our date-nut bread made its debut. Everybody enjoyed a sample, and plenty remained for later (and larger) family gatherings.

By 10:30, it was time to get things rolling. Driss went outside to hire two professional butchers – teams readily available at the nearest street corner – to prepare the sheep. Rain drizzled in the home's compact courtyard where the sheep would be sacrificed. The scene presented a unique photo opportunity, and I had the ideal vantage point from an adjacent bedroom window.

Absolutely no time was wasted by the two men. The sheep was thrown off its feet and its throat was quickly slashed. It bled all over the courtyard, like a garden hose filled with a thick red liquid. Less than two minutes later, the men removed the head, while Driss' sister Rania used a squeegee to steer puddles of blood into a nearby drain. The speed of the men's work impressed me. One worker cut a small slice of skin from a hind leg. Then, as if the carcass were a balloon, he inflated the sheep! His special cut had enabled him to blow air between the sheep's hide and carcass, simplifying the skinning process. They hung the carcass on the clothesline, then simply peeled away the hide using a small knife. It looked like a set of wooly long underwear coming off of a pinkish torso.

The final step was to remove the entrails and sort them for later preparation by Driss and his sisters. The intestines looked like an endless rope coiled up inside the sheep. The butcher casually coiled them in his hand as if he were a cowboy with his favorite lariat.

Driss paid the two men about $5 each. They left, probably to repeat their routine across the street. The sheep had cost 600 dirhams or about $150, a major expense for the family.

Hadifa, another sister, had received special training as a young girl to prepare the different parts. She divided the main delicacies – heart, stomach, liver, intestines, lungs and testicles – into separate bowls. With containers of boiling water beside her, she washed and cut up the organs. After witnessing the courtyard butchering, I was surprised at the amount of hygiene and cleanliness that prevailed in that stage.

Meanwhile, Driss and his brother were busy with the head. Removing the horns, they split the skull to remove the brains. We would later find them in a tomato-sauce dip served as a spicy condiment next to the main course. The head remained intact and was set aside for preparation the following day.

The two-day feast involved four main meals – two each day. Starting with the internal goodies, everyone dining with the family gradually worked up to the choice meat of the sheep.

I knew Meal Number One would be the real test. The menu featured the heart and stomach of the sheep that had greeted me the previous night. Eight of us sat around a small table while the bite-size chunks were placed on metal skewers and cooked over a charcoal fire right in the living room. Called a *mijmar*, the stone bowl-shaped receptacle contained the white-hot charcoal and supported six to eight skewers across the top. The weather remained very cold (below 40 degrees) but the windows had to stay open due to the smoky charcoal fire, so the meal resembled a wintry cookout.

My preconceived strategy to handle the main course was to eat lots of bread, but I didn't need to worry. The meal was actually pretty good, like other exotic meats I had eaten before – tender medallions of zebra and water buffalo steaks while in Tanzania.

An afternoon trip to the hammam with Driss and Mohammed gave us a chance to recover from the day's initial excitement. Washing with steaming buckets of hot water warmed me up, too.

By a strange coincidence, two clean-cut Americans – a few years older than me – joined us there, pulling off sweatshirts labeled University of Michigan and University of Minnesota. I enjoyed some friendly conversation – all in English, for a change. Originally from Seattle, they were traveling from Sweden, visiting Morocco, before heading back to Canada where they lived. They had many questions about my work in the Peace Corps and asked, "Why did you volunteer?"

"I like the food!" I replied with a chuckle. After relating the cultural adventure of my day, I recognized their reluctance to say much about their backgrounds or why they lived in Canada. My suspicions were piqued. Details built up in my head, and I surmised I was entertaining two bona fide draft dodgers. I felt quite the contrarian in their company. Our interaction turned rather awkward and certainly memorable. I was relieved to part with their company.

Tuesday evening, the large extended family of cousins, aunts, uncles and other relatives arrived to socialize. I witnessed the string of greetings close relatives and good friends shared. It was one "La bes" after another – a fascinating cultural demonstration of the lesson we learned during training. Abdou One had prepared us for that extended greeting practice by teaching us *Kulshi la bes?* It meant "Is everything fine/OK?" and could be used as the question or the response. The phrase became my customary comeback line when people opened with "La bes." It worked at the office, in the shops and restaurants – even with a taxi driver. Many Moroccans thought we actually spoke Darija when we used that phrase. They appeared impressed or even shocked as they asked, "Ah, so you speak Arabic?" We could only offer *"Schweeya l'Arabia"* (a little Arabic) before diverting the conversation to French. It was a valuable icebreaker.

More relatives arrived. The family reunion was a three-ring circus in itself. The TV blared with a soccer game; a wild card game began in one corner; and more clusters of men and women stood in the center of the room to see who could outshout the others (in Arabic, of course). Since women sat on one side of the room and men grouped on the other, Becky and I found seats on separate banquettes to observe all the activity.

Becky had earlier been prepared for the event by Driss' sisters who dressed her in a beautiful floor-length kaftan. Her hands were decorated with traditional henna designs. She blended right in. The sixteen-and-under crowd surrounded me and discussed my background, America and what I thought of Morocco. When I started doodling on some paper with a pencil, one little boy insisted I draw his portrait right there on the spot. I amazed them with how I could draw a simple face starting with the letters b-o-y.

I'll never forget the noise level of those 30 to 40 people. Some left, but others remained for the late-night Meal Number Two of stomach and lungs, prepared in a spicy sauce. I had to take a pass on that one ... not very tasty at all. I occupied myself with a lot of bread and a bit of the gravy. Seventeen people crowded around the same table where eight of us had dined earlier.

Settling back with after-dinner mint tea, we watched an old *Medical Center* on TV, dubbed in French. By 11:30, the crowd cleared out and we were off to bed. What a day! The last of our date-nut bread disappeared during the wild evening. Becky received multiple requests for the recipe.

Wednesday was another full day. Driss and his brother spent nearly two hours carving up the sheep carcass, still hanging on the clothesline. Since it was barely above freezing most of the day, they had no need for refrigeration.

Around 2 in the afternoon, Meal Number Three arrived at the table in a covered dish, unlike the previous two. When the cover came off, the sheep's entire head – minus horns – was laid out like we might present a turkey at Thanksgiving. All family members were excited about the reveal and started tearing off pieces of the furry hide still on the head. Surprisingly, they didn't eat that part ... but, boy, were the lips and cheeks ever good!

Eight people were around the table, but the tongue could only be divided five ways. I was one of the lucky five. Cut up in bite-size chunks, it looked and tasted like a swollen hot dog. The only thing that really bothered me at that meal was having to look at all the teeth sticking out of the main course.

Soon, only the skull remained – along with what looked like two cue balls stuck in the side pockets. I wasn't eager to draw straws to see who got the eyeballs. Driss and his mother scooped them up and devoured them in one quick bite. Was I ever relieved!

Following that meal, Driss suggested we partake in the promenade, a daily activity of urban Moroccan social life (generally between 6 and 8 p.m.) when most everybody in town strolls the main boulevards primarily to see and be seen.

I couldn't believe it: outside of Rabat, I still ran into people I knew (Moroccans, even). We met Moustaffa, who was working in Fes. He had helped me during training, mostly with French technical language. The streets were crowded; I was freezing and wearing everything I had brought. We sat in a café for more than an hour, while I drank coffee and tried to thaw out.

We returned to the house around 8, and more relatives arrived. We watched another soccer match on TV and prepared for the final event – Meal Number Four, a jumbo lamb tajine that contained the best meat. A little surprise was included. I remarked how much I liked the chunky vegetables (I thought) – something like potatoes – included in the tajine. Driss informed me that my choice delight were the testicles from the sheep ... and quickly added that he also liked them very much.

Certainly, those two days included a lot of firsts.

As it turned out, half of Morocco had the same idea we did – taking the 1 a.m. train to Rabat. No reserved seats for trains, unlike the CTM buses, so each station along the way could conceivably fill up the train. I ended up sitting on my luggage in the aisle. We finally got to Rabat around 6:30 and somehow made it to work that day.

Like the day before Aid el-Kbir, the day after the big feast resulted in very little accomplished work. Everybody had stories to tell of their family experiences.

Back in our apartment, every room was chilly – like experiencing one continuous power failure. Winter made a Moroccan out of me. I bought a heavy wool djellaba, the hooded overgarment every Moroccan wore. Mine was strictly for use around the frigid house, though.

### one volunteer remembers...

I got up at 7:30 a.m. on Aid el-Kbir. I had to be at the Cheshire Home at the foot of the Koutoubia Mosque in Marrakesh by 10, the traditional time to kill a sheep for the day's festivities. First, though, the king would kill two sheep on national television, signaling the time to start mass slaughter around the country.

As I was leaving, I ran into the owner of the house where I rented a room. She shook her finger at me and then her head, looking glum. What was wrong? It turned out that yesterday afternoon someone left the door open and the sheep ran away. I thought of inviting her and her family to the Cheshire Home celebration, but it wasn't my place to invite them. There was nothing I could do.

At the Cheshire Home, Dave, a volunteer, put up three tent poles in the courtyard and hung the sheep upside down. Not all Moroccans can kill a sheep. It is a learned skill. Si Moulay, a neighbor, came over with a set of knives and got to work. With blood gushing all over the floor from slitting the sheep's throat, he pulled out the intestines and then blew into its asshole to clean out the interior.

The meal was great. First, there were liver brochettes wrapped in stomach lining served with a salad and fries. In the evening we had a stew made of tripe and lungs with the sheep's head served on a plate. The last part of the meal was eating the sheep's eyeballs. They tasted like liver and, dipped in cumin, they were quite good, but not as good as the wild boar brain jelly I had tried in the Middle Atlas Mountains.

*Mike Kendellen*
*TEFL Instructor*
*Khenifra*

## Turkey Day

Country Director Paul Hare held a Thanksgiving party at his residence. The event was our first opportunity to socialize with Paul. We met Robbie, his Australian wife, and their young son, Emmett. Their two-story home in an upscale neighborhood of Rabat was comfortably furnished.

Through the embassy, Paul had arranged to have four 20-pound turkeys flown in from the States. Ham was also served. We just did not see turkeys over 10 pounds in Morocco … and certainly no ham or bacon.

I pitched in to man the carving station in the dining room. TEFL teacher Brady from Meknes carried one of the turkeys from the kitchen to the table. Impressed with its enormous size, Brady quipped, "Moroccans would have cut up that bird years ago!"

Plates soon overflowed with slices of turkey, mounds of stuffing and mashed potatoes with gravy and an assortment of other vegetable dishes. Volunteers brought several pies and cakes. One counter next to the refrigerator was reserved for the fully stocked bar featuring cold American beer. Ice cubes in our drinks were a holiday treat.

Larry Berube made the trip from Beni Mellal, where he was assigned to manage a surveying crew for the Ministry of Agriculture. In the course of catching up, we compared job situations. Larry had been faced with nothing to do when he arrived at his office.

"Once I got there back in September, the office wasn't providing me with work, and I was just sitting around at my desk all day ... not what I had in mind," Larry recalled. "I talked with my buddy Joe, the mechanic ... he worked next door in the motor pool there. I told him I was bummed out with my 'nothing job' and that I was thinking of asking for a transfer to someplace that could really use me. Joe surprised me by making a phone call to Phil Hanson at the office ... he and Phil had a good relationship. About a week later, I was shocked when Phil appeared at our office and we had a meeting with the provincial supervisor, my boss. As a goodwill gesture, Phil brought with him a couple of boxes and donated to the office about three dozen engineering books. It was like a mini library, a gift to the province's engineering office as an incentive to keep a volunteer – me in particular – busy. No telling where Phil got the books or whether they were in English or French. I just knew my boss was happy to accept them. Sure enough, since Phil's visit, the boss has kept me pretty busy, and I'm officially a happy camper. Sitting around with nothing to do was no fun, believe me. I couldn't thank Joe and Phil enough for salvaging my job there."

I sympathized with Larry, explaining how shortages of art supplies and other materials had been frustrating as I tried to complete assignments during my early days.

About 80 volunteers had made the trip into town for the party – more faces I hadn't seen since training. It was a great get-together. There was more news to exchange, more gossip to absorb from other regions of the country. The network of communication among volunteers in the field never ceased to amaze me.

After a dozen weeks in challenging classrooms, a few TEFL teachers appeared shell-shocked while expressing their determination to stick it out and cope with assorted adversities. For everyone there, the gathering could not have come at a better time. A half dozen of them followed us home to crash – typical.

Meanwhile, some 350 kilometers away, another Thanksgiving celebration was underway, sponsored by TEFL teachers Mark Postnikoff, Steve Long and his roommate David. Some three dozen volunteers at the far end of the country assembled in chilly Midelt. It was a convenient alternative for those unable to travel all the way to Rabat. Mark had been corralling a pair of Moroccan turkeys on his rooftop for a few days in preparation for the rural feast.

"If it snowed and the roads to Midelt were closed, I could start a turkey ranch on my roof," he told me later.

A nearby public oven was kept busy cooking the turkeys, pumpkin custard and date bread. Delivering the birds and baked items back to Steve and David's house was the highlight of what was, for most of them, their first big holiday away from home. With fresh bread, wine and assorted goodies received in care packages from home, a slice of Americana had landed in Midelt.

---

***one volunteer remembers ...***

Our first Thanksgiving in November 1977 when many of us gathered in Midelt ... for most first-year volunteers, it was the first time we had been away from home, college, comfort zones and support networks. Just as the loneliness, the isolation and demands of a "real job" combined to knock us out, we had an opportunity to get together with people going through the same thing. When I got off the bus in Midelt that November day and walked down to Steve and David's place, it was like "Ahhhhh!"

Rich Eckert
*TEFL Instructor*
*Settat*

---

## December Weather, Letters & Life

Rabat weather had turned much cooler and more rainy. The interior of the country was freezing. Snow covered the mountainous areas. (And people thought Morocco was one giant desert!) Coming from Denver, Becky still hoped it would snow on Christmas. She had never experienced a Christmas without snow. She found her Christmas music, so we were all set ... couldn't have Christmas without Mitch Miller and the boys!

My friend Dennis from New Jersey was making plans to leave for good January 1. He couldn't tolerate the persistent problems with his housing, the food and unruly students in Khemmiset any longer. For all of us, the adjustments had been a challenge. For Dennis (as I had expected), they were impossible. Nobody was really surprised.

Other TEFL friends dropped by while schools were out for 10 days to two weeks. Many volunteers, mostly from the small towns, hit the road for a taste of city life in the capital.

My mailbox at the Peace Corps office started collecting Christmas cards. Besides family, I heard from neighbors and former co-workers – people who hadn't written to me previously but wanted to extend their holiday wishes of support. A small desk and a few chairs were scattered near the library at the office, so I took a break to read my cards.

Denise Schickel came in, collected her mail and joined me. I had briefly spoken with her during training. She was the one in our class who had visited Morocco as a tourist after college, becoming interested in Arabic. She had a degree in political science and history from Western Carolina University where she had also studied French. Peace Corps offered the travel opportunity she wanted, and her language experience made Morocco a good fit. Teaching English in Khouribga was her assignment; and, like many others, she admitted that her first year teaching was a challenge.

"When I arrived at Lycée Ibn Abdoune, I was surprised how little interaction I had with the school's administration. When the school year began, I checked in, got my class and room assignments and was basically left on my own. To start with, I had four classes of beginning English – three of them all boys and one all girls – with about 30 students in a class. I have to say, the classes of boys were easier to manage," she explained. "Sometimes, the students would get excited and start talking and laughing. Not knowing how to impose discipline, I would start talking to them in Arabic. We weren't supposed to; all instruction was to be in English – 'audio-lingual,' it was called. The Arabic worked; they would stop talking immediately and look at me, surprised. Normally, the French didn't learn Arabic, and Moroccans were not used to foreigners speaking to them in Arabic. Once I discovered its magical properties, I used Arabic when I needed to control the class or get a point across. The students love it."

I asked her how she was coping with winter weather.

"We don't have heat in the classrooms, so we all just bundle up. So far, it has never been quite freezing, so it's manageable. I can walk to my school from my apartment."

Denise checked out two paperbacks from the library and departed. She was staying at the Hotel Grand across the street from the office, which was popular with visiting volunteers.

One day for lunch, Raquia surprised us and cooked a delicious lamb tajine. Preparing the meal was her special Thank You for the extra money we gave her for Aid el-Kbir – like a Christmas bonus. Our clothing and the whole place had been spotless ever since.

---

**one volunteer remembers ...**

Ed and I finished graduate school at Central Washington University in 1976 and did not know what we wanted to do. My oldest sister had been in the Peace Corps in Honduras. Ed had finished his military service, so Peace Corps seemed like a logical choice. We had the choice of Guam or Morocco, and Ed chose Morocco. Probably not a good choice for a Jew (although raised Catholic). Throughout my entire time in Morocco, they recognized me as Jewish, even though it was never obvious in the United States.

Our jobs in Morocco were different. I was given "Letters" students who had to take three years of English, so they were very motivated to do well. I also had a degree in school administration, so I was assigned that job as well. Ed was given "Science" students who had to take one year of English to graduate, but the grade meant nothing to them.

Our biggest problem was that corporal punishment was expected but not practiced by us ... took a while to get that straightened out. We were both teaching kids (mostly young men) who were 15-17 years old. I had already taught TESL (Teaching English as a Second Language) for two years in a migrant labor town so I had experience working with a different culture.

Trish Henderson
*TEFL Instructor*
*Ben Slimane*

## Some Holiday Cheer

I decided to take a weekend trip to Tangier to visit Aziza and buy a few things that were proving hard to find in Rabat. I left on a Friday afternoon in a light rain and stopped off at Ksar el Kebir to visit Maura and Jackie overnight. A week of rain there had turned the town into wall-to-wall mud.

Since I was traveling with limited clothing, I rolled up my pants legs to avoid soaking them in the mud. A wooden plank led to their front door. Once inside, scraping the caked mud from my shoes was a priority.

We enjoyed a nice, though brief, visit together. We opened a bottle of wine and traded work-related stories while dinner simmered on the stove. Jackie had been busy all afternoon drawing up the English dialogues for exercises they used in their classes. Apparently, for the teachers, pictures really were worth a thousand words.

Maura was convinced anyone who could draw would be a great teacher. She declared, "And Jackie can draw!"

I told them a free Sears catalog loaded with helpful pictures was waiting for them at the Peace Corps office. Jackie was already drawing pictures for the next term since tests had to be prepared far in advance to make certain they could be mimeographed.

"The school calendar is very unofficial here," Maura explained. "I suppose we'll start teaching again whenever the kids decide to come back to class."

The women appreciated my visit and promised to drop by our apartment if they ever made it to Rabat. I reminded them that Didier had a car.

Leaving early Saturday morning, I arrived in Tangier around noon and immediately looked for a particular store that sold all kinds of liquor at rock-bottom (black market) prices. Becky had given me directions and a crude map, but I still had a terrible time finding the place.

I was instructed to wander up to the counter and casually mention to the merchant, *"Je sais"* (I know), indicating I knew about the alcohol stashed beneath the counter to be sold at discount prices only upon request. I secured premium rum and gin at prices below American – not a bad deal. Our bar stock in Rabat was complete. It was nice to have an occasional change from wine, even without ice cubes.

Room rates had dropped at the Hotel Paris since the tourists who packed the streets during the summer were long gone. After washing up, I was off to see Aziza. Her family's large house was not far from my hotel, but the hills of Tangier made good exercise out of any walk.

Over a delicious lunch of chicken, peas, bread and fruit, we enjoyed lively conversation. Even though we had exchanged a few letters, we still found plenty to talk about – mostly of mutual friends and her current teaching job in Tetuoan.

I needed to buy some shoes – my once-new Adidas were shot. When I mentioned my need, Aziza suggested I first look at her brothers' boot shop down the street. Three of her brothers were involved in an import-export business of handmade leather products – mostly footwear. I knew I could get a good deal if they had what I wanted.

After lunch, she escorted me to their shop, which featured upscale merchandise and sky-high prices, and left to do her own shopping. The brothers were most friendly toward me. We settled on a good price for some stylish handmade boots. They even let me pay half then, half later as a friend of the family. I made arrangements to meet one brother later at the Ranch Bar near my hotel.

A big U.S. Navy battleship, the USS *South Carolina,* was in port for the weekend, so American sailors were all over town. With a crowd of them filling the Ranch Bar, combined with the American music playing there, the place reminded me of my old hangouts in Atlanta. Waiting for Aziza's brother (his name was too long to remember), I enjoyed talking to the crew-cut sailors. They were full of questions about the Peace Corps and Morocco. I surprised them by ordering my beer in Arabic.

Once Aziza's brother arrived, we discussed current events and his boot business. He had been in New York, California and Florida only three weeks earlier. It was a fun evening with a successful Moroccan businessman.

Sunday got off to a late start. Leaving the hotel at 10, I picked up a few small items I needed and then found a sidewalk seat at my favorite café. Enjoying my café au lait as I wrote some letters, I could hear four or five languages being spoken by passersby.

During an enjoyable afternoon in her garden, Aziza and I found still more to talk about, including towns visited, adventures with the food and updates on other volunteers in the Ag group.

Another big lunch with tea arrived, and we used more French as the afternoon wore on. The family had to attend a wedding reception later, so I left around 4:30 to catch a late evening bus back to Rabat. Aziza and I became regular pen pals throughout my stay in her country. Ever the teacher, she insisted I write a portion of each letter in French – subject to her review and corrections.

Mr. Goodbar sells me and Becky our lunch: fresh bread, a can of tuna fish and a two-liter bottle of Coke.

Four flights up: the Ocean Hotel on the top floor.

Theatre Days: Producer Becky joins me, the director, before a rehearsal of "Arsenic & Old Lace".

Country Director Paul J. Hare visits me at my drawing table.

Medina merchant: a cooperative subject sells his single product – snails.

Carpet merchants at the souk in Azrou, willing to pay me for a picture with their merchandise.

The impressive Roman ruins at Volubilis.

Mom is intrepid, climbing aboard a camel, while my dad *(below)* meets a snake charmer in Jemaa el-Fnaa, the main square in Marrakesh.

"Miss Lillian" Carter visits the U.S. Embassy in Rabat.

On location in the Mamora Forest near Rabat, under the direction of Marc, the Belgian leader of our department.

The hide is removed from the sacrificial sheep, beginning the annual feast of Aid el-Kbir.

"Marlboro Man" Paul Huntsman surveys bone-dry farmland on the road into Rabat.

On the road near Beni Mellal – a popular photo spot.

## 'Twas the Season

Back in Rabat, Becky had made stockings, and I had bought some lights in Tangier for our little potted pine tree. A package of goodies arrived from home on Christmas Eve. Inside was a world map – we were officially an international household. Mounted on our living room wall, it proved to be quite handy and generated plenty of conversations.

Country Director Hare had invited all those in town over to his house for an elaborate Christmas Eve dinner. He also extended invitations to teachers from the Rabat American School, plus the Marine guards and several embassy staffers.

We dressed up for the occasion and walked across town to Paul's house. Everyone was in a festive mood, and we all enjoyed the generous spread of traditional American food. Once again, the fully stocked bar was a popular gathering spot.

After dinner, holiday tunes played on the stereo. Director Hare danced with Becky, and I danced with Kathy. Many volunteers arrived who we had not seen at the Thanksgiving event. I detected an overall sentiment of happiness (and plenty of good cheer) among those attending – an upbeat crowd with plenty of stories from the field. I was impressed with the creativity of a TEFL teacher from El Kalaa.

"No time left to be homesick around our place," Eric boasted, suggesting it was one adventure after another in the tiny town. "We've been having some fun with our beginning English students. After Aid el-Kbir, we discussed with them the American holidays of Thanksgiving and Halloween. We found a pumpkin in town and had the best time carving it like we did back home. The kids were fascinated. My roommate Jerry plays guitar, so we are working in a few songs in our classes too. When our classes don't overlap, Jerry will come over and play for my kids. We started with 'Row, Row, Row Your Boat.' I'd write the lyrics on the board, and the kids could follow along. I tried introducing them to Mitch Miller and following the bouncing ball routine, but that got a little too complicated for them."

Dave – an athletic guy I had not seen since training – arrived from Marrakesh. He was in our technical group during the stage, learning French. I remembered Dave was often jumping rope at the lycée. We'd see him in the courtyard or up on the third floor of our dorm jumping his rope like he was some prizefighter in training.

He worked in a social services program as a physical therapist at a treatment center for handicapped children and adults. Following our welcome to the party, a few of us admired the colorful scarf he wore around his neck – ideal for the chilly nights.

"Omar makes these. He's one of my patients, about forty-five years old," Dave told us while we felt the smooth knit of multi-colored camel wool. "The money he makes from selling these covers his treatment at our center, plus some extra income for his family. And he makes them with his feet! He lost the use of his hands as a child. He is quite an artisan; isn't this beautiful work?"

Looking at the lighter side of Omar's craftsmanship, Dave quipped, "I would say his scarves were handmade, but they're really 'feet' made."

Dave offered, "I can ask Omar to make one for you. Tell me what colors you like, and I can put him to work. I think he sells them for around 25 or 30 dirhams – might take a few weeks to make."

I found a sheet of paper in the kitchen and listed my color choices for Omar to make three scarves, thinking they might make nice Christmas gifts to send home next year. Two others at the party also handed Dave their orders.

"Still jumping rope?" I had to ask him.

"Every chance I get," he responded, laughing. "It's an easy workout and a great way for me to unwind after working with my patients all day."

Before we parted, Dave mentioned the snow piling up in the mountains near Marrakesh and that ski slopes would be opening soon. He extended an open invitation to visit him.

"Come down to see us and catch a little skiing while you're there – maybe late January or February. You can pick up your scarves then," he suggested.

I was interested to see his town and had heard about the house Dave shared in the medina, near the city's famous square, Jemaa el-Fnaa.

He left us with one bit of travel advice and a laugh: "When you come down, don't take the train. That Crosby, Stills & Nash song 'Marrakesh Express' does not tell the whole story. There's nothing 'express' about it. It's actually the slowest damn train in the country – makes tons of stops out in the middle of nowhere. Take the bus."

By 10 p.m. the party was winding down. Like the Thanksgiving feast, the evening was a fun get-together. Not a single volunteer followed Becky, Kathy and I home for a free place to lay their bodies.

# Holiday Thoughts

Landing on a Sunday, Christmas Day was full of activity – opening gifts, endless cooking (featuring a 6-kilogram turkey baked in the ferran down the street) and the arrival of six guests.

As the end of 1977 neared, I reflected on my personal progress through those first months on the job and my co-ed living situation.

I had finally settled in. The effort of the previous six months was immeasurable, hard to define. A new home, a new language, a whole new world actually – plus the ultimate discovery of what humankind was all about. And I had thought Calculus 207 at Georgia Tech was the hardest concept ever proposed to me! I accepted the whole experience as an experiment – and its parameters were well-defined, though, as I had discovered, subject to change.

Daily life was most interesting. Though we operated on limited funds, Becky and I lived comfortably. We had managed to maintain cordial but separate personal lives, though we shared the same front door. I had learned so much by living with another individual. Becky liked to discuss *everything*. As a result, I found myself becoming more open-minded, and free to express my views on a subject. Rather encouraging, I thought.

At first, work at the office was a struggle due to lack of materials. Once I managed that hurdle, I completed several animated sequences for films, designed an emblem for ministry cars and redesigned both the interior of a ministry grocery store and the cover for the ministry's bimonthly magazine.

Concern over the season of all our American holidays (beginning with Thanksgiving) was relieved by the constant activity we had developed in our overseas life. The transition was successfully made to accept the absence of family and familiar faces and replace them with new ones.

Santa was good to me. I received two sweaters, some socks and a nice desk set for my writing endeavors. I gave Becky an umbrella (she always borrowed mine) and some colorful bloomers. Our neighbor, the history professor, recognized our holiday and gave us a colorful ceramic plate to decorate our table.

As I headed out the door for 7 p.m. Christmas Mass at the Cathedral, my co-worker John requested, "In all seriousness, please say a little prayer for me too." He had seemed content with the approaching end to his two-year service; most likely, he would not extend for a third year.

As of Christmas Day, all I really had to pray for – other than John – was continued good health and a meaningful living situation. Things could not have worked out better for me than they had in the previous two months. New directions, new goals and a somewhat brighter outlook on my job had all appeared. I only hoped I could make the most of new opportunities.

I was inundated with a stack of Christmas mail right after the big day. People sent me all kinds of 1978 calendars. I put one in every room of our place, then started giving them away at work. Our Moroccan co-workers got excited whenever we gave them the smallest things from America. I also gave each of them a small candy cane from my Christmas package, but they just couldn't figure those things out. Their reactions were comical.

I enjoyed all the Christmas mail – more than 20 cards – a real morale booster.

### one volunteer remembers...

Rich Eckert and I were in Taroudant over the first winter break. We had spent Christmas in Ouarzazate with Debbie Beck and John Schroeder and had taken a bus from there to Agadir. We had gone to Taroudant on our way back home and had heard there was a New Year's Eve party in Marrakesh. We decided to take the shortest route to get there, which was over the Tizi-n-Test pass. We took the CTM bus from the hotel at 6 a.m. and expected to be in Marrakesh by noon. But it was raining, and on the way up the mountains, sleet started, then snow. Finally, a few kilometers below the pass, the bus driver stopped at a café that was hanging off the side of the cliff. When he stopped around 8 a.m., the bus slid into a ditch in the snow against the hillside.

We all got off the bus and huddled on the floor of the heatless café without anything to eat or drink until around noon. At that point I got up, went outside and saw that the situation was hopeless because so much more snow had fallen. Finally, around 4 p.m., with the sun starting to go down and the prospect looming of us freezing to death overnight there, Rich and I, a couple of German tourists and a Canadian all looked at each other and decided to see if we couldn't dig the bus out. We did so with our bare hands and a broom that

> the café owner lent us. As the sun set, the driver came out, looked at our work, got in the bus, and then all the passengers helped him push the bus out of the ditch. We got on, rode back to Taroudant and had the best meal of our lives – pot au feu and dijon mustard with some frites on the side – in the CTM hotel restaurant while we watched a review of the year's events on Moroccan television.
>
> Mark Dressman
> *TEFL Instructor*
> *Kasba Tadla*

# 1978 Arrived

Happy New Year. Earth was ready to make another trip around the sun with us aboard – our feet firmly planted on the northwestern tip of the African continent. The Islamic Calendar remained stuck in the year 1398.

The holidays were behind us. What a relief! Three weeks of running a hotel at our place for the vacationing TEFL teachers was winding down … or so I thought.

Often, volunteers from the stage just showed up. Becky knew some of them; I knew some of them. We couldn't possibly know everybody in our class. How did these people find us? It wasn't like we were down the block from the Peace Corps office – we were a good 20-minute walk across town, then a climb up four flights of stairs. Turned out, directions were well-known. Staffers at the Peace Corps office sent some guests, and the gossip chain broadcast directions to our door.

One Tuesday evening – with some invited guests over for dinner, plus our usual three or four traveling friends – I cooked dinner for 10 people, my biggest accomplishment so far in the kitchen. The following evening, sitting down to a quiet meal for two was a real relief. We did enjoy seeing the visitors; some we had not seen since the stage. But it was also nice to watch all the activity around our apartment subside. The entire holiday period had made for an expensive month, so we were stretching our dirhams until the next payday – January 20. It would be close.

Unlike the TEFL teachers, we did not get any extended time off for Christmas from our ministry's office. We had managed an occasional morning or afternoon off.

The early weeks of January produced significant turning points that would impact my assignment. On January 9, Paul Huntsman informed the Peace Corps office that he wanted to terminate his service and return to the United States on January 22. His disappointment with the job (ministry operation, minimal equipment) and a serious female interest back in Idaho were the main reasons for his decision. I tried not to appear overjoyed when he told me, but he realized, too, that his departure would improve my job satisfaction. His decision had been in the works since October when he first expressed frustration with the situation at the office. Productions moved along slowly; the equipment was somewhat makeshift; lab work for films was done in Europe; and long delays were common. I thought Paul had hoped for Morocco's version of Hollywood to be there in Rabat, but it simply did not exist.

### one volunteer remembers...

I was almost totally unprepared for the experience. Two things saved me: 1) I had had some teaching experience, so standing up in front of students and teaching English was very comfortable for me; and 2) I was too dumb to know how completely bad I was at learning languages and navigating a foreign culture. My lack of self-awareness helped me to persist because I just didn't know I was supposed to give up. The first months were hell, but by December when I started to hear about people leaving and I was still there, I realized I was going to make it through at least the first year. That gave me strength, and then gradually, as my language skills did improve, I was able to communicate with students and people in the street, and that was when I realized I might be more competent than I thought or others gave me credit for.

Mark Dressman
*TEFL Instructor*
*Kasba Tadla*

While I was busy drawing pictures at work, our apartment walls remained bare. With back issues of *Time* piled in one corner of our living room for our visitors to peruse, I decided to make a collage using the covers. Taping 30 different covers edge to edge (six across and five high), we wound up with a colorful decoration for our living room. Plus, the montage tracked the international news-making issues and trends of our months since arriving in Morocco.

One of Becky's Moroccan friends struck a deal for a huge poster (in French) from the movie *All the President's Men* for our living room – another colorful addition to our décor. Hanging or mounting anything on our concrete walls was always a challenge, though, and we tried all sorts of tapes and adhesive strips. As it happened, the adhesive tape from our Personal Medical Kits worked best.

Meanwhile, at the office, I officially joined Marc and John on the crew as the assistant cameraman, which meant I got to carry a lot of the equipment. Paul was busy packing and handling paperwork for his imminent departure.

Before we left to shoot some sequences required for a TV spot about fixed prices for potatoes, John alerted me about the temperamental latches on the case holding our extra film magazines. When we loaded up the car, I made sure all latches were securely closed.

We bounced around on muddy rural roads for an hour to reach the location where farmers were planting spuds. Initial filming was going great when John dispatched me to the car to retrieve another loaded magazine of film. As I slid the problem case out of the car, the lid flew open and our last full magazine plopped into a giant mud puddle. The classic rookie mistake, I assured myself. We had to make do with two short rolls of other film. I spent most of that afternoon in the office cleaning the magazine – no serious damage done.

With photo projects at a standstill at her desk, Becky decided to take a week-long trip with Kathy, our temporary boarder. Kathy would be making inspections of TEFL teachers located in the southern part of the country.

As the new year got started, the weather turned much colder. Contrary to my assessment of the prevailing climate, Dan and Ray – two visitors from the frigid inland areas – declared Rabat had sunbathing weather compared to where they came from.

Dan reported, "I got to Rabat and immediately took off two layers of clothing!"

I guess we were lucky after all. The daytime temperature hovered around 40 degrees ... still chilly. Seemed odd seeing your breath in front of you at the dinner table. We drank a lot of hot chocolate.

**two volunteers remember ...**

Our house in Khenifra was of such construction that, after a few days of rain, the walls on the inside were wet. There was no heating except for a small fireplace in the kitchen which did not radiate heat for more than a few feet. We had to prepare our lessons and correct homework within a couple of feet of the fireplace. Elsewhere in the house, our fingers got too cold to hold a pen.

Winter overnights often went down to the freezing point, and obviously there was no TV or internet, so getting a bit high and listening to music was the sole solace from the misery of the damp cold.

The next winter, a French couple who were leaving the country kindly left us their wood stove which we installed in the living room: heaven!

Piotr Kostrzewski<br>
TEFL Instructor<br>
Khenifra

---

That first winter, the temperature in the house was in the 40s.

Piotr was right ... that fireplace in the kitchen was useless. During our second year, we sat on rugs near the stove at night and wrote lesson plans, listening to Piotr's music – Frank Zappa and Patti Smith were favorites – and we played word games.

We had a stairway to the roof that proved useful in the winter when the sun came out. It snowed in Khenifra ... not as much as in Azrou or Midelt, but enough.

The "living room" was the open space in the middle of the apartment, maybe 20 feet by 20 feet, with nicely tiled walls. We had two bedrooms, a kitchen, and a bathroom plus one long room which was impossible to heat so we kept the door closed all winter. I stashed a box of Mars chocolate bars in that room and rationed them all winter, as a personal treat.

I coped with the cold by wearing a jacket and hiking boots indoors at all times. I slept in a down sleeping bag with a Moroccan wool blanket over me. I drank a lot of tea.

> It was cold teaching too. Wind would blow the door open and snow came in through the windows. My students wore only socks and sandals. I rarely wore gloves in the classroom. We had fun with exercises using American music; I taught my students "Forever Young" sung by Joan Baez. I heard about another TEFL teacher using the Eagles' "Hotel California" in their classroom.
>
> Mike Kendellen
> TEFL Instructor
> Khenifra

A bunch of us fought to stay awake one Sunday night to hear Super Bowl XII on the Armed Forces International Radio Network. Kickoff was at 11 p.m. The Dallas Cowboys clobbered the Denver Broncos, 27-10. I won a bet (dinner out) from Becky. During halftime, we heard of Vice President Hubert Humphrey's death. The embassy's flag was lowered the next day.

I finally received a generous shipment of extra clothing sent by my parents. Some comfortable, familiar attire: my favorite green-and-gold-striped rugby shirt, two pairs of corduroy pants, plus more handkerchiefs, socks and other items were stuffed inside a compact vinyl travel bag, then packed into a cardboard box for shipping by boat to Rabat. It took three months for the box to arrive, but it was worth the wait.

Receiving large packages from home was a process. I got a notice from the post office to visit the *Colis Postal,* or postal package station, conveniently located a block from the Peace Corps office. There, I was left to the discretion of three rather grumpy customs agents as to the amount of import duty I might have to pay them before they handed over the goods, following their inspection. I had directed my mother to specifically label the contents as Used Clothing. Once the men got through the layers of tape my dad (the packaging professional) had used to seal the box, they were satisfied I could accept the package with a payment due amounting to barely $2.

My dad had also crammed three issues of my *American Cinematographer* magazine into the box, as my subscription had expired after I left. With nothing better to do, one of the agents carefully paged through them, hoping to find pornography or other objectionable material, I guessed. Not noticing any offensive content, he tucked them back into my box without comment. Mom had added a paperback copy of *The Fanny Farmer Cookbook* to help us in the kitchen.

Becky returned from her trip around southern Morocco, and she was not in a good mood. While stopped during lunch one day, their car was vandalized. Thieves stole her camera and seven bottles of wine.

"Stupid people, they left good stuff – lenses and my down parka," she told me, still very upset, while recapping the details. "I swear, anything that should take an hour to do takes five hours here! I went to the police station to write a report, and they made me wait almost an hour. When I finally met with the officer, he actually told me, 'Come back tomorrow.' It was clear he did not want to deal with a woman. I could just tell he hated women. He started asking me all these questions about my living situation and what I was doing in his country in the first place ... all bullshit. I wrote down what happened and left, totally disgusted. I'll make a claim with the insurance we have and see what happens."

I could relate to the theft experience after losing my boots at the end of the stage.

Earlier that same day, Paul had flown out from Casablanca, having terminated his Peace Corps service. Changes had occurred ever since.

Monday night, Becky took me out to dinner at the place we called The Hole in the Wall – officially El Bahia – to settle our Super Bowl bet. We entered the restaurant through a large opening in the medina wall and chose our usual table on the upper level.

Brahim, our regular waiter, was a cross between Duke Ellington and Andy Devine – a real character. He asked about Becky's mother and taught us a few new Arabic words each time we dined there. Without asking, Brahim brought us the customary Ramadan soup, harira; they had the best in town. He had an idea what we wanted but asked us anyway. Typically, we each ordered the standard Moroccan salad and three or four brochettes – a miniature shish-kabob with meat only.

As usual, the meal was all very good and cost only about $4 for two. Since it was a Monday night, the place was virtually empty. Becky and I had the opportunity to discuss (and possibly resolve) minor points of tension that had grown out of our living situation. Our discussion also covered the changes in the office situation resulting from Paul's departure and how that development would impact my work. More film production work would come my way – great.

Leaving around 8, we paid Brahim (adding a generous tip), and he quickly reviewed our new Arabic words: a more intimate form of *hello*, as in "Hello, good friend" *(spa-CLAIR)*. If we needed a reason for something, we could ask "Why?" *(al-LESH?)*. And our favorite, meaning "nothing, zero" – remember, can't use "zip" – *WAH-loo*. We already knew the word for telling him "Goodbye" – *B'slemma*.

We stopped by the apartment to pick up a few things and left again to visit separate friends in the neighborhood. Her friend was male, mine female. As we left and I locked the door behind us, Becky jokingly remarked – "Now this is what I call an open marriage!" The situation was worth a laugh.

## This Play Could Be the Thing

A set of unforeseen circumstances presented a new project to me: I was given the opportunity to direct the play *Arsenic and Old Lace* for the Very Little Theatre Group of Rabat. I never knew a band of aspiring thespians existed in Rabat, comprised of embassy staffers, American School and Cultural Center faculty, assorted spouses, plus a few Peace Corps Volunteers. Members had chosen the play months ago, but I hadn't known about it. My interest only began when I walked into the Peace Corps office after work one afternoon and a staffer friend, Linda, was typing the script before she made copies.

The planned production had a problem. Linda explained the regular director was too busy with job responsibilities, so the group had an urgent need for a new director. I shared my experience with two previous productions of that play in high school and college. I agreed to direct if somebody else would coordinate the production aspects – set construction, lighting, costumes and props. Folks were available for those duties.

I never thought I would go to Morocco and direct a play! And of all plays, the group had chosen the one with which I was most familiar. My theatrical experiences on stage began in Atlanta with my high school's Senior Play, a fun production of *Arsenic and Old Lace*. Two years later at Georgia Tech, the student theater group, DramaTech, managed another four-performance run. In both productions, I played the role of Dr. Einstein.

Bonus features of the new project were the opportunities for me to meet people and to remain active in my spare time.

Showing up for tryouts over two evenings at an American businessman's posh home, acting hopefuls read for the 14 parts. The group was mostly from the older generation. They were all excited about the new face coming in to direct and were fairly responsive. From my vantage point, it was like handling a cast of players from my parents' bridge group.

With three rehearsals a week, we were shooting for March 9, 10, 11 performance dates at the Rabat American School's auditorium, amply equipped for the show. The group actually had a long history of packing houses for every performance. The whole project struck me as a most interesting challenge. Becky was recruited to help out as producer.

Due to the limited number of men who read for parts, I assumed my former role of Dr. Einstein. I hoped the double-duty arrangement would work out. Production crews were organized, and rehearsals began with a read-through of the entire play. One English-speaking Moroccan, Rachid, had a small part. As with any group of people, the cast contained one know-it-all, Helen, playing a leading role ... I thought she might be a challenge to handle from a directing standpoint. Complicating matters, I cast her husband, Robert, in a key supporting role; and he had a terrible time learning his lines. I was confident, though, that we could construct a reasonable production. Previously unknown to me, Rabat's English-speaking community shared quite an interest in theater.

## Adjustments Were Possible

Meanwhile, we experienced an uptick of overnight guests. I was happy to see my friend Rich Eckert again from his small southern town of Settat. Rich was the only volunteer (and only English-speaking person) in his town. He had come back to Rabat for further assistance with his TEFL teaching situation. He appeared agitated, nervous and upset. The isolation, complicated by his challenges in the classroom, was creating a rather unpleasant Peace Corps experience.

I met Rich for lunch at the Café Renaissance, one of our favorite diners during training, and tried to cheer him up. He recounted how he had first heard about the Peace Corps from a high school friend; the friend's older sister and husband were serving in Afghanistan and loved it. Rich had left South Bend, Indiana, a month after graduating from Notre Dame with a degree in English. He was excited to be in Morocco and only hoped his job situation would improve.

Before returning to Settat to try some new teaching methods suggested to him by the TEFL program coordinator in the office, Rich left us a note on a tiny sheet of paper:

> Dear Rich, Becky & Kathy,
>
> I want to thank you all once again for putting up with me. It came at a time when I needed to be put up with. I don't have any change now, so I will send a mandat to cover meals and extraneous expenses. Thanks again for your company ... hope to see you all soon (in a somewhat more sedate state of mind).
>
> Rich

Two days later, Rich returned to Rabat, admitting further problems and not much optimism for future improvements. Rich was interested in a transfer out of Settat.

Fortunately, he was able to relocate to Rabat and help administer a grant from the U.S. Department of Health and Human Services to support a local clinic for girls with heart disease. The clinic was in a Moroccan Croissant Rouge (Red Cross) facility. His new job entailed some accounting, gathering patient data and filing reports. And he would not be working alone – Rich could work alongside George, a third-year Peace Corps Volunteer we knew in town. Things could not have worked out better for him.

We heard of similar instances where volunteers could shift their assignments and remain focused on completing their two years of service, rather than terminate. Some flexibility among the Peace Corps administration certainly helped matters.

### one volunteer remembers...

Kasba Tadla was a friendly town. Mark Dressman from my class and Robin, a second-year volunteer, were also there. We all lived in small "houses," rather like apartments, built around the same city block with one shared central courtyard. We could go in and out of each other's back doors and share dinner most evenings. There was camaraderie amongst the three of us and Robin's French roommate, plus the frequent socializing with the many volunteers who traveled back and forth from the towns scattered throughout the center of the country.

> The first volunteer in our town, who had been there before Robin came, was greatly loved. So, people liked us and had high expectations. We tried not to disappoint, but I doubt we ever lived up to the glowing memory of that first volunteer.
>
> As an additional service, we taught night classes in English to working people who wanted to try to pass the baccalaureate*. They were very appreciative. Many of our students were boarders from the mountains, since there were few high schools in the Berber villages at the time. Sometimes, we would go home with students on the weekends to stay with their families. There were also several Romanian teachers as well as French cooperants. Life was pretty full between teaching, socializing with volunteers and hanging out with other foreign teachers. None of the three of us had a shower in our little houses, so we went to the hammam every week, whether we needed it or not!
>
> Tinker Goggans<br>TEFL Instructor<br>Kasba Tadla
>
> *Passing 'the Bac" was required for entry into the university. It is based on the French educational system and served as a means of limiting admissions, since the university was publicly funded. The adults we coached, like our students, were hoping to improve their lot in life by obtaining a seat at the university. - TG

## Game Nights

Outside of our jobs, we always had something going on around the apartment. We had been playing a lot of Scrabble with our latest parade of visitors. The English teachers proved to be talented opponents. Popular card games included Canasta, Pinochle and Hearts.

For some game-time variety, I created a Moroccan version of Monopoly I called MOROCCANopoly. Pilfering art supplies from the office, I recreated the same board design of property spaces, changing all the names.

The 22 streets became Moroccan towns. Rabat replaced Park Place; Casablanca filled in for Boardwalk. You landed in a Souk where the four

Railroads would be. The notorious SMD stood in for the Electric Company. A Water Bucket (for flushing) replaced Water Works. The Medina was everyone's suggestion for Jail.

Each player started with 1,000 dirhams. Go was the Peace Corps Office – pass it and collect your living allowance of 200 dirhams. Three spaces each were designated Chance and Community Chest.

Landing on a Chance space, players took a handwritten card and found, among others: the valuable Get Out Of The Medina Free card or payments to make such as, "Your new apartment requires a deposit of 200 dirhams. Pay the Banker." and "A stray dog bit you. Pay the Banker 75 dirhams for rabies shots."

If you hit Community Chest, the top card delivered payment notices such as: "Aid el-Kbir is next week. Pay each player 100 dirhams toward the cost of their sheep." and "Ramadan started today. Pay each player 10 dirhams for their first bowl of harira."

The game was an instant hit; and, with a few bottles of wine uncorked, visitors would play it for hours. Game pieces were trinkets we found around town – a tiny camel, a donkey, a car (grand taxi), a bus and a small locomotive. Nobody wanted to be the donkey.

## Read All About It

Some unfortunate news arrived about our friend Bob, an architect stationed in Ksar es-Souk and a member of our French-learning technical group during training. He had already been pickpocketed, losing his wallet while he waited at a crowded bus station. More recently he had been bitten by a dog and was undergoing the required series of painful rabies shots. People started calling him Bad Luck Bob; daily life was challenging enough in the small towns without experiencing such mishaps.

Ned brought along the latest issue of the monthly volunteer newsletter. The front page noted the publication was looking for more material from volunteers.

"They're starting a new column called 'What's Bugging You?' In 20 words or less, we're supposed to tell about our pet peeve," he told anyone listening. "And here's something we've all experienced: boredom. They want us to share our knowledge of the subject with others for a new column next month, 'How I Beat Boredom' ... I can certainly do that!"

That January newsletter issue also reprinted an article that had appeared in *The Christian Science Monitor* in November. Chris Kenrick, a staff correspondent, wrote the article titled, "The New Face of the Peace Corps." It was an informative recap of what was happening in Washington.

Under President Carter, the senior leadership of ACTION was undergoing a substantial overhaul from the practices of previous administrations. Following years of stressing recruitment of degreed professionals or technically skilled graduates and watching enrollment steadily decline to about one-third its former size, a reactivated push to recruit the B.A. generalist commenced.

Sam Brown was President Carter's choice to head ACTION and reshape the Peace Corps. With a rather colorful background as an antiwar activist and later state treasurer in Colorado, Mr. Brown – the article noted – came to Washington and "... is convinced that the B.A. generalist can help revive the Peace Corps in both numbers and spirit." He criticized the Nixon administration's efforts to stifle the Peace Corps while focusing on recruiting skilled volunteers with advanced degrees – "... folks that were increasingly hard to find and a strategy that avoided many applicants who were dedicated, committed and with a humanitarian spirit, but without a Ph.D."

We learned from the article that Sam Brown was the origin of the latest Peace Corps mantra to address "basic human needs" – the mission introduced to us when we first landed in Rabat. He strongly felt liberal arts graduates would benefit from restructured training programs that better prepared them for their assignments.

Six months after Sam Brown landed at ACTION, a new director of the Peace Corps was appointed. During the Nixon and Ford administrations' efforts to scale down the image of the Peace Corps, the position had been technically vacant for five years. The new director, Carolyn Payton, was a psychologist at Howard University and had worked overseas as a Peace Corps administrator during the 1960s.

Typical of any government agency policy change, the new trained generalist direction that Sam Brown and Carolyn Payton were endorsing had its share of critics. The article concluded: "[Sam Brown and Carolyn Payton] are convinced that their new breed of 'highly trained but not necessarily highly certified' volunteers will be able to make an enormous difference in the poorest communities of the developing world. Equally stressed around Peace Corps headquarters these days is the need for volunteers to learn from their host countries."

The article generated lively discussions among the cross section of volunteers who wandered through our apartment. It was interesting reading about the so-called "new direction" the Peace Corps was heading. Were we part of the new breed? All of us, having arrived in Morocco six months before, thought the operation was functioning as well as could be expected – at times saddled with its fair share of government bureaucracy and red tape. I was certain we all had preconceived ideas about what the experience might be like. Living it was proving to be quite an education in itself.

A farewell message from Paul Huntsman closed the newsletter:

> "Contrary to popular opinion, I have not terminated ... I've simply left Morocco. I'm sorry I couldn't hang around to enjoy more good times with you all. And so it goes ... Happy Trails!"

Below his signature was a P.S. asking us to keep in touch and including his home address in Idaho Falls.

During the week, my younger sister Mary Claire had sent me the full section of comics from their Sunday paper in Jacksonville, Florida. One weekend, John from the office dropped in and started paging through them.

"Now this is Sunday – complete with the funnies!" John said. He was also a big fan of the *TV Guide* crossword puzzles I got in my mail.

In an ideal (Moroccan) world, January should have seen the beginning of the government's second Five-Year Plan – an ambitious scheme covering all aspects of national development. We learned from people at our office and others around town that getting that plan off the ground financially proved impossible. In reality, foreign firms supplying personnel, construction and materials of all kinds to Morocco weren't getting paid. Continued dealings between the two parties (foreign suppliers and the Moroccan government) depended on immediate settlement of all accounts and better arrangements for future transactions. For a time, the standoff was a tangible one – construction projects came to a halt while warehouses at the ports became clogged with materials awaiting final payment.

## Chalk Up Another Month

February shaped up to become a most unusual month. Our life of constant activity continued.

Somewhere, somehow, Becky contracted a skin irritation caused by microscopic bugs. I had no idea where she picked that up. Since I didn't catch it, I knew it wasn't from our reasonably clean living quarters.

For her month-long itch, Becky finally saw Nurse Dolores. Becky's unusual case resulted in a special trip to Kenitra to visit an American doctor. She came home with a load of lotions and orders to disinfect her clothing and bedroom; a sore throat and slight fever complicated her recovery.

Work at our office became fairly active, thanks to more moderate weather. Our latest films for television covered potatoes and sugar beets. Several Moroccans who worked in our office said they saw our spot about potatoes on TV, so it was good to know our efforts were getting noticed.

The flow of productions varied, though. If we had the needed materials, every day was different. We looked forward to a week-long trip photographing cotton plants.

Our Belgian supervisor, Marc, took care of a lot of administrative work and was interesting to work with, plus he spoke English. Between Paul's departure after five months and John leaving in July, our crew was shrinking. No trainees for the Ministry of Agriculture would be arriving in June. I learned Peace Corps might add one or two positions but not until next January.

I looked forward to being in charge of the camera work by summer. John had been a big help in showing me how the total operation worked. A lot of possibilities remained with the job.

Another work week wrapped up. The weekend left time for a few home repairs around the apartment. The frames for our living room banquettes needed attention. To decorate our kitchen, we started a postcard collection – a collage of postcards received from all over the world. In our letters, we encouraged our correspondents to send us a postcard when traveling. Several visiting volunteers contributed their postcards too. Before we knew it, we had over 100 postcards from all over the United States, Europe and parts of Africa taped together for a colorful wallpaper display. It became quite a conversation piece while preparing dinners.

Our friend Driss stopped by, surprising us with our first invitation to a Moroccan wedding. His sister Hadifa would be getting married in early July. It was quite an honor to be invited and we were excited about attending. Before the actual ceremony, the event included a feast to be held in neighboring Salé.

Meanwhile, our theatrical production was shaping up for Opening Night in two weeks. The old folks in the cast and I were getting along. My Dr. Einstein lines were coming back. Much work remained to be done, and I kept telling myself, "The show must go on." At that point, I wasn't sure it was worth the time and energy, but I'd soon find out.

---

**one volunteer remembers...**

In Ben Slimane, our town, there was no electricity most of the time, so cooking was often impossible. On Thursdays, our souk day, there was a man who made the most amazing harira. However, you did not want to look too closely to see what was in it. We would take a big pot down to the souk and buy enough to last us a few days... probably cost us just a few dirhams. We usually had a bowl while there at the souk. All the locals watched us eat, and we seemed to be really good for his business.

Of course, the town also had no running water most of the time. So, to clean the bowls between customers, he just swished the bowls in this murky water and then dished up the next helping. Hmmmm ... my husband Ed went from 230 to 165 pounds. I wonder how. Yes, Ed lost more than 60 pounds and lost his hearing due to severe infections ... his condition resulted in his medical discharge and our return home. We ended up in Vancouver, Washington, since there was an opening teaching middle school, which was my specialty.

*Trish Henderson*
*TEFL Instructor*
*Ben Slimane*

---

We were scheduled to film on location in the coming days. I hoped we wouldn't get rained out.

Noticing a break in the weather on a Tuesday, we packed our equipment and ventured out to an agricultural area about two hours east of Rabat. A German agribusiness company sponsored the production, promoting their experimental seed treatment for growing disease-resistant sugar beets. Two company representatives met us at the site – an assortment of outbuildings where seeds were stored – and explained the type of coverage they were most interested in. One building resembled a greenhouse where young sprouts were started in small pots, then transplanted to the field by a crew of four Moroccans. The translucent ceiling provided plenty of light for us to get shots of the seeds going through the treatment process using a chemical sprayer.

Marc directed our camera placements, collecting the treatment process from various angles. John would slip on his wire-rimmed glasses to peer through the viewfinder and nod his tight-lipped grin to signal a shot was successful. An accomplished cameraman, he always envisioned the best shot, careful not to waste precious film stock with unnecessary takes. When working away from the office, he typically wore a baseball cap sporting the Goodyear logo – he was an ardent fan of auto racing. I carried and adjusted the tripod in various setups, plus kept up with film magazines as we used them.

The Germans appeared satisfied with our teamwork. They were aware of our production about the gypsy moth. While at the location, one of them mentioned an upcoming film festival back in Germany for agricultural films and suggested we enter that production. It was worth considering.

Following our afternoon spent with seeds, we chased the setting sun back to Rabat. It had been a productive day on location.

## The Curtain Rises

A long, rough week launched the month of March as we ironed out all the details involved with the play. For the last week before opening night, Becky and I went straight from work to the school and worked on the set for a while, then I managed the rehearsal. One night, we ran the whole play to the tune of saws and hammers finishing the stairs and the window seat.

"Just pretend it's a noisy audience!" I told the cast. Turned out to be one of our better rehearsals.

Fortunately, the production involved a single set, and John was in charge of building and painting it. For furnishings, a local antique store let us pick out anything we needed. Costumes were fairly easy to come by, though we had to improvise for the three American police uniforms. A few lighting tricks were mastered, and we all chipped in to collect the list of required props.

As the number of rehearsals dwindled, I worried whether certain cast members would learn their lines. I was relieved when we whipped out three acts in under three hours, including stops and prompting, during our all-acts rehearsal. We gelled as a group toward the end.

Finally, we made it to Opening Night. Everything looked ready for a big show on a stage flanked by portraits of President Jimmy Carter and King Hassan II. Some 220 chairs were arranged for the audience. Three performances, and it would all be over. The whole project had been quite an experience.

After the Friday night show (the best performance in my opinion), a short chubby man ran up to Becky and me, shouting, "That was great! Just great! What a show! I have seen this play done five times before, and this was one of the best productions! Great show! You were all just great!"

Shaking my hand, he added, "Oh, by the way, I'm John Duncan, the British Ambassador. My pleasure, really." He was quite funny. He grabbed a broom and helped us sweep up after the audience left. What a sight – Becky and I and the British Ambassador sweeping. Turned out, cast member Shirley Mordin was his personal assistant.

Ambassador Anderson missed our show since he was in New York City. His wife and his Number Two man at the U.S. Embassy, Mr. Moffett, attended our final performance. About 20 volunteers also made it to Rabat that evening. We planned a big Peace Corps/cast party that didn't start until nearly midnight at our place. We had prepared a tub full of sangria using 10 kilos of oranges and put together three giant pizzas at the public oven. People in our building probably thought we were opening a restaurant up there on the fourth floor, so much food was coming in.

Becky went straight to our apartment after the show to crank up the party. As director, I felt obliged to drop by a first-class celebration at our prompter's house – the plush place where we had tryouts. So, we were at opposite ends of town, both going crazy with relief that it was all over. It had been a true test of our relationship, but we retained our sanity.

About 30 people crowded into our apartment. I ran out of gas around 4:30; the good times continued until nearly 6 a.m. Our place was a disaster. The maid came in Monday morning and couldn't believe it ... and that was after we had cleaned up a few hours on Sunday!

Celebrations continued with a 4 p.m. Sunday strike-the-set party. By 6:30, we were at the home of our German makeup lady, Beate Schlueter, for coffee and German cakes. All but one of the cast members showed up to help.

It was a memorable gathering; everybody was all smiles, enjoying friendly conversation. A few of us stayed for a fantastic German dinner. I thought the hosts asked us to stay to practice their English, but they spoke it rather well. Discussions on photography, classical music and art were popular topics around the table. I hoped for more good times ahead with my newfound friends.

We were back home by midnight. Broadway Moroccan-style would be shut down – at least until the next fall. At the time, I couldn't decide whether or not I would become involved with the group again.

## Can't Live Without Me

Our living situation had become strained again – and not because of the play. For the first time, I was considering moving out in June or July. Becky and I had been on divergent trajectories. The regular stream of overnight guests was getting to be a bit overwhelming for me. When it came to household expenses, we argued too much over who was paying for what. Something had to give.

Becky and I no longer seemed to be as compatible as before. Maybe I was looking for more of the quiet life, too, which I thought living elsewhere could provide.

Was I forgetting the Peace Corps Way – that open-door policy Kathy preached when she first joined us? Certainly, if you wanted to combat the loneliness we heard about from volunteers posted in small towns, just get a place in Rabat and enjoy a new set of visitors for dinner three or four nights every week.

We finally sat down for a long talk, resolved a few things and decided a split would cause more logistical problems (setting up separate households) than either of us wanted. Our conclusion was "We're sort of stuck with each other." We agreed to try a few new methods for making the place more pleasant for people of different lifestyles. Working and living together had many drawbacks, obviously, but I thought it could work and was willing to try.

## Second Thoughts, Again

Springtime had come to Morocco. Everything was green; the sky and the ocean were again beautifully blue. A day of showers might sneak in, but then a week or two of perfect weather joined us. The fantastic summer weather I remembered from the past year appeared about to return. I was ready for it.

I was slipping out of another two-week slump in the dulls – not much excitement about anything, especially the Peace Corps life. I didn't know why it hit me at that time. I hadn't felt like that since October when I had considered pulling out altogether; the lack of mail from home didn't help matters.

Out of our class of some 90 trainees, about a dozen had left Morocco. That was considered very good; typically, 30 percent left during their first year. Like most everyone, I had thought about leaving, but my job became more tolerable once materials were made available. I considered what I would have when I finished two years: pride in my accomplishment.

I began to see my position in perspective with what I really wanted to do – what I was capable of doing. I realized the immediate importance of strong self-discipline and confident attitudes. I had already discovered that a pessimist didn't survive in Morocco. Since the play was behind me, I was optimistic things would take a turn for the better.

Meanwhile, Washington transmitted a brief bad-news telegram: no Peace Corps countries would receive living allowance increases. Our Peace Corps office was trying to negotiate a deal for helping Rabat and Casablanca volunteers because those two cities were the most expensive. Becky and I stretched our allowances, but nothing was left over at the end of the month. An increase would help us cope with soaring food prices.

Becky took matters into her own hands, penning a lengthy editorial for the March 15 issue of the newsletter. Her editorial, "I Just Can't Understand," tried to rationalize Washington's actions (or lack of them) in light of rising prices for everything.

"Are they saying: we have greater priorities than the welfare of the volunteers?" she asked. "All volunteers should take personal offense and issue with the terse reply of Washington to our appeal for an increase in the living allowance."

Her editorial, complete with illustrative examples comparing costs in Morocco of ground beef, chicken and eggs with prices in the United States, filled two pages in the newsletter. Her closing remarks urged volunteers to cut it out, sign it and send it to their representatives in Congress or, better yet, to Director Carolyn Payton herself (she included the address). Becky had discovered her newest vocation – activist.

## A Roundtrip Tour

Every quarter, we received an extra check (about $54) for travel expenses. These vacation checks were distributed at the ends of December, March, June and September. Peace Corps staffers encouraged us to roam the countryside, visit other volunteers and fully experience the culture. So, I decided it was time to take a trip.

A Georgia Tech friend, Peter Hampton, arrived from Germany where he was studying. The year before, we had casually discussed getting together on that side of the Atlantic. I never thought we actually would.

I took a week off from work so we could travel around to Beni Mellal for a big St. Patrick's Day celebration. With visits to Meknes, Fes, Azrou, Khenifra and Kasba Tadla, the trip would be a chance for Peter to meet other volunteers and see what the Peace Corps was all about. I was certain the bus travel alone would provide a memorable cultural education for him.

While in Meknes, we made a side trip farther north to a small village – Moulay Idriss. It was a gorgeous blue-sky day. Leaving our bags at a hotel there, we walked a few kilometers out of town to the impressive Roman ruins at Volubilis. I had never seen anything like it.

Surrounded by wheat fields, excavations and restorations had created the most well-preserved Roman ruins in Morocco. Volubilis dated back to the second century A.D. when it was home to some 20,000 residents. It was the most remote city within the Roman Empire; the Romans withdrew in 285 A.D.

Sections of whole buildings still stood. Floors featured intricate tile. It was somewhat eerie walking though the site. Peter and I split up and made solitary strolls through the ruins, a place with the ambience of a cemetery. Visitors were left to absorb Roman vibes and imagine what life was like there all those centuries before.

A few years earlier, Volubilis was a featured location in the movie *Patton*. I walked down the road lined with Roman columns that a Jeep carrying George C. Scott had driven. I took pictures of that most impressive scenery, beautifully set in the late afternoon light that produced some inspiring shadows.

We walked back to our hotel, impressed with our trek through Ancient Times.

A pair of souk bus rides later, we joined about 20 volunteers in Beni Mellal for the party held at Joe and Lou's place. Tales of winter survival and the latest gossip were popular topics. Peter chimed in, adding his impressions of our adopted country, while meeting a diverse assortment of personalities.

The next day, during his lunch break, Joe took us on a tour of Beni Mellal and his garage. When French teachers returned to France, they would let Joe use their cars in exchange for a tune-up or maintenance.

Riding 20 kilometers south, Joe drove us to see the Bin el Ouidane dam – an impressive arch dam on the El Abid River. Completed in 1953, the dam provided hydroelectric power to the surrounding provinces and irrigated nearly 200,000 acres of the Tadla plain – some of the country's most productive farmland. Stopping near the top of the dam to take in the view, we heard the hum of electricity above our heads.

The dam and its surrounding infrastructure stood in stark contrast to the Moroccan farmland we saw from the overlook. Below us was a land of souks, mosques, mint tea and couscous, steeped in centuries-old traditions. French colonization had built many of the roads, that impressive dam and the national networks that kept the country out of the dark.

Peter and I hopped on a late afternoon bus to Kasba Tadla to visit Mark and Tinker and savor a delicious tajine prepared by Zohra. The next morning, we managed to catch the 4:30 bus back to Rabat.

Upon arrival in Rabat, we had time for an afternoon walk around the Tour Hassan and tomb of Mohammed V. Becky informed us that Country Director Paul Hare was hosting a party that evening for a visiting Washington official. I was bushed from a week on the road; but, as Rabat residents, we were expected. Peter got a big thrill out of seeing more of our active social life.

Overall, Peter seemed impressed with the Peace Corps life, both in Rabat and in the towns we visited. He indicated he might be interested in seeing what the Peace Corps had to offer after he graduated.

Peter departed the following day on the 9 a.m. train to Tangier. We had the day off for Easter Monday, one of the few holidays Morocco recognized for Christians. It was optional for us to show up at work. It wasn't hard for me to decide – the tour guide needed a day off.

# Entering the Lap of Luxury

I prepared to house-sit at Paul Hare's residence while he and Robbie ventured off to London for 10 days. I would move in on a Thursday and could not wait. The roomy four-bedroom semi-modern house included a refrigerator, kitchen with normal appliances, a good stock of American supplies bought through the embassy and a nice stereo system. The only catch was I had to feed Zany, their cat. That particular cat required fresh liver every two days. Some pampered cat, I thought.

That most interesting assignment looked like a good deal. I would certainly enjoy the change of scenery. Khadija, their live-in maid/cook, would be on vacation but the 24-hour guardians would still be around. That was a good idea because there were no keys to the house. Strange for Morocco, I thought, but that was the setup. All day and all night, a guardian sat at the front gate and occasionally walked around. The property was not large – simply a tiny backyard and a small front yard with a fountain.

The office was slow that week. We had planned to go all the way to Oujda, near the Algerian border, for a week of filming sugar beets – a follow-up to the German-sponsored pilot program featuring seed treatments. Marc delivered the news that the trip was delayed two weeks because the stars of the film weren't yet sprouting. So, we had to occupy our time with fill-in work.

Back at our apartment, a long, involved talk with Becky stretched past midnight – we reinforced our decision not to split up. More direct communication was suggested as a potential source of more peaceful cohabitation for both of us.

Thursday was move-in day. I went over to my new pad during our lunch break. Paul gave me some final instructions: "Feed the cat. Pay the gardener." He handed me 100 dirhams and added, "Feel free to have a few people over for dinner or maybe a get-together." He left me with a case and a half of Heinekens (my favorite brew) and a big bottle of vodka, plus all the accessories.

That first night in the spacious house was an experience – all those furnished rooms and just me and the cat. Something told me Friday and Saturday nights would be a different story. And they were.

Becky and I had planned a Saturday night dinner party for eight, so Friday evening I intended to take it easy, maybe read a book or a magazine.

By 11:30, the word was out: "Open House at the Hare's!" A flood of Peace Corps people arrived. School vacations meant the TEFL teachers were out – quite a few of them in Rabat. Before I knew it, more than 20 people were greeting me; somebody cranked up the stereo, and the party started.

Becky led the way with the six teachers staying at our apartment in tow. Kathy was back in town and joined the crowd. John arrived with Melanie, his girlfriend visiting from Fkih ben Salah. Sandy came with Carolyn, Brenda and Connie, followed by Robert, Don and David. I quit counting heads. The chummy Brits Mandy and Rory dropped by too.

A bunch of us found our way up to the rooftop terrace, taking in the slight breeze and the full moon over Rabat. Finding a quiet spot, I enjoyed a friendly chat with Sandy, a second-year TEFLer stationed in the tiny dustbowl town of Souk Sebt. She told me all about her serious boyfriend back in Ohio, a volunteer who had finished his two years and left Morocco when we arrived. Sandy made no bones about it – she missed the guy and was lonely.

I tried to lighten up the conversation by recapping the latest Peace Corps newsletter that included results of the recent survey, "What's Bugging You?" Besides missing her boyfriend, maybe Sandy had some ideas along those lines, I thought.

"I remember three responses were: lack of privacy, eating alone and not being around American men," I told her, framing my summary as a clever "did you know?" factoid. She smiled.

We held hands; I gave her a hug; and she surprised me with a most passionate kiss and lengthy embrace. I was taken aback ... damn right, that lady was lonely! We enjoyed our evening on the roof, stargazing and hoping for a shooting star. Honestly, I didn't even care that my stash of Heinekens was probably dwindling that night. Way past midnight, I wondered what the neighbors must have been thinking, hearing the music and excitement that consumed the house.

I started to rest up for Saturday night when the crowd finally left around 3:30 a.m.

Saturday was quite a day. Our planned dinner for eight grew to a banquet for 12, and Becky and I spent the entire day preparing it. She wanted to try a Jell-O salad and dessert to make use of the refrigerator. I was involved with a mass of chicken paprika and enough rice to feed 50 people. Rice and noodles – I could never figure out the right amount to cook. All around, great results; everybody enjoyed it. Making use of the nice silverware and table fixtures gave the meal an extra touch of class.

Finally, Sunday provided me that day of R&R I had wanted. Becky came over to help clean up for a few hours in the afternoon. The volunteers staying at our apartment had departed for their towns that morning. School would start again the next day, so most volunteers would be back at work. I was looking forward to a week of true peace and quiet. I hoped to catch up on my letter writing. Possibly, Becky and I would team up for one or two small dinners that week – for four instead of 12.

Paul and Robbie returned late one evening. We spent a couple of hours exchanging stories of our adventures from the previous 10 days. They saw 11 movies and five plays while in London. And they brought a genuine Panama hat from Harrod's for their favorite house-sitter. Robbie also brought me the issue of *Variety* – the TV & movie trade paper – that covered the Academy Awards; it would take me a week to read it all.

During our time together that evening, Paul and Robbie shared the news that Robbie was pregnant with their second child. Robbie preferred to keep the news low-key, so she asked I not add it to the prolific gossip chain.

By Tuesday, I had moved back across town to resume living a more typical volunteer life. It was a bit of a shock – no carpets, no fancy kitchen and no refrigerator. My stay at Paul's house with their cat Zany did not change my opinion of cats … I still didn't want one.

A fun break in my routine was over.

## We Can Work Another Month

Tear off another month – March simply flew by and April kicked off with good news: Becky had made a full recovery from her skin affliction. In other apartment news, Kathy, our part-time roommate, had departed. She was heading for an administrative position at Peace Corps headquarters in Washington, D.C.

Meanwhile, we were enjoying quite a response to our campaign to collect postcards. A correspondent in San Francisco sent us six from all over California. Cards from Memphis and Daytona Beach arrived too; the collage in the kitchen continued to grow.

One evening, I decided to listen to a little Moroccan radio for a change. From 6 to 8 p.m., American pop music played. They were crazy about Fleetwood Mac and the Eagles. A little James Taylor came through too. And then, it finally happened – the music from *Star Wars* played on Moroccan radio. We had heard it was all over the United States. I was sure the movie wouldn't get to Morocco for some time, though.

Despite an unusual cool spell and some big downpours, we returned to the Mamora Forest to film segments for a project about reforestation. I was chief in charge of the umbrella to cover the camera. We made it through most of the day, sitting out occasional showers in the car. Our last setup of the day was in the middle of the woods, a good 300 yards from the car. The three of us got stuck huddling under the umbrella with our best (and largest) camera during a sudden hailstorm. Finally, we gave up, broke the camera down into three pieces, wrapped them in our clothes and made a run for the car. We all got thoroughly soaked. What a day!

We had a relatively active week at the office. I was busy tackling an editing job on a film about the agricultural school system in Rabat. In the process, I became more familiar with our film operation. In two months, John would complete his service and return to Philadelphia. That would leave only Becky and me to handle all photographic assignments. We would have our hands full.

Out of the blue, I was bumped from our long-awaited trip to Oujda to film sugar beets. Originally, the plan was to send me and Becky by train and John and Marc in the ministry car with all the equipment. The ministry nixed the cost of the train and the car could only take one more person, so John and Becky went with Marc. The bottom line: I would be working solo for a week in the office.

Those days on my own were interesting. Before I left for lunch one day, Mr. Jebbor came in, escorting three men from A.I.D. (the U.S. Agency for International Development). The trio was visiting our office to see how the United States and Morocco were cooperating. I got a kick out of showing off the place, telling them what we did and explaining the equipment we used. The three guys were rather dull, dry G-men – gray suits, too – and could only manage a few stupid Carter jabs when they learned I was from Georgia.

I was pressed to make our operation look impressive while Mr. Jebbor (understanding some English) hovered over my shoulder. My biggest challenge was answering "How many films have been completed in the last year?" I said 18 – the number in production – when, in fact, only three were completed and distributed. After barely 15 minutes, they scooped up their black briefcases and marched out, almost in step.

While he was at my editing console, Mr. Jebbor gave me another date for moving to the new building. "Only two months away," he declared proudly. I would believe that when I saw it. The place was nowhere near completion. We would get a sound studio and a better layout of our production space if we ever did move. Becky would get a darkroom too.

At last, I got around to cleaning my personal camera equipment after the trip with Peter Hampton and found all my batteries either dead or corroded. The full set of replacements I had brought with me were also corroded. Luckily, no equipment damage. That ocean air and dampness ate into everything. I salvaged one good set from my light meter.

Meanwhile, Becky was getting hassled by the insurance company over her claim for the camera she lost while traveling with Kathy down south. Reading the fine print, she discovered the theft was a covered loss if it occurred during a burglary "within your premises" or a robbery – described as the "unlawful taking of property by violence or threat of violence." Becky authored another editorial for the April newsletter, "Insurance: No Assurance," citing the injustice and encouraging volunteers to take a second look at their policies.

"I realize now the policy is virtually worthless. I signed up for it while being bombarded with papers and information in Atlanta," she confessed.

## Do We Have the *TIME?*

Another batch of *Time* magazines arrived at the Peace Corps office, expanding my colorful collection of covers on our living room wall. The collage sparked lively political and environmental discussions among visitors.

Stopping by the office to collect mail one Monday, I learned of three more terminations from our class. A married TEFL couple left after the husband simply quit going to his school to teach. It was common knowledge he hated the assignment and his bossy wife had talked him into coming to Morocco in the first place. He was actually *fired* by the Ministry of Education. I heard he was the first volunteer in Morocco ever to be fired! The other departure was a guy who couldn't seem to do anything right.

"I'll be the first one terminated for ignorance," he was heard telling anyone who would listen to him. After weeks of private tutoring plus our initial training, he could not handle the basics of a foreign language. If you couldn't talk, you couldn't work. He went back to Indiana all shook up about it. He said he would try VISTA but never anything overseas again.

## Off to Iberia

While John and Becky were in Oujda, I decided to play hooky from the office for a few days. I headed for an adventure in Spain. I had heard from many visitors to our apartment how easy it was to get there.

"You can be there overnight, and it costs only $7" was the enticing suggestion to get a break from the Moroccan routine.

I caught the special 11 p.m. CTM bus from Rabat all the way to Ceuta, the Spanish enclave on Morocco's coast facing the Strait of Gibraltar. A long, bouncy seven-hour ride permitted very little sleep. Patches of fog added a veil of mystery to the trip.

Arriving in Ceuta, I walked right on to the 11:30 ferry. I was excited about my 90-minute skip across the Strait of Gibraltar, spanning between the mythical Pillars of Hercules. Legends told of ancient mariners sailing westward across the Mediterranean in search of new worlds. The Pillars of Hercules – the Rock of Gibraltar and the Moroccan coast – signaled the edge of a world many considered flat. Sail past the pillars, and your ship was doomed to fall off the world – into oblivion. Eventually, the ancient Greeks figured out our planet was really a roundish orb.

Our ship, the *Victoria,* was not filled to capacity, and I found ample seating on the top sun deck to relax. The stiff wind up there made wearing my hat impossible, though.

Since land was visible during the entire voyage, I never felt totally at sea. Our approach to the Rock of Gibraltar was interesting. What first appeared on the horizon as a rocky stump became a massive outcropping covered with the full complements of civilization: high-rise hotels, a busy port, a beach and a sizeable commercial district.

Docking at Algeciras with Gibraltar directly across the small bay, the separation between the two seemed hard to comprehend. At that time, Spain did not appreciate the British control of Gibraltar and, for that reason, had closed the mainland's border with that English-speaking possession.

Algeciras was prepared for the wide-ranging stopover trade with many hotels, transit terminals and places to eat. Every third storefront was a travel agent. My lunch experience introduced me to Spain's inexpensive prices and the fact that beer or wine came with just about any meal. A Coca-Cola cost more than a beer. After lunch and a brief walk through town, I left Algeciras for Malaga – a scenic three-hour bus ride up the Costa del Sol.

Billboards. All the way up to Malaga, the highway was lined with billboards – something that did not exist in Morocco. We arrived in

Malaga in the late afternoon, and I found a hotel in the center of town. At dinner, I discovered the epitome of Spanish cuisine: paella. Before calling it a day, I strolled through the main train station and learned I could catch an early morning express to Madrid. Why not? I was working without an itinerary.

The Spanish capital was everything I had heard about – a huge city, complete with subways, traffic jams and massive department stores. I found it surprisingly easy to navigate. The Plaza Mayor and Retiro Park were ideal places to relax, unwind and people-watch while enjoying the pleasant spring weather.

Shopping was a priority. I resupplied my camera batteries and bought new tennis shoes. I treated myself to a nice chess set, thinking we could graduate from Scrabble to a brainier game at our apartment.

I did almost everything in Madrid but see a bullfight. I decided to save the Prado Museum for a later visit. Evenings were spent in movie theaters watching a total of five movies (all in Spanish), including *Star Wars, Close Encounters of the Third Kind* (my favorite) and the Madrid premier of *Saturday Night Fever* – the locals went crazy over the music.

That was quite a trip! The change of scenery boosted my mood. Views from the train heading south generated mental notes of other locales in central Spain I wanted to explore on future visits. Recollections of the trip occupied my mind all the way back to Rabat. Two train rides and a direct CTM bus from Ceuta brought me back to reality, landing once again in the middle of the Arab culture.

## Meeting Friends of the Forest

May 1, 1978: I'd spent 10 months in Morocco; a quick 14 to go. My father's birthday was coming up. May Day – a big Moroccan holiday, something like our Labor Day – meant another day off work.

We had been quite active over the past six weeks, mainly because of the improving weather. Our latest production highlighted an effort to control erosion, fertilizing fast-growing ground cover plants in the forests near Kenitra. Marc had several people lined up to participate, including the local forest ranger and workers.

Early one Thursday morning, we loaded a ministry car with our equipment and left the office, heading northeast. Less than an hour later, our driver pulled over at the edge of the forest where we met Karim, the provincial ranger. Despite the warming weather, he was dressed in a navy blue wool uniform, complete with a pressed shirt and necktie. With his military-style captain's hat, he reminded me of a skycap at the airport back home. Fortunately, he spoke French, but our driver was standing by to handle any Arabic, if needed.

Following brief introductions, we followed Karim in his vehicle to a location along a rutted roadside area where planting ended three weeks earlier and needed to be fertilized. It was a convenient location close to the road. A crew of three Moroccans, wearing jeans and baggy shirts, were tossing handfuls of granulated fertilizer across the soil. After more introductions, Karim asked them to take a break while we set up our equipment and discussed the shots we needed. The overcast sky presented no lighting problems. Once we were ready, Karim directed the trio to move in one direction, fertilizing the ground about 10 yards in front of us. John took the camera to ground level for some closeup shots of the granules landing in the dirt. Becky collected plenty of still photographs. Three passes of their repetitive action and we had what we needed.

The lunch hour was approaching as we packed up our equipment. Karim relayed an invitation from the workers to visit their nearby homes for tea. Driving 10 minutes down a dirt road into a clearing, we came upon a small settlement of concrete buildings with corrugated metal roofs. A crude, barn-like structure for livestock had a thatched roof. As we climbed out of our car, two Berber women and eight excited children surrounded us, amazed to see three Americans and one European visiting their communal habitat. Plenty of Arabic flew around us.

A third woman carrying a silver tea service joined us. Seeing the silverware amid these folks of rather modest means surprised me. The woman placed the tray on the hood of our car and poured us glasses of mint tea. Some fresh bread and small cakes were passed around. We were showered with a generous dose of Moroccan hospitality. Throwing out our one-word Arabic compliments and expressions of gratitude, we were handicapped language-wise from contributing much to that impromptu celebration. Karim and our driver were helpful translators. The visit was a memorable glimpse into rural Moroccan life, plus we remained dry the entire day.

### one volunteer remembers ...

*'If you have much, give of your wealth; if you have little, give of your heart." – Arab proverb*

My work as a Peace Corps Volunteer took me to many small villages in the Atlas mountain region of Morocco where, on a daily basis, I was humbled by the gift of Arab hospitality.

I was a land surveyor working with a Moroccan survey crew on preliminary survey work that would improve the supply of potable water for out-of-the-way places with names that were hard to find on a map ... names like Tanogha and Ait Yakoub-Taftouit.

My Moroccan team and I were invited twice a day into simple mud brick homes where we were served some of the best meals of my life. We sat on carpets that were spread out on dirt floors. The villagers didn't have much, but they gave us their all and then some. In the morning, we were treated to mint tea – the liquor of Moroccan hospitality. In the afternoon, we were served great meals which usually consisted of a tajine piled high in a pyramid shape. But before we ate, we had to wash our hands. This hand-washing ritual involved our host carrying a basin to us and having rose-scented water poured over our hands into the basin. He then supplied a towel for us to dry our hands. Our hosts were typically village elders who humbled themselves to serve us. I had heard about Arab hospitality, but it was a level of openhearted generosity that this Yankee from New Hampshire was unfamiliar with, and it was very humbling to me.

I experienced another level of a traveler receiving courtesy and graciousness which is at the core of Arab hospitality. This originated from a conversation I had with one of my survey crew when we first met. He asked me about my family, which Moroccans are want to do. Upon further questioning, I mentioned that I was a Vietnam veteran. I only said this in passing and thought no more about it; I certainly wasn't bragging. Little did I realize at the time that he would mention this to every host who invited us into their homes, and I was accorded instant respect, which I had no reason to expect. After all, I was from the U.S.A., and they were from a Third World country. But that didn't seem to matter to these village elders. Some of them had served in the French army,

> maybe even Vietnam, but I never asked because it seemed of small importance. All they cared about was that we shared a comradeship in arms, and I was treated with a dignity and respect I seldom received in my own country.
>
> I was exposed to many memorable sights during my Peace Corps service. But the picture that is most indelibly imprinted in my mind was the image of one of my elder hosts abruptly taking the wash basin from one of his sons and gruffly grabbing the towel from him which he ceremoniously slapped over his shoulder as he pushed the son aside. He then proceeded to assert his role as the head of the household to humble himself by helping us wash our hands. It was an example of Arab hospitality that has stayed with me and reminded me of Jesus stooping to wash the feet of others in a ritual act of humility and service.
>
> Larry Berube
> *Surveyor for the Ministry of Agriculture*
> *Beni Mellal*

## The Week for Spring Cleaning

Monday started the week with a full day of shooting in a Rabat biological lab as part of the ever-growing epic gypsy moth film. Tight quarters and harsh lighting made it a challenging day.

Tuesday, I met Bob, the dog-bite victim and architect from Ksar es-Souk, for lunch at the American Embassy – cheeseburgers and a beer. Bob was on his way to meet family arriving the next day in Casablanca. Staying at our place, he was bothered by the steady traffic noise through the night. He admitted that, in his town near the Sahara, he was more accustomed to passing camel trains!

After a dull day at work, I made my way to the main post office to call home Wednesday evening. Letters exchanged well in advance prepared everyone for the trans-Atlantic call. Family members were gathered at my brother Bill's house. It took forever to get the call through.

At the telephone and telegraph station inside the post office, I turned in the number I wanted to call and took a seat along a wall facing a row of phone booths. Operators placed my call and waited for a call back from a U.S. operator to complete the connection – could be 30 minutes ... could be two hours.

I dozed off several times while waiting. Finally, just before midnight, the connection was made; the operator at the desk pointed me to booth number eight. We talked for barely five minutes; though, it was a very good connection. I told my dad a belated Happy Birthday. It was a boost to hear familiar voices in person. My Aunt Kaki, a regular correspondent, was visiting from Memphis, so she got in a few words too.

My taxi driver was not at all sympathetic that I had to wait two hours in that drab post office to speak with my family for five minutes.

I arrived late to work Thursday morning. We drove around the corner and did a few inserts of a government building for another film. We were back in 30 minutes – a rather routine morning on location.

Moroccan students simply quit going to school once the weather turned nice, I had heard, so our summer barrage of visitors began. Visitors just appeared, mostly arriving in the evenings.

Two of our most favored guests were among the latest arrivals – Patty Balch from Azrou and my buddy Mark Postnikoff from Midelt. Patty was on her way to the Casablanca airport to meet her mother. Patty had dyed her hair red for the occasion, ready to shock her mom with a new look along with the obvious cultural jolt.

Mark was happy to report his latest culinary successes. He had arrived in Morocco with a cookbook his mother had given him – how to make all kinds of dishes from scratch. Mark combined corn syrup with maple flavoring and created a reasonable facsimile for maple syrup. He taught his maid Malika how to make pancakes.

"Now, whenever Malika does a great job cleaning my place, I'll tell her 'Let's make pancakes!' and she gets all excited," Mark told me.

Patty and Mark obliged us by vacating our place for the afternoon so we could undertake a big spring-cleaning project. We brought Raquia in for an extra day, and the three of us tore the place apart.

Mopping the smooth concrete floors was a laborious process; our idea of a mop did not exist. Raquia bent over at the waist and, with arms outstretched holding a wet towel, she walked backwards and made wide sweeps of the floors, from the back of a room to the doorway. She would rinse the towel in a tub of water and go to the next room. Once the floor dried, results were impressive.

Our apartment had never been cleaner, and it looked great when we finished a few hours later.

# Keeping Busy

Another week flew by, capped by a stressful Friday. I spent the entire day shooting a complicated animation sequence. In total, my entire day's frame-by-frame patience might have occupied less than a minute in our ever-growing gypsy moth film. We finally made arrangements to shoot the last scene for that project the following week. I was also handed the post-production editing job; it looked like I would be busy for a while.

After a beautiful Saturday, Sunday turned rainy. I was supposed to be in charge of filming a special assignment, though working on a Sunday was rare. The agricultural college was sponsoring an equestrian exhibition and competition, and they had requested our services. The rain cancelled everything, until Marc came by around 3. The weather had cleared up, and he estimated we could still catch the final parts of the event if we hurried.

We grabbed equipment from the office and headed to the location on the edge of town. On our way, I learned the prince of Morocco would be there to hand out awards. The course looked like a steeplechase – a course of 14 jumps on a small field. Some 300 spectators were there, along with the national newsreel crews. Police were everywhere due to the scheduled appearance of the prince.

Early shooting went great. It was my first solo assignment, and I was still getting used to the heavy 16-millimeter camera we used. It weighed close to 20 pounds with its battery and the film magazine fully loaded. My right arm would be sore the next day; John had warned me.

We were able to get surprisingly close to the prince's portable throne – a royal grandstand. The kid did not look at all interested in the horse show; he sat there and looked bored. Suddenly, while the course was being changed for a new class of jumpers, the prince decided he wanted to take a break. The royal honor guard snapped to attention, and all the security guys suddenly looked busy. That was quite a sight!

Distant showers produced a rainbow on the horizon. As the prince returned across the track to his seat an hour later, I collected some choice shots of him walking with the rainbow framed in the background.

Fortunately, despite a camera jam ending our day prematurely, the film was not officially part of any big project. I looked upon it as a practice day for me. The ministry would get a scrapbook record of the event. We called these *actualities* on our production list at the office – an actual event of record. The ministry kept a library of these films.

Four hours after I had left, I was back home. Two more visitors had dropped in; two others had left. When Marc came by earlier, we had been in the middle of a Scrabble game and (miraculously), I was ahead of Becky for once. I had just scored 33 points with G-U-Y when I left the game to one of our visitors to finish for me. Becky won by six points. She remained undefeated by me.

> **one volunteer remembers...**
>
> It was during the spring, a Friday with no school in the afternoon. I took my bike and headed out into the wheat fields and olive groves toward the mountains, coming to a very small settlement right at the base of the mountains, with a mosque and a hanoot. I stopped and went into the hanoot to get a Coke. I guess my Darija was pretty good by then – or at least my accent was – because as I was asking about the Coke, an old man who was all dressed up for services at the nearby mosque approached me. He had on glasses with really thick lenses, and I don't think he could actually see more than my outline.
>
> *'Ouild Hussein!'* he shouted at me, raising his arms. *'Nta Ouild Hussein!'* (Hey, you're Hussein's boy!)
>
> *'Sma-ha-li, Asidi?'* (Excuse me, Sir?) I explained, *'Ana meshi Ouild Hussein. Ana Amerikan."* (I am not Ouild Hussein. I'm an American.)
>
> Before I could finish, he grabbed me and started hugging me, to the absolute hilarity of the other men in the hanoot and the shopkeeper. We all had a good laugh and tried to explain to the man who I really was. I don't know if I ever felt more Moroccan, more fully part of the culture, than at that moment. I glowed for the rest of the day, and the memory has stayed with me ever since.
>
> Mark Dressman<br>TEFL Instructor<br>Kasba Tadla

## Coming Soon: A New Class

Hanging around the Peace Corps office after collecting the mail, I learned a group of 65 trainees would report June 27 for 10 weeks of training. Most of them were English teachers, along with a few engineers. Their preliminary meeting would be in Philadelphia. The Class of 1978 would arrive on two commercial flights, changing planes in Paris.

With our location in Rabat, Becky and I would be busy meeting many of them. We planned to hold two or three basic cooking classes at our apartment as part of the trainees' cross-cultural program. I looked forward to meeting some new faces.

In just 34 days – we were counting – we would inherit a refrigerator from John's house. I couldn't wait – ice cubes for my vodka-tonics. And cold tea and beer!

Coming home from work in the evenings, I never knew who had established camp in our living room during the day. One of our favorite visitors was Marjie, Becky's best friend. She was on her way to Casablanca to catch a flight home for her sister's wedding. Marjie hailed from Boston – two words from her would confirm the fact. Often, the two of us compared accents and shared a few laughs.

The night before she left, we took our homemade pizza to the public oven, and I discovered Marjie walked faster than I did. It was a challenge to keep up with her. Tall and thin with short hair (à la Dorothy Hamill, 1976 Olympic champion figure skater), Marjie was always smiling, upbeat and ready to laugh at her favorite Moroccan misadventures. She was stationed in Midelt, teaching English with Mark and Steve Long. The Peace Corps experience obviously agreed with her.

After seeing her off, Becky and I celebrated another anniversary – 11 months down and a quick 13 to go. The months kept flying by. I had already celebrated, downing three Oreos and a liter of Coke that afternoon, then we enjoyed dinner out at the popular Hole in the Wall.

## On the Job Training

Memorial Day arrived. The Peace Corps office staff enjoyed the official U.S. holiday – just another workday for Moroccan ministry offices.

The nationalized radio-television network, RTM, had been developing some of our color film. The last rolls we took in for processing had days' worth of my animation work on them, and I was eager to see the results. Moroccan bureaucracy crept in again, and the officials at RTM demanded some slip of paper (with the proper stamp and signatures) before they would return our processed film to us.

Marc was angry about the sudden twist in the rules. I had gotten used to it – more bureaucracy to deal with; leave it to somebody to screw up the works. RTM released the film to us a week later. Good results captured on film of my tedious animation efforts.

With June approaching, our summer office hours would become 8 a.m. to noon, then 4 p.m. to 7 p.m., giving us a four-hour lunch break.

That schedule would continue until Ramadan when our routine shifted to working only 9 a.m. to 2 p.m. – Becky and I looked forward to that!

John's departure quickly approached. I had some slipups at work that had not made the upcoming transition all that encouraging. He had been a little wound up about leaving too. I was gradually regaining confidence that everything would work out.

Our film supply was nearly exhausted, and another shipment was not due to arrive until June 20. We were trying to put a few short segments needed for several projects on our last roll. All we had scheduled for the week was to be out locally – filming trees being sprayed with anti-gypsy moth insecticide.

With our large office windows always wide open, we often heard a distant military marching band practicing routines. The Moroccan rendition of "Seventy-Six Trombones" really woke us up one morning. We assumed a royal visit or big parade must be coming up. On a daily basis, we found another cultural experience to appreciate.

## We Sprung Forward

Morocco switched to Daylight Savings Time – and didn't bother to tell us. Becky and I waited as usual for the work bus at 8:10, but it was actually 9:10. We got to the office around 10, new time. One Moroccan co-worker insisted the time had not changed. A pleasant result was daylight lasted until 9 p.m.

The early days of June marked my first weekend adventure to Casablanca. We lived only an hour and a half away, but I'd never gotten around to an extended visit. Faced with the prospect of my only friend there leaving at the end of June, I packed a big lunch bag (I felt like I was going around the corner) and hopped the hourly bus to the big city – and a big city it was. At that time, 10 percent of Morocco's population lived there.

My host was TEFL instructor Lynn – around thirty, and from the heart of New York City. She had modeled for fashion shows and Revlon print media ads; her specialties were her eyes and hands. Her complexion and facial features confirmed her Lebanese heritage. She was a unique beauty who was very nice. I didn't know Lynn until our play in early March. She attended the final performance and raved about it. She had a theater background at NYU and hung out on the theater beat in New York. How she transgressed to the Peace Corps to teach English in Casablanca, I would never understand. She had been living quite well in New York.

Arriving in "Casa" (we never used the "-blanca") around 10:30 and finding her apartment, I nearly got Lynn and a visiting girlfriend out of bed. Lynn came to the door with giant rollers in her hair and a towel wrapped around her, à la Barbra Streisand. Quite a sight! A cassette tape of the *Saturday Night Fever* soundtrack played in the background. The tape had just arrived for sale in Casa the week before.

Lynn's visitor, Marla, was traveling around the country from her TEFL assignment in Taza. Marla spent much of the weekend talking about her Moroccan boyfriend, Hassan, who lived in Rabat. I had met him ... a nice guy. Marla was from an old Italian family, and her folks were not too keen on the prospects of a Moroccan suitor. Marla had recently decided to extend for a third year, and that news really shook up the pasta back home. She had plans to transfer to a new Peace Corps program in Rabat – and to see a lot more of Hassan, no doubt.

By 1 p.m. we were off to the Seaman's Center at the port where all the ships' crew members congregated for imported American food at great prices. I enjoyed the standard burger and fries with a flat Pepsi. No ships were docked at the time (the evening hours were more active), so the place was virtually deserted. We headed for the port.

The docks were guarded like a prison – high walls, lots of barbed wire and few gates. We had to get a pass from the police station to walk in and look around. The effort was worth it; all the mystique and adventure of travel on the high seas appeared in the activity around the docks. I took pictures like crazy. Great photo subjects all around me, I thought. A Russian liner was docked and, we later found out, was heading around the world. The two women did not seem as excited as I was to be walking around cranes, docks, trucks and tugboats, so we headed back into town.

A row of shops pushing Moroccan goods was strategically positioned right outside the port. All merchants thought us to be tourists (my two cameras didn't help), but a subtle flash of the right Arabic identifying us to be expat live-ins immediately slashed prices. Nothing in the way of handcrafts was made in Casa. It was all shipped in – mostly from Marrakesh – and affixed with highly inflated prices. I picked up some small jewelry items just so I could say, "I bought that in Casablanca." Those and six postcards were my total purchases. To be different, I bought a unique whalebone ring made in India.

We prepared dinner at Lynn's place, recapped our marathon trek and discussed the things we missed most while living in Morocco. Marla missed driving her car everywhere; Moroccan taxis were not her favorite mode of transportation. I mentioned missing my daily heaping bowl of cereal with real milk. Lynn missed the trappings of New York City, even though she lived in the largest city in Morocco. She especially missed experiencing live theater. She admitted she occupied her spare time around her apartment humming or singing her favorite show tunes. Then Lynn pulled out her copy of the latest Peace Corps newsletter containing responses to the survey "How I Beat Boredom."

"I'm never bored," Lynn declared. "My students remain interested in learning English, and I lean on a great network of friends here when the going gets a little bumpy; plus, I'm able to enjoy staying healthy. Not much spare time left for me. I got a kick out of reading some of these survey responses."

"I jump rope," signed Anonymous – though every volunteer in the country knew it was Dave in Marrakesh.

"Counting mud puddles" was reported as a seasonal activity.

The editor's choice for the contest winner was a married couple stationed in Guercif who created a numbered listing "101 Uses for the Bidet." Utilitarian ideas included using the bidet as a home for your pet turtle, making it into your own personal wishing well or soaking tired feet while on the head.

Fatigued from the day's hike around town, we hit the sack early.

Sunday, we slept late and headed for Lynn's favorite seafood restaurant, the Restaurant Dolphin, right next to the port. Unbelievable seafood at great prices – all fresh, too. I ate all I could – fried calamari, plus a huge salad Niçoise. Later, we visited Casa's main market right in the center of that busy, modern city. It retained the essence of Morocco. We walked forever, it seemed, and saw most all the sites – big trade buildings, fountains, nice parks, even stores that took Master Charge … one mark of civilization, I thought!

Marla was also headed for Rabat that afternoon, so we acquired tickets for the 5 o'clock bus. I was bushed. Marla wanted to talk family all the way. I inadvertently mentioned my Aunt Kaki's family tree project, tracing the Wallace family; she was full of questions about it. The trip went by fast, though. We were back in Rabat by 7, and I was home a half hour later.

I filled out my six postcards, washed up – and it was lights out by 10. What a weekend! I didn't go far but still saw and did so much.

When I left for Casa, Becky took off to Marrakesh for the annual Folklore Festival. That meant I would live solo on the fourth floor for the remainder of the week.

> **one volunteer remembers ...**
>
> Social life for a single woman in Morocco had its challenges. The town knew everything that happened, and there were the obvious cultural differences. So, I made the choice to basically live like a nun while I was there.
>
> As an American woman, I was viewed as sort of a neutral creature; not exactly like the Moroccan women and certainly not a man. I went home with my students for tea or for dinner. I could have a meal with the family and hang out with the women in the kitchen.
>
> I had one student who was very bright in math and physics. He invited me home to visit his family in another village. We took the bus to his town and then walked to where his family lived, in the country. Their house was rather simple, made of stones. We slept on mats on the floor; something was biting me all night. His mother was so kind and gracious, feeding us some couscous when we arrived and serving bread and coffee in the morning. There was a small stone enclosure for their animals – chickens and a goat – located on the side of the house. We walked around the hillside a little and then returned to take the bus back to El Jedida.
>
> Denise Schickel<br>TEFL Instructor<br>El Jedida

## Who's Paying the Bills?

By some bureaucratic good fortune, we finally received a 150-dirham raise to our monthly living allowance. That was welcome news. More short trips, a few gifts and meals out would be possible.

Supposedly, Morocco paid to the Peace Corps office in Rabat a portion of each volunteer's living allowance check. At one time, the deal was fifty-fifty. But over time, increases in living costs meant higher allowances. Morocco didn't want any part of such increases. The result was that – as Peace Corps periodically granted cost-of-living increases – Morocco's contribution to total volunteer support began to represent less and less of the original fifty-fifty arrangement. With the recent raise, I received 1450 dirhams a month. Sticking to the original agreement,

Morocco contributed only 400 dirhams toward my total allowance. That was the deal: 400 dirhams per volunteer serving Morocco, nothing more. Unfortunately, the government – the Ministry of Foreign Affairs – had failed to make any monthly payments to the Peace Corps office in Rabat since the previous October. Our living allowance had come totally from U.S. funds, due to Morocco's default on the agreement. Hopefully, a complete settlement of back payments would occur soon.

A recent speech by our royal boss, King Hassan II, confirmed earlier hints that his kingdom was falling apart economically. He had abruptly canceled his cherished Five-Year Plan for commercial and economic development and initiated a three-year tighten-the-belt campaign as an emergency measure. We had seen it coming. Construction on our new building had all but stopped, and our office had been strapped for the most basic operating funds since January when the bottom had really fallen out.

Since the new order, operating funds for our film operation had become scarce. We were forced to cut corners and eliminate certain production steps to avoid spending money. A contract for our new sound studio equipment – previously negotiated and approved – had disappeared from ministry records. No telling what would happen next.

## Life Continues

With the apartment emptied of visitors, I found time to start reading a paperback from the Peace Corps library, *The Great Railway Bazaar* by Paul Theroux. Many volunteers had been talking about that travelogue by rail – an epic four-month journey – packed with cultural insights. An admitted slow reader, I was hooked from the opening pages and determined to finish it.

Work at the office became repetitious. I spent more than three days shooting an animated sequence frame-by-frame, only to discover the camera was not functioning properly. The film came back with scattered black and blurred frames in the middle of my colorful segments – I couldn't believe it! I spent more days getting it set up and reshot using a different camera. Those things would happen, I assumed.

I wandered over to John's house one evening to pick up some items he was selling. At garage sale prices, I acquired his electric blanket for the chilly months of November to February (I could easily resell it next year) and his field boots – perfect for filming in muddy potato, cotton and sugar beet fields.

## A Visit to a Small Town

I got up early Saturday morning and walked to the dusty lot where souk buses collected and deposited passengers all day. Roaming through the rows of red and green buses, I found one with Souk Sebt – the terminal point for that particular bus – hand-painted in yellow on the side, amid a long line of Arabic characters and roundtrip departure times. The owner/driver/baggage handler was happy to sell me one ticket for his daily 11:30 run through central Morocco.

Souk Sebt was a tiny village, about 225 kilometers from Rabat. Sandy and three other female volunteers, all English teachers, lived there. I was lucky to have a direct souk bus available, but it would be a long six-hour ride.

Following breakfast back at my apartment, I returned to the bus lot and found one of the last seats available ... on the last row. I knew a very bouncy ride was in store. We pulled out a little before noon. The bus was equipped with the luxury of a cassette tape player, and the driver was constantly changing selections of Arabic music. It seemed his only volume setting was high. The music easily drowned out the engine noise, the screaming babies and scattered shouting matches between passengers. Like in America, popular recording stars and performances entertained the masses. Music was a vital part of life. Weddings, births – all social events – were surrounded by it, and a bus ride was certainly a social event.

I recognized familiar landmarks on that road into central Morocco. Passing through Rommani, we stopped at the small rest station, the classic brochette stop, where drinks and snacks were available. I didn't eat anything. With my seat on the last row of the bus – like bouncing on the end of a diving board for hours – I was aware of what could result. Besides, the person next to me had been vomiting sporadically for the last 30 kilometers. Gradually, the hours and the kilometers started to add up. I thought we would never get through the rugged hill country east of Rabat – very slow going.

Approaching the halfway point, the other passenger next to me (a healthy one) decided he didn't like the music blaring over the speaker system. He casually pulled his own portable tape player from his bag and dropped in his favorite selection. To be sure he could hear his music over that of the bus, he set his machine on extra-high volume. Sitting in the middle of all that, I obtained a strange mixture of Arabic music in a version of stereo.

Luckily, a number of people disembarked at the first town, Oued Zem. As seats emptied, I gained the luxury of a window seat closer to the center of the bus and a smoother ride. I was the sole foreigner on the bus. That distinction earned me extra attention from all the vendors, beggars and peddlers who wandered through the bus at each stop.

After Fkih ben Salah, few people were left on the bus. Souk Sebt, the end of the line, was finally within 20 kilometers. By 5:30, I had arrived and started looking for Sandy's home.

Seven years before, the government of Morocco decided to build a sugar processing plant in the middle of nowhere. To encourage people to live nearby, land was given away for homesteaders; and, thus, the town of Souk Sebt was created. About 3,000 people lived there at that time. During the long, hot summers, it was a dustbowl. In the rainy months of December through March, it became a mud bowl. Only a few main streets were paved.

I stopped at a hanoot and asked about my friends. The town was so small, everybody knew the four Americans. I feared no one there would speak French – only Arabic or the Berber dialects of neighboring mountain people, such as Tamazight or Tashelhit. But the man behind the counter spoke French and gladly dispatched his son to show me where my friends lived. I was very close. A three-minute walk and we were at their door.

Sandy shared a second-floor apartment with another volunteer who happened to be away for the weekend. The four-room place was roomy and rustic but comfortable. The only hitch was that their water supply – available off and on at varying times – came from a spigot at the base of the stairs leading up to their apartment. So, every climb upstairs meant shuttling up another container of water for cooking, washing and flushing. Empties were returned with every trip down the stairs.

A relaxing, somewhat lazy weekend followed: walking around the town, visiting local friends and eating plenty of excellent Moroccan food. Sandy was packing up to leave – she had completed her two years – so I helped with that project. She gave away jars, old books and other items we would classify as attic junk. But the locals receiving it acted as if they had acquired some rare artifact. Sandy handed a worn *Ladies' Home Journal* to a 10-year-old boy who was most impressed with the pictures. A little girl took home an issue of *Better Homes and Gardens*.

That evening, we savored steaming couscous with vegetables that Sandy's downstairs neighbor had delivered – the remains from her large family's meal. Spiced to perfection, leftovers never tasted so good.

After sunset, a veil of darkness and quiet fell over the town. I had experienced the same phenomena in Ksar el Kebir. A distant dog barking might be the only sound from outside – such a contrast from Rabat. Quite relaxing, actually. Also like Ksar, the small windows and limited interior lighting kept the place rather dark, even during daylight hours. At night, electrical service was often rationed in the small towns, so an assortment of candles was kept at the ready.

Sandy and I played a few hands of gin rummy while listening to her favorite Seals and Crofts tape on her battery-powered cassette player before retiring to separate rooms. Reading by candlelight was a challenge; I managed a few more pages of my Theroux paperback. Through her cracked door, I noticed Sandy was writing a letter by the glow of two candles – most likely penning tender thoughts to her boyfriend back in Ohio while the tape played Carole King's "So Far Away," a suitable accompaniment.

On Sunday, we visited two Syrian couples and enjoyed some terrific Lebanese cakes and cookies, served with tea and coffee – sort of a late brunch. Most impressive, interesting people; they also spoke a little English. The husbands had contract jobs to teach Classical Arabic at the school there. Another TEFL volunteer, Erin, joined us. Erin was bummed that Sandy would be leaving soon. She expressed her appreciation for all she had learned about both teaching and Moroccan life from Sandy during her first year in the tiny town. I grabbed my camera and shot a few candids of the two volunteers posing for me under the late morning light; I could tell they were the best of friends. Erin was artistic, spending a lot of her spare time with calligraphy and mastering the minute details of Arabic characters. She was the first volunteer I came across who had successfully written her name in Arabic with help from other teachers at her school, Lycée Sidi Mohamed.

While we visited a neighbor's house, Sandy's maid brought over her specialty – a huge chicken dish called Treet. The maid's Arabic name was shortened to Ruby, so I was told we would enjoy Ruby's Treet while dining outdoors in their courtyard. Delicious and filling – I didn't need to eat anything the rest of the day. I had brought along some Oreos for dessert. What a sight – watching that old Berber woman eat her first Oreo. She seemed to enjoy it. Later, I was told the wrinkled, thin woman who could pass for seventy-five was actually thirty-eight! A rugged life sure put the years on her.

Another Berber woman, a friend of Ruby, arrived with three small children. I noticed the kids were well-dressed, faces scrubbed, hair combed and apparently ready for some special occasion. Turned out, the special occasion was me. Like everyone else in town, that woman knew about the red-headed American visitor ... and his camera. She arranged the children along the chain-link fence in the small courtyard. As they stood at attention, smiling on their mother's cue, I collected a few memorable portraits of our HCN's younger generation.

Sunday night, we sat on the rooftop and stared at the Milky Way arching across the clear, moonless sky. You couldn't see stars like that with Rabat's lights – quite a treat for me. Sandy was not overly excited about something she had seen nightly for the last two years. We shared a bottle of wine and enjoyed the twilight, exchanging stories of what we thought our respective futures might hold. Where would we be in, say, five or 10 years? Sandy hoped to be happily married, starting a family and continuing to teach someplace. I anticipated employment involving any version of photography, willing to relocate just about anywhere. It was fun forecasting our futures.

In order to experience all of Sunday in Souk Sebt, I had decided to take Monday's 4:30 a.m. direct bus back to Rabat. John had been visiting Melanie in nearby Fkih ben Salah, so he hopped on our bus there. Surprisingly, it was full by the time we reached Oued Zem. We got a little sleep. Making a stop on the outskirts of Rabat, we hopped off and took a taxi to our office. We were at work by 10. Another long, adventurous and interesting weekend was committed to memory.

Recapping my weekend for Becky, I was glad I made the effort to see that side of Moroccan (and volunteer) life. It was quite different from what we experienced in Rabat.

John's last day at the office soon arrived. Becky made a cake, and we enjoyed a makeshift celebration with other co-workers. The following week, I would become the sole cinematographer in the office. I was looking forward to my promotion.

## Another Busy Week

Dozens of Peace Corps folks gathered at John's place for his going-away party. We had eight people staying at our place. Once again, I felt like the desk clerk at a popular hotel.

A few evenings later, Becky and I hosted our official last supper for John. Three others came along – dinner for six at our place. John announced he was off to the Grand Prix circuit in Europe before making his way back to the States. He was excited about that. All the celebrating was apparently catching up with him – he later fell asleep at the table.

The next day, we produced another big dinner for the Hares and their Australian visitor to experience a sampling of the Peace Corps life. House guests and Marine Staff Sergeant Landry, who had enjoyed a recent birthday, added to the total.

For after-dinner entertainment, Staff Sergeant Landry, athletically slim with muscles in all the right places, announced he could better the total of all sit-ups and push-ups from everyone else in the apartment. Most everybody – even Paul's Australian guest – did their duty. After a heavy meal of beef stroganoff, I managed 14 push-ups. We collected a total of 200. Our bold Marine took the floor and whipped off 200 reps as if he were warming up. No problem for him to top our combined total. A different kind of evening, certainly memorable.

After our guests departed, I stayed up late finishing a Rabat city map for the new trainees who would arrive in a few days.

Friday evening meant a meeting of the Rabat welcoming committee for the new trainees. I planned to help with medina tours and late afternoon trips to the hammam for the guys. Becky and I scheduled a pair of Friday evenings for basic cooking classes at our apartment. Locations preferred for homestay visits were discussed, and we created a master list of where 65 trainees would be heading on their first exposure to travel in Morocco.

I was home by 11:30 and sound asleep in seconds. What a week! Becky and I considered alternatives to avoid that hectic routine from happening again. Two big dinners back-to-back were the killers. In the future, we would try to space out large social events at our place.

# PART THREE

A Changing of
the Guard

## The Class of 1978 Arrives

The week arrived for the annual changeover – new trainees landed, while others finished their service and departed. Lots of people would be passing through Rabat.

Through most of June, I had waited eagerly for some new faces to show up and to observe how we must have looked the year before. The preliminary info was interesting – average age was a young twenty-two to twenty-three. Representation from the state of Georgia would be growing, too, with the arrival of Louis, a recent Georgia Tech graduate (a civil engineer) from suburban Atlanta, and Debbie, a TEFL trainee from the northern part of the state.

For training, they would be using the same girls' boarding school we did. It was interesting to see their reactions to their initial encounters with Morocco. Returning to Rabat with the first busload, I casually pointed out the medina wall, and half the bus lunged for a view out the left side windows. They got terribly excited over a tall, thick wall. Wait until Aid el-Kbir, I thought; that event would shake them up.

I returned Monday night to get the second batch of trainees – a late night at the airport and a two-hour ride with the new group back to Rabat. The ones who were not half asleep peppered me with all kinds of questions about life in an Arab culture – the food, best places to live, even the weather. A few of the women expressed safety concerns. One guy was disappointed he would not be permitted to drive.

The highlight of our week was using our newly acquired refrigerator! We were living in high style – cold beer and wine, ice cubes and the ability to keep leftovers were all possible. Along with the refrigerator, we acquired other Peace Corps hand-me-downs from John: a living room rug, a massive cutting board and – of all things – an ice-cream maker. Our home entertainment center grew, too, with two new speakers and a slide projector. We enjoyed looking through our stockpile of slides. Our white walls made convenient projection screens.

Our maid, Raquia, came in one day to find the refrigerator and rug. We were just waiting for her to hit us up for a raise.

Meanwhile, work at the office was slogging along. I endured a challenging on-location filming job at the Royal Stables where ministry workers were spraying trees against the gypsy moth. That film was shaping up to become a Moroccan version of *Gone with the Wind*. I honestly thought we had finished the film weeks earlier. Marc and I worked well together, and he was receptive to my ideas. Next on our production list was more editing work. Like the remaining calendar days of June, our film supply was nearly exhausted. Our long-awaited resupply of film stock was due to arrive any day.

> **one volunteer remembers...**
>
> During the vacations, I would travel around Morocco on the bus. I loved going through the mountains, seeing the beautiful desert landscape and the brilliant sunsets – the shades of red, orange and purple. The quiet of the desert at night is profound. I felt safe there. My knowledge of Arabic was a tremendous help. Many times, Moroccans would speak to me in French because they knew I was a foreigner. But I would answer them in Arabic and tell them I did not speak French ... I was an American and spoke English. They were surprised and had a positive response to me. I did this in order to develop rapport, and it helped me feel safe there.
>
> Denise Schickel
> *TEFL Instructor*
> *El Jedida*

## The Wedding Celebration

As a foreigner, to be invited to a Moroccan wedding was quite an honor. Becky and I had waited six months for the event. Our friend Driss was in charge of an elaborate production. Becky and I showed up at his cousin's house around the corner from our apartment and waited for a ride to the big feast that preceded the traditional ceremony. The activity in the house was fascinating – relatives in and out, sisters of the bride loading cars with suitcases full of the many wardrobe changes that would occur during the main events and kids trying to stay out of the way. We waited in a salon next to the front door – an excellent vantage point. So much was loaded into cars, it looked like a family was moving out of the place.

Finally, we got into a relative's car and headed for the groom's family home across the river in suburban Salé. We arrived to find the place packed with people. Three large rooms were being used to serve everybody. Each room had four round tables and around each were crowded 12 to 15 people.

Becky and I were lucky to arrive when rooms were being completely emptied and set up for a fresh platoon of guests. One room was for women only. The color was unbelievable – vibrant reds, bright yellows and golds. There seemed to be a contest to see how well the women could outdress one another – lots of heavy gold jewelry too. The appearance of the two Americans drew a lot of stares and some smiles; many tried to impress us with scraps of long-forgotten English. One well-dressed man addressed me with a very cordial, well-meaning "Good morning. How are you?" even though it was past 8 p.m.

We got reacquainted with some friends of the family we had met during our Aid el-Kbir experience in Fes the previous November. A few folks remembered our names.

The scene would put Morrison's Cafeteria to shame. People shoulder-to-shoulder squeezed around tiny tables, seated on thick cushions on the floor. Think of a table the diameter of an average card table. Ours was set for 12; Moroccans liked cozy settings.

A team of uniformed young men delivered the many courses. How they got to each table through that mass of humanity I would never know. Becky and I picked a spot in one of the co-ed rooms and started with handwashing. Too many witnesses there – as a lefty, I was going to make every effort to use only my right hand for eating. Most washed only their right hand at the table.

The only disappointment of the meal arrived first; the pastilla, a pastry/casserole dish of chicken with almonds was served cold, probably due to the large number of people present. Lots of conversation centered around the two Nazranis at the table. They were surprised we knew a little Arabic and spoke reasonable French. More of their entry-level English came our way.

One of the servers removed the pastilla platter and peeled off one of four layers of tablecloths; that arrangement saved wiping the table of food particles between courses. Next came a big plate of four roasted chickens – more than enough for 12 people. I thought that was the main course, so I really dug in and was soon full. That plate and another tablecloth layer left, and I was surprised to find the main course – lamb – set before us. I had only a little room left for some. So far, my right hand was functioning as well as could be expected. A plate of fruit finished the menu (and the last tablecloth). Fresh cherries, plums, peaches and apricots were still in season – an excellent selection. An extraordinary meal, purely Moroccan, a real feast.

Our group left the room and made space for the next shift. Driss told me later that 34 tables of invited family friends with 12 to 15 persons per table were served at that feast.

Around 11 that evening, Becky and I arrived at the Rabat Court Building's *Salle de Fete,* which had been acquired for the main ceremonies; the groom was a prominent judicial figure in town. Imagine a huge room paneled like a courtroom but as big as a cathedral. Near the center, a bandstand faced the special seating arrangement for the bride and groom. The rest of the room was filled with tables and chairs. Colorful bottles of orange Fanta ringed with small glasses served as centerpieces.

Those who had not been invited to the feast were already arriving. The groom, dressed in white, greeted all guests at the door; no sight of the bride, yet.

The band started playing – popular tunes mostly like what was heard on the radio. Finally, the bride and groom entered together and took their special center-stage seats. Female guests danced in front of them. Others greeted them individually. They sat there virtually motionless for more than an hour, then left the room and prepared for what I called the bucket dance.

The bride wore the heavy bejeweled, traditional hooded wedding gown. The groom had changed to a dark suit. They sat in individual, colorfully decorated round wooden boxes that were hoisted onto the shoulders of their respective attendants – equivalent to our bridesmaids and groomsmen. They were paraded through the crowd for at least half an hour. Everybody cheered. Lots of excitement throughout the room. The band played on. A folklore band joined in and the resulting commotion was deafening, even for such a large place; four to five hundred people must have been there. In the middle of all that, the marriage service was performed. There was nothing left to do but celebrate some more. Snack cakes and those glasses of orange Fanta were served – no chance of anyone leaving drunk!

I left the scene around 3 a.m., and the celebration was still going strong. My ears were ringing for hours. The festivities finally ended around 6.

The next day, activities continued in a less formal fashion. Back to the site of the feast, we enjoyed glorified leftovers from the night before, a smaller crowd and conversation with family members. The bride and groom made their appearance, but even that occurred with little ceremony. Actually, that day was something like a family reunion for all those attending from out of town. A smaller Moroccan band showed up for entertainment. The day was definitely low-key compared to the previous night. Most people were a little worn out too. The women's colorful wardrobe show continued, however.

Becky and I took photos of all the festivities as our gift and arranged them in a nice album. I got a stern "They had better be good!" from one relative – and he meant business. I could have made a small fortune taking family portraits; everybody wanted their picture taken by the two Americans.

## Back on the Job

After John's departure, it was strictly me and Becky when it came to photo work at the office. Our Belgian supervisor, Marc, planned to take off for a month in September, so things would remain slow. At my editing table, I stayed busy conforming a final cut on a film about the new Agricultural Institute in Rabat. A trip down south beyond Marrakesh to film sequences for an irrigation film was rumored. If our long-awaited shipment of film stock didn't arrive, we wouldn't be able to go.

The film I had shot of the recent equestrian exhibition, including shots of Prince Mohammed VI, was returned from the lab and looked OK. That project required preliminary editing. So, I easily had three weeks of work to keep me occupied. That was encouraging; we heard some volunteers, mostly engineers, had no work – money had dried up.

Hanging around the Peace Corps office after work, we learned the Ministry of Agriculture had failed to request new volunteers to replace Becky and me the following year. Our boss at the office, Mr. Ben Saiid, was not too encouraged about our program continuing.

One Friday afternoon, Marc explained a few things to me. Our ministry (like most other government agencies) was broke – any big film projects would require elaborate proposals and some fancy footwork. He was optimistic that outside sponsored projects, like the German and U.N.

productions, would continue to occupy our time. That was fine with me. We had managed to always have something in production to justify our presence.

On top of all that, King Hassan II had recently announced some unreal import restrictions that could really screw up Morocco. Essentially, he wanted everything used there to be made there. The king wanted to prohibit imports of essentials like cheese and coffee. Other basic food items could disappear, and we heard people had started hoarding staples like sugar. That decree could become a critical problem for our office as well. We were out of film, and a shipment of Agfa film stock was apparently held up somewhere in transit (most likely at the port). People I knew in private business were going crazy. Many hoped the "Land of Insh'Allah" would prevail and the king would forget about the whole plan in a week or two.

Nobody really knew how Morocco would survive without its imports. The price of many everyday items had gone up 10 to 15 percent too. Our raise had arrived just in time.

## Showing the Trainees Around

The weather in Rabat had returned to the mild days I remembered from the previous summer. Many volunteers from our class were in Safi (south of Casablanca, on the coast) for an optional in-service language school Peace Corps organized for improving skills. I decided not to attend, but Becky went down for it. So, I was living the life of a bachelor once again. The new group of trainees was busy traveling all over Morocco, visiting volunteer homesites. I enjoyed a quiet Sunday afternoon at our apartment, for a change.

> ***one volunteer remembers...***
>
> My neighbor across the street was married to a much older policeman and had a cute little boy. Her husband was an alcoholic and sometimes I could hear him beating her. During the summer, she mentioned that she was going to visit her family in Safi and invited me to visit while I was there to attend a Peace Corps "language stage." We met up and went for a stroll along the ramparts. There she revealed that she had escaped her husband and would never go back. Her brothers were policemen and could offer protection. I was not to speak

> of this back in Tadla. When I returned, the house across the street was quiet. The old policeman sometimes sat on his front stoop and occasionally was even sitting drunk in the middle of the street.
>
> One day, weeks later, I saw the little boy playing outside ... and then I saw her again. The father's paternal rights had pulled the child and, so the mother, back to Tadla. She would look at me with a defeated expression but never spoke of her fate.
>
> Tinker Goggans
> TEFL Instructor
> Kasba Tadla

With our abbreviated summer work hours during the week, I could be at the training site around 3, meeting more trainees. The new class continued to work hard and ask many questions about the Peace Corps lifestyle. With Becky in Safi, I enjoyed meals served at the training center on Monday and Tuesday evenings.

One afternoon, I led a group of a dozen men to the local hammam. Wearing our swim trunks, we sat on the tile floor with buckets of steaming hot water around us. Following my brief demonstration, the trainees got a kick out of scrubbing themselves with the customary porous stones. I hadn't been in months. We all left the place feeling super clean.

Becky returned on Friday in time for us to host our first cooking class. Shopping for the ingredients offered trainees worthwhile cultural and language orientations. Getting a grip on the metric system of measurements (buying grams of butter) proved to be an interesting lesson. Four trainees – Debra, Laurie, Randy and Jeff – joined one of their Arabic instructors to prepare a basic main dish in our kitchen: a tajine featuring chicken and olives. The results were delicious. The trainees had already discovered Moroccan wine, so the meal became something of a celebration of their first-time success emulating the local cuisine. They were full of stories recapping their homestay adventures from the previous weekend. I got the impression they were all enjoying Morocco so far and were gradually absorbing the culture.

Of the group huddled in our kitchen that evening, I remembered meeting Debra Snell at the Casablanca airport. She had walked off the plane with a broad smile, wearing a sun hat with an extra-wide brim and toting (of all things) a tennis racket. I wondered to myself: was she a Peace Corps trainee or looking for Club Med?

"I've wanted the Peace Corps since I was in the eighth grade and heard about JFK's idea," she told me. "Where I lived, nobody traveled."

Debra lived in Birmingham, Michigan, with her three sisters. A French major at Michigan State, she knew she wanted to live someplace else after graduation.

"Originally, I turned down the Peace Corps offer – don't really know why. But I changed my mind. A friend convinced me to accept the offer, telling me 'everything here will be the same when you get back.'" Her smile told me how satisfied she was with her decision. "I'm having a great time, so far. Learning a lot. It's an interesting group of people we have here."

Debra impressed me as being very intelligent, personable and funny. Out of the blue, she asked me, "Do you play backgammon? I brought a game."

"I played some in college a few years back," I replied, kidding her about bringing her tennis racket too.

We agreed to play a game one evening at the lycée. She was on her own to find a tennis court. I learned later that Phil Hanson and Debra arranged to play tennis after class one afternoon over at the Rabat American School. Along with the good meal, another lifelong friendship was cooked up that evening.

After the cooking lesson, Becky and I walked back to the lycée and enjoyed a Bon Voyage party underway for Sandy, the departing volunteer I had visited in Souk Sebt the month before. So many people I had known over the last year had completed their service, packed up and left. It was time to replace old friends with new faces.

The coming weekend allowed many in the new class to explore the country and check out potential teaching sites.

## Halftime Reflections

During one of his visits, Larry the surveyor remarked, "This is the beginning of the end." In more ways than one, he was right.

The first day of July marked a turning point in the way we (and I) thought of our Peace Corps service. I felt more intelligent, more assured that the decision to come to Morocco was a good one. I had survived the life of a foreigner for a full year. Another period of now-familiar customs and practices, food and climate, pressures and excitements was ahead – with fewer surprises in store. Some language was learned, and I had that to build on and certainly improve.

Two letters from Paul Huntsman since he left us in January revealed he had rejoined his former employer, Sun Classic Pictures in Salt Lake City, and had more or less picked up life in the United States where he had left it. Paul had mixed feelings about his decision to leave Morocco. Surely, the thought of leaving was a natural inclination for me and several other volunteers. No contract obligated us to stay. At times, I had thought of what I might be doing for that production company in Chattanooga – an offer I turned down two weeks before leaving for Morocco. But that position lacked the foreign experience opportunity; and I usually concluded, "I wouldn't be seeing as much of the world had I stayed in Chattanooga." Besides, that offer or others like it might be waiting for me when I returned.

I realized later that the first half of 1978 initiated a period of significant economic change in Morocco. Those six months revealed a Third World country gasping for its very financial life. Everybody was taking a wait-and-see attitude since the king had complicated matters by imposing unbelievable import restrictions on foreign-made goods. Some believed such a near-total embargo on imports was impossible for a country like Morocco.

Motion picture film could be included under the order too. We were still waiting for a shipment of film from Germany to restock our supply. We had one can of film left. Any delays in receiving more film stock would really slow things down for us.

Our work emphasis had taken a decided shift, too. With ministry projects at a standstill, we had concentrated on foreign assistance programs. The United Nations, through its Food and Agriculture Organization (FAO) branch, was working with us on a reforestation film. A German chemical company was allowing us to film – and later promote – their test treatments for improved sugar beets. The people from both groups were top-notch professionals and a pleasure to work with. The coming months would tell a lot about what sort of workload we could expect. With the slower pace, I had a lot of energy building up; I only hoped I would get an opportunity to use it.

I assumed I would finish my Peace Corps service at the same office location where I started it. The new ministry building – to house our Audio-Visual Bureau – had yet to be completed. The original completion date had been October 1977, but the building stood nowhere near completion. Over the past six months, supervisors in our office kept insisting, "Two months more, just two more months." At times, it was funny; it was obvious to see, day after day, that nobody was there working on the building.

My accomplishments over the past year were hard to pinpoint. Certainly, I had met a lot of interesting people, faced a new culture and discovered so much about myself. The distance from familiar faces and places was real. I had produced a few pretty pictures about gypsy moths, dropped a caseload of equipment in the mud and traveled 50 kilometers to film on location only to discover I had left a vital camera part back at the office. Those things would happen. For a while, it was difficult to establish that professional credibility the original job description talked so much about.

The past dozen months had received my best shot. I played by all the rules and gained sufficient reward. My Moroccan co-workers were considered my friends. Mine was a relatively comfortable life. I never really ran out of money, had several nice (though brief) trips and held on to good health while gaining self-confidence. The independence was great, even with my responsibilities, and I could manage things on my own. I had become more receptive to other people's feelings as well. The slight uncertainty of what was to come was often concerning, but I had my past experience to lean on and to learn from.

### one volunteer remembers...

It seemed that Moroccans in small towns accepted and protected individuals who were different, whether they were cognitively impaired or mentally ill. One of my favorite things about Tadla was the way everyone, including the kids, embraced our "town fool." He was an older man who had been in the French army in Indochina. His delusion was that he was a field marshal and was married to the daughter of Charles de Gaulle. (At the time, there was a quaint vestige of the French protectorate visible in town. Most every café still had a portrait of Charles de Gaulle above the counter.)

Le Marechal, as everyone addressed him, wore a French army cap and always carried a telephone receiver which he explained was needed to communicate with his troops. He saluted everyone in town, including the little kids who would chime in and say, 'Bonjour, Monsieur le Marechal!"

Once I had to go to the mayor's office and, upon knocking, was greeted by Le Marechal. He announced proudly to the mayor, 'C'est l'americaine!" (It is the American!) The mayor calmly replied, "Very good Monsieur le Marechal, show her in."

> No doubt Monsieur le Marechal thought that Tadla would cease to function without his careful stewardship.
>
> Tinker Goggans
> TEFL Instructor
> Kasba Tadla

## Miss Lillian Visits

I had started buying French newspapers every Monday, Wednesday and Friday; reading them helped my understanding of the language. I could read the bare facts of what was happening in the world.

One brief front-page clip reported that President Carter's mother, Mrs. Lillian Carter (affectionately known as Miss Lillian), was to pass through Rabat on August 2 and 3. Truth be told, you couldn't believe everything you read in the papers – she arrived July 23 and left the next day.

The visit was a big event in Rabat; the embassy was abuzz with activity. Paul Hare was trying to swing a personal visit by Miss Lillian to our office. She had asked to see some volunteers, and our office was right off the road going out to the Royal Guest House where she was staying. All day Sunday, embassy staffers worked on arrangements.

Mrs. Carter flew in from Rome to begin a tour of African capitals. Rabat was a 24-hour rest stop and not an official visit to the government of Morocco; she did not visit with the king. She mostly made social visits and greeted Americans in town.

Her tight schedule did not permit her to visit our office, but she was set to speak to the new group of Peace Corps trainees at the embassy at 11:30 a.m. Becky and I went to work that morning before skipping out at 11. Everybody at work wanted to know why we were all dressed up. There had to be a special occasion for me to wear a coat and tie on such a warm day in Rabat. We provided a reasonably successful explanation.

The trainees and Peace Corps staff had arrived, and we awaited Miss Lillian's entrance in the embassy courtyard. Paul wanted to have an authentic Georgian there, so he had me up front for a handshake. I was joined by Louis and Debbie, the two trainees from Georgia. Both had pronounced Southern accents. No mistake about it, they were Southerners.

Mrs. Carter's entourage was impressive. I noticed two female Secret Service agents, plus four large men. She had a press corps of about six reporters and some kind of youth group traveling with her. The total crew added up to around 30 people.

Paul was the first person to come out of the side door. All the trainees cheered. Paul, at forty, could act like a kid sometimes. He was smiling, waving and enjoying a moment of celebrity at the event. He found us three Georgians in the crowd and pulled us aside.

"She does not like that European kiss on the two cheeks," he told us. "And go easy on her hands – she doesn't like a bone-crushing handshake. She's eighty years old, so speak up. She's very funny. Ask a question if you want but keep it short."

In the meantime, the press (now including Becky, my personal photographer) had formed a line opposite our Peace Corps delegation. A minute later, Ambassador Anderson entered, escorting Mrs. Carter.

Miss Lillian's short stature and silver-white hair were the first things I noticed. She wore a striped mint green pantsuit, very light and casual and a contrast to all the near-formal dress around her.

Paul quickly guided her in our direction. She was prepped for our meeting and all excited about seeing somebody from the home turf. Light handshakes and a few words followed. She wanted to know where we lived. I said Atlanta. Louis, for some reason, said Sandy Springs. She looked puzzled. I offered Atlanta as a substitute for Louis, but he kept saying Sandy Springs. Finally, she came back with, "Oh yes, that's up near Roswell, isn't it?" I was impressed at her knowledge of suburban Atlanta.

The other trainee, Debbie, managed to get her two cents in. "I'm from Rome" came out in a long Southern drawl unlike anything I'd ever heard.

Mrs. Carter seemed pleased and genuinely excited to meet us. She asked us if we had stayed healthy and what our general impressions of Morocco were. Cameras clicked away like crazy. You would have thought that lady was the president. The air of a politician was missing, though. She was an amiable, down-home country person.

Next, she addressed the group, told of her earlier travels through Paris and Rome and wanted to answer some of our questions – many concerned her Peace Corps life in India. A dozen years before our meeting, at the age of sixty-eight, Miss Lillian took her nursing skills to India, aiding patients afflicted with leprosy.

She spoke for about 10 minutes and closed her remarks by announcing Chicago's plans to honor her August 15, India's Independence Day.

By noon the big event was over. People wanted to shake the hand that shook the hand. A bunch of us headed for the Café Jour et Nuit for lunch in the garden since we were all dressed up.

## Chat with Phil

A week later, I arranged a visit with Phil so I could discuss ongoing problems with my co-ed living situation and supply some company for Phil, who was recuperating at home from his recently discovered case of hepatitis.

Phil was moderately helpful. I explained my situation – a combination of personality conflicts with Becky and the steady stream of overnight visitors. He immediately suggested I move out, but that was not in my game plan. Further explanation and discussion resolved a few things. With Phil's advice while enjoying two beers, the subject was quickly wrapped up.

As an odd parting gesture and attempt to cheer me up, Phil handed over a box of Uncle Ben's Converted Rice and a carton of carrot juice. At an earlier dinner visit with Phil, I had raved about the rice – he was able to procure it through the embassy. The carrot juice was one kind of drink he didn't consider a tonic for his illness. I agreed: the stuff was truly horrible.

Certainly, a strange afternoon. To make it even more bizarre, 30 minutes after I left, Becky arrived at Phil's place to perform her own corporal work of mercy.

Over a late dinner at our apartment, Becky and I talked about a few issues. It seemed she formulated the impression that I was cracking up and needed pure compassion. I took the view that our lifestyles simply were no longer synchronous or even marginally compatible. Nothing much was resolved. A lot of loose ends were left hanging.

I decided it was time to get away.

## Road Trip

Since I self-mandated that a change of scenery was required, I tagged along with Mark who was returning to his home in Midelt from the in-service language school in Safi. Mark was a congenial travel companion. Others passing through town allowed us to take a grand taxi, and by 10 a.m., we were headed for Meknes. Nothing was pressing at the office that Friday, so I gave myself a holiday. That trip was important. I needed a break in my Rabat routine. I would never make it working straight through until September 16, the target date for a planned visit by my parents. The destination wasn't really important. My finances weren't in the best shape, but I could worry about that later.

Once we arrived in Meknes, I felt the heat of inland Morocco. I couldn't believe the difference from the coastal area – it was at least 10 degrees warmer. We changed taxis and took off for Azrou to the south; Patty Balch lived there.

By 2 that afternoon, we were in Patty's house. Azrou had long been one of my favorite places, though I hadn't spent much time there.

The crowd at Patty's house began to grow. A group of trainees arrived from Rabat. Azrou was a potential teaching site for them, so they had come to look it over. An hour later, another group of three appeared. By 6, Patty had 10 people staying at her house. She really didn't know what to do. With my newly acquired skills in hotel management, I gave her a few pointers.

Amid the commotion, Patty's maid, Fatima, dropped by. She was a well-known character among Peace Corps people. At thirty-seven (she looked sixty-seven), she smoked, drank and generally had a good time with us Americans. Fatima was tall and slim, almost toothless, and had the traditional Berber facial tattoos. Though she had long worked for Peace Corps English teachers, she was lucky to get beyond *hello* and *very good* from her limited vocabulary. She also served as Patty's Arabic tutor.

By 9:30, Fatima had prepared the best couscous I'd ever consumed in Morocco. A huge dish for 10 people, covered with vegetables and chunks of lamb. Cabbage was a new addition to the dish, and it made the difference.

An after-dinner walk around town took us by Patty's school, Lycée Tarik – the largest one I had seen in such a small town. A late stop at a café for conversation with some of the trainees ended the long day. To top it off, we slept under a cloudless, star-filled sky on Patty's roof. The surrounding hills made it all a beautiful, peaceful setting. Quite a switch from the congested, concrete jungle of Rabat.

Saturday morning got off to a much earlier start. Mark wanted to try for a 7 a.m. bus to Midelt. We packed up and walked to the station, only to find the 7 o'clock and two later buses all filled. I decided to stay in Azrou for the remainder of the weekend. Mark decided to get an early start at a hitchhike attempt, so we parted. He eventually made it home to Midelt.

> **one volunteer remembers...**
>
> To collect our monthly living allowance, we received a paper – a mandat – more like a telegram than a check and cashed it at the post office in town.
>
> One month, I remember cashing mine, while being terribly ill with some kind of virus. As soon as I pocketed the cash, 1,200 or so dirhams, I passed out. I came to on the floor of the post office surrounded by concerned faces ... one of them being a Moroccan English teacher from our school. She was kind enough to be sure I wasn't robbed, and then she drove me home in her car.
>
> Mark Postnikoff<br>TEFL Instructor<br>Midelt

A relaxing day followed. The afternoon heat was bearable. I enjoyed catching up with Nora from our group who was visiting Azrou from her teaching station in Sidi Slimane, north of Meknes. Nora and I visited the well-known cooperative where local artisans displayed and sold their handiwork.

A late-afternoon climb up one of the surrounding hills gave Nora and me a scenic overview of Azrou and the surrounding territory. Some great sunset photo opportunities there too. Two young boys joined us; they were returning home with loads of firewood collected from the hillsides. The pair was excited about having their picture taken. A late arrival to the group insisted he was worth a 1-dirham fee (25 cents). He wanted the money up front, too – a real hustler, he was. Surprisingly, the boys spoke a little French. Nora handled the Arabic.

Saturday night, I made a point to hit the sack early. By 10 o'clock I was, once again, under that terrific night sky I never saw in Rabat. Several falling stars streaked across the sky. Local dogs and an agitated donkey provided annoying sound effects.

Sunday was souk day at nearby Khenifra, one of the best markets for Moroccan carpets, tapestries and other woven items. Our Peace Corps entourage had dropped to eight. We hopped on the 8 a.m. bus for an hour-long ride – the rolling hills and neighboring mountains flattened onto the Tadla plain, Morocco's principal agricultural area.

We met more trainees in Khenifra – another teaching site available to them. The souk grounds were dotted with young Americans all day. I ended up buying a selham, the hooded Berber cape made of heavy brown wool, for my winter overcoat; I paid about $35 for it. I didn't think I would ever be in that area again on a Sunday morning, so I decided to make the trip worthwhile.

### one volunteer remembers...

The Sunday market in Khenifra, one of the largest in Morocco, had everything from vegetables, fresh meat, carpets, furniture, tools, clothes, school supplies, bug spray, shoes, goats, chickens, rabbits, donkeys, ducks and turkeys. A menagerie of life, the market was also a place to get healthcare.

One Sunday, I witnessed dentistry. A man wearing a white smock sat under an umbrella with a couple dozen teeth and a scissor, displaying his work, skills and authenticity. To make his point that he could get rid of both pain and evil he had a rubber snake hissing at the display. A teenage boy sat on the ground with a wool cap over his mouth writhing in pain. Next to him, two bloody molars indicated success, in some odd way. I stopped to gawk, along with about 20 Moroccans. The dentist told the boy to open his mouth so he could swab his mouth with a pain reliever before continuing. After the boy spit on the ground, the dentist took a scissor and said "Open" and poked around. I left before the boy lost more teeth.

Wandering through the market, I came across a man sitting on a carpet. He had a few vegetables piled in front of him but was making no effort to sell them. I didn't know his purpose. He gestured for me to sit, presumably because I was a foreigner and, if he was lucky, French. I took up his offer and sat down, crossing my legs. He poured me some tea. We tried conversing in my terrible Arabic, non-existent French and made-up hand gestures. I had been in Morocco only five months; it's all I had to offer.

With the effort in verbal communication failing, he handed me a bottle and pointed to the label which was in French. It looked like a medicine. I asked what was wrong with him. He pointed to his groin and then made a circle with his thumb and forefinger, and with his other hand moved his forefinger through while saying, "Madam, madam." I assumed he had contracted a sexually transmitted disease from madam. With

> my French comprising nothing but everyday pleasantries I couldn't read the label. But I didn't tell him. Instead, I suggested he see a doctor, which I said in French, *docteur*. He looked disappointed, maybe even very disappointed. I got up, shook his hand, thanked him for the tea and continued walking through the market, looking to buy vegetables for the week.
>
> Mike Kendellen
> TEFL Instructor
> Khenifra

The project for the afternoon was to return to Rabat. Heading back to Azrou, we picked up our things and had a group of six traveling together – the magic number. Six passengers filled up a grand taxi, so we thought we would have no problems. We were wrong. By that time, it was 4:00 and no taxi driver in Azrou wanted to drive to Meknes and be stuck there overnight if he couldn't get return fares. We ended up settling for a 5 p.m. bus.

I was due for a nap, and the ride to Meknes was the perfect opportunity. But, of 60 others on the full bus, the Moroccan seated next to me happened to speak English. He was a fat, smelly book merchant from Meknes who had learned English from Christian missionaries and was all excited about the opportunity to use it. For once, I couldn't claim ignorance of the language – as in the case of French or Arabic questioners. The nap idea was quickly forgotten. "Where are you from?" "Do you like Morocco?" "Are you married?" "How much money do you make?" That guy covered every imaginable topic.

I would call him a marginal Muslim. He talked at length about the contradictions between our Bible and his Koran; he had decided not to follow either one. Reminding me of his large girth, he concluded that if he didn't eat all day, he would die – so practicing the fast during Ramadan was not for him. He didn't particularly appreciate the intrusion of Christian missionaries into a Muslim society either, though he did learn English out of the deal. He also learned to play games – Clue, Sorry and Monopoly ... Clue was his all-time favorite. He was almost funny. Luckily, the bus arrived in Meknes ahead of schedule, and we parted company. An interesting person, he was.

By 7:30, we were in a taxi heading for Rabat. What a weekend! I never made it to Midelt, but I enjoyed seeing more of an area I had only passed through on previous trips. I spent a lot of the money I was trying to save, but the getaway weekend was worth it. I was glad I went. By 10 p.m., the bathtub and I were reunited. I was so dirty, I left quite a ring.

## Another Year Older

We reached another tear-a-page-off-the-calendar event. July was history; August 1978 had arrived. Thirteen down, 11 to go.

August 1, my special day, started late. Becky and I discussed the night before that the Ministry of Agriculture could surely do without my services on my birthday. Simple plans evolved into a celebration to cut the cake with about 40 invited friends.

Some of our in-house guests had made enough sangria to fill our laundry tub. The cake filled the large cookie sheet we used for making pizzas. We acquired a block of ice to float in the sangria. Others arriving brought assorted drinks and small gifts.

By 11 that evening, the place was wall-to-wall Peace Corps people and local friends. I was most impressed to see Phil Hanson; almost fully recovered from hepatitis, he made it all the way up our four flights of stairs. We laughed when I started opening the wooden sculpture he gave me – the only wrapping paper he could find read Your Wedding.

Paul Hare brought two bottles of Taylor champagne – good New York stuff – plus a huge bottle of Chianti. He was definitely ready to celebrate. His wife, Robbie, and her visiting Australian mother came. My favorite French teachers from the past summer dropped by. All enjoyed our great view of Rabat at night; several found the rooftop terrace much less crowded than our apartment.

We cut the cake around midnight; everyone heartfully sang the standard tune, and I popped open a bottle of the champagne. By 1:30, the crowd started to leave. It was a birthday party I would never forget! Somehow, I managed to get to work the next day around noon.

## Ramadan Returns

Following my birthday celebration, I enjoyed a casual, lazy weekend around the apartment and finished reading my Paul Theroux paperback. Years later, I learned that Theroux was himself a Peace Corps Volunteer, serving in Malawi (1963–65).

The Muslim lunar month of Ramadan had begun, which meant total fasting sunup to sundown for our Host Country Nationals. The streets were virtually deserted at sunset. People made a beeline for the nearest bowl of harira, their traditional Ramadan soup. One day at our office, a co-worker justified his participation.

"I starve my body to feed my soul" was his personal Ramadan credo.

Our favorite restaurants and cafés were closed all day, but we had solved that problem by going to the embassy snack bar for hamburgers during the normal lunch hours. I missed our regular hangout across from the main post office, the Café Renaissance, for weekend lunches.

Taking a break from the stage and enjoying those summer breezes off the ocean, a bunch of trainees joined us for long strolls down the main drag. I introduced several of them to banana splits at the Restaurant Italia.

During the training stage, I had hung out frequently with Julie from the San Francisco Bay area and Tracy from Phoenix – both TEFL teachers. Julie had just graduated from UC-Davis with a degree in education. Tracy attended a small liberal arts college in Arizona, picking up French with a minor in language studies. The pair had enjoyed weekend trips to see more of the country and collect ideas about where they would want to spend their two years teaching. They had to turn in their three preferences that week and were hoping to be assigned to towns in central Morocco – places like Midelt, Azrou or Beni Mellal. Both preferred an authentic cross-cultural experience away from the larger cities. Their visits with in-service volunteers had included generous servings of couscous and mint tea, and they were anxious to try their skills in the kitchen making their first tajine. Their tales sounded similar to my experiences of the previous summer.

The class of 1978 would soon blend with the existing volunteer population.

With no students attending schools during the summer months, TEFL program administrators promoted guidelines for all TEFL volunteers to complete a summer project.

The Peace Corps cookbook we all received during training was hailed as an example of a successful summer project. From our group, aspiring chef Mark Postnikoff assembled a supplement to the cookbook featuring his favorite recipes. I heard two musically inclined women produced a basic songbook for classroom use. Two others worked together creating simple word games teachers could use to help students build their vocabulary.

Like everything else, completing a project was voluntary. Helping out with the stage in Rabat constituted a practical summer project for more than a dozen volunteers. With six weeks for their project, TEFL volunteers were still allowed 30 days leave during the summer.

The late weeks of summer also recorded transfers in TEFL assignments among those completing their first year. Several English teachers decided to relocate and teach at a different school their second year. Maura Murray and Patty Balch had become good friends (and Maura's French friend, Didier, had completed his service and departed), so Maura arranged a second-year transfer from her teaching spot in Ksar el Kebir to a TEFL position at Patty's school in Azrou. Denise Schickel transferred from Khourigba to a similar teaching post in El Jedida, a coastal town about 50 miles south of Casablanca.

With other volunteers extending for a third year, there would be some 170 Peace Corps Volunteers in Morocco once the new class was sworn in.

---

***one volunteer remembers...***

My second year in El Jedida, Morocco, I was teaching three second-year English classes, which was fun because they knew enough English to read short stories. We were reading Arabic folk tales (Nasruddin) in English. They knew the stories and were excited to learn the English versions. They would often repeat the English lines when they learned them, talking and laughing with each other.

They also wanted to learn the lyrics to songs by Bob Dylan and the Beatles. I took a cassette recorder to class, played the tapes for them and wrote the lyrics on the blackboard. They enjoyed shouting out "Here comes the sun." One day, when I was walking down the street in the town, one of my students yelled at me from across the street: "Miss, how many roads must a man walk down?" They were very excited about learning English.

Denise Schickel
*TEFL Instructor*
*El Jedida*

## Planning for Parents

September 16 was the planned arrival date for my parents' visit to Morocco. Over the course of the spring and summer, about a dozen letters had crisscrossed the Atlantic outlining what to do, where to stay and what to see. My parents also wanted to combine their visit to Morocco with a tour through Spain. We merged features of two itineraries I had drafted and came up with what I thought was a doable schedule, ending with time to travel to Madrid and join a motor coach tour they had booked with their travel agent in Atlanta.

Using a rental car, we would make the well-traveled loop around central Morocco. We planned to stay at Mark Dressman's house in Kasba Tadla for a sampling of volunteer living, then enjoy a lunch stop with Mark Postnikoff in Midelt. Two nights each in Fes and Marrakesh would be in nice hotels; volunteers stationed there would be our personal guides.

Anticipating their visit and knowing full well the culture they would be experiencing, I was confident they could tolerate a measure of roughing it and going along with the prevailing circumstances. They had no foreign language skills; I knew they would depend on me for everything. Mom and dad were veteran travelers holding well-worn passports, so I framed their visit as a unique cultural experience – stepping back in time a bit and not having every modern convenience readily at hand.

With my letters devoted to planning their visit, I suggested items they could bring with them. It would be like a little Christmas with all the goodies I had requested – mostly clothes, plus more film and camera batteries; my supplies were dwindling.

## Problems?

I was learning every relationship had its share of problems. And my living situation remained an issue.

Becky was more tolerant of the stream of overnight company than I was. I felt like we were housing and feeding half of Peace Corps Morocco. Our budget had been really shot up the past two months due to all the visitors. Our shared finances became the spark igniting too many arguments. She was heading to Spain for two weeks, so I would get a little time off. A split remained a possibility. But with all the time coming up during which we wouldn't have to cohabitate, it seemed unreasonable to contemplate an immediate change of address.

One Sunday in mid-August proved to be a quiet day in Rabat – no overnighters. What a change! On that overcast, gloomy day, the sermon at Mass was all about the legacy of Pope Paul VI who had passed away the week before. The news had earned plenty of coverage in the newspapers too.

Work at the office was winding down. Marc would be leaving for Europe August 27, so not much would be in production until we all got back together sometime in late October. I had two small editing jobs remaining. Unless some film stock was delivered by late October, we could be out of commission for quite some time. The situation did not look good. It was impossible to see realistic objectives for the job when you didn't have film, the most basic of our materials.

## Another Chance to House-Sit

Late one Sunday, I took an afternoon stroll over to Paul and Robbie Hare's house to arrange another house-sitting job while they ventured off to Spain. In jest, I made my usual requests: a case of beer, bottle of vodka, bacon, hot dogs and one surprise item. Robbie agreed and only asked me to pay her American Express bill when it arrived in the mail. We got into a long discussion of my domestic differences with Becky, and she agreed I may be right to find other living quarters soon. That was encouraging.

A few days later, I stuffed a straw basket with some clothes and my toothbrush and moved over to the Hare's house. My surprise items were a box of Bisquick and a bottle of Log Cabin syrup. Too bad they didn't own a waffle iron, but pancakes sure were tasty.

An added surprise was that Khadija, their cook/housekeeper, would be staying over one day to straighten up the house. That meant one evening of the royal treatment – a meal that was hard to top. I ordered steak and fries. She turned out a banquet with enough food for four. I ate for more than an hour. I needed to walk it off, so I headed over to the training center. I explained my new setup to Julie, and we arranged to have dinner there the following evening, complete with china, nice silverware, the works – quite a switch from the basic Peace Corps Volunteer lifestyle.

The short office hours during the last days of Ramadan allowed me to enjoy the 11 days of pure luxury living at the house even more. My expertise in the kitchen continued to improve. So far, after a week there, only one disastrous meal. The two cats (they had received the second one as a gift from Australian friends) and I were getting along OK. One required fresh liver; the other preferred canned tuna fish. Those were some spoiled felines.

I enjoyed having more of the trainees over for deluxe (non-cafeteria style) dinners. Our gatherings became impromptu cooking lessons featuring the fresh vegetables and bread from the hanoot around the corner. They were impressed with their results. Seated at the dining room table, I told them I didn't live like that all the time. I did enjoy having help doing the dishes.

Somewhere along the line, I had lost five pounds and was down to a skinny 145 – all the walking to and from the training center probably did it. I certainly had not cut down on eating. My pants had become a little roomy. Maybe I would recoup my losses with some Spanish cuisine the following month.

Becky was off on her two-week vacation in Spain and Portugal. In the back of my mind, I believed the timely separation provided me a valuable sampling of what living on my own would be like.

## More Volunteers Dispatched

Training was wrapping up for the new class. Surprisingly, the group had remained fairly intact through the summer, with only three departures. One guy had a bad reaction to Morocco and exited, and a woman had a family situation back home that required her attention. Rumors swirled among trainees why the third one – considered a loud, obnoxious creep – was no longer around. He just didn't show up for breakfast one morning. Gone. Everyone I spoke with was glad to see him leave.

The level of excitement around the lycée peaked when the TEFL assignments were announced. Julie was both relieved and happy to learn she got her top preference of Midelt. She would be joined by her newfound friend Debbie, my fellow Georgian. The pair was already making plans to find housing together.

Tracy was an emotional opposite; she was upset with the news that she would be posted to Oujda – clear across the country near the Algerian border and not one of her three choices. As with our class, it all came down to a numbers game – placing a certain number of volunteers in a limited number of towns.

During the last week of training, Tracy joined me for dinner at my favorite place for crepes, the Café Français. Thoroughly disappointed with her TEFL location, she needed a pep talk but pledged to make the most of it. I suggested she get to know Jane and Louise from my class. They had accompanied Larry and me to the beach during our training and lived in Oujda. They would be helpful contacts for getting oriented, finding housing and setting up her classroom. I could tell Tracy was determined to stick it out.

Becky had returned from her two-week vacation visiting Spain and Portugal. She and I were recruited to take a group photo of the 1978 class a few days before the swearing-in ceremony.

The trainees assembled on the dusty playground, arranging themselves with their teachers and staff members all around a large steel playset. Folks were layered on the slide, and others perched on swings and the climbing bars. Becky had brought a tripod and the medium format camera she used at our office. We managed to get up on the roof of the adjacent classroom building for the perfect angle, considering how the light was falling. I assisted, using my trusty light meter. With more than 60 trainees and all the staff in the photo, the black-and-white image was a memorable keepsake.

A few days later, the class of 1978 was officially sworn in as Peace Corps Volunteers and integrated into the Moroccan population.

## The "Divorce"

The first Monday in September – Labor Day back home – was another day to remember. Becky was back from vacation, and I had returned to the apartment having completed my house-sitting project. During our time apart, we had both done some serious thinking and come to the same conclusion.

September 4 saw the end to the made-for-Peace-Corps-living marriage Becky and I had conjured up exactly a year and a day before. That evening, both of us ended up in the kitchen.

"I think we'd better end this living arrangement finally," I simply told her.

She got the message and admitted a split would best serve her interests as well. The challenge of working and living together was a key factor in the split. There was no need to rehash our issues or our conflicting opinions of each other. We considered the breakup a result of those irreconcilable differences that people living together often experience. Arguments over household finances stoked the fire, and the regular stream of overnight visitors didn't help matters.

I had spent much of the day looking for new housing. We had a two-day holiday, Monday and Tuesday, due to the end of Ramadan. I needed the time off to do all the necessary running around. I was lucky to find an apartment available – one recently vacated by another volunteer. Whatever I chose, I realized moving would be expensive.

Events happened quickly. Wednesday morning, I met with the agency handling the new apartment and arranged the finances for it. The landlord lived in Casablanca. Luckily, the agency could reach him by telephone, and he approved my contract for the one-bedroom place. It would never match the spaciousness of my former residence, but for the remaining 10 months, it would be sufficient.

The following week, I arranged the services of the Peace Corps van to move furniture. I didn't know I owned so much. Three loads were required. The night before, Becky and I managed to work out the property settlement. It was kind of fun; no problems at all. Becky had plans to move in with other established volunteers, while I was starting from scratch. I acquired the stove and refrigerator, the dining table and three nice chairs. We flipped a coin for which pair of matching banquettes each would take; neither of us had a preference. I ended up with the softer foam-filled ones. Becky got the heavy, extra firm straw-filled pair.

Wednesday night, friends came over at midnight – the only time we could have use of the van. Four flights of stairs proved to be our biggest problem. We felt like crooks, moving out in the middle of the night. It was easier; we avoided the almost certain barrage of questioning neighbors and had no street traffic to contend with. At the new place, a very tight two flights of stairs were negotiated. The bed was a close fit.

For the last time, I climbed down those four flights of stairs at Number 39 Abidjan. Becky made plans to move out by September 15 so a Moroccan family could move right in the next day. Apartment Number 11 looked as barren as we had found it just over a year earlier.

Two more truckloads were required to move Becky's things over to a Peace Corps staffer's house where there was an extra room. She seemed satisfied with the arrangements, though I couldn't calculate her exact feelings on the subject. Sure, we talked, but it was not like it used to be.

The logistics of our split could not have gone better; all concerned parties were satisfied with the results. I could not begin to measure my relief that it was over and done with. Relax and enjoy – that was all I had ahead of me.

News of our separation alerted readers of the monthly Peace Corps newsletter:

### Coming to the Capital?

> The "Ocean Hotel" has officially closed and the proprietors, Becky Mangus and Richard Wallace, are living elsewhere. Mr. Wallace, now living in rather confined but comfortable quarters, can no longer accept guests due to the size of the new premises (other than invited, that is). Miss Mangus has taken up residence in an old, traditional home in Diour Jamas sharing proprietorship with two others. Guests are welcomed but they request that confirmed reservations be made in advance so as to assure room or avoid any embarrassing situations. Your cooperation is appreciated in this matter. Write Becky, Mike or Greg at the Peace Corps office.
> 
> Thanks.

My new home was in an upscale neighborhood, just off one of Rabat's busiest boulevards. Phil Hanson lived around the corner. I also had a distinguished next-door neighbor – the Egyptian Ambassador to Morocco. His villa came complete with 24-hour security guards; they got a kick out of watching us move in at 2 a.m. My building only had three apartments, one per floor. Bulgarian and Romanian couples lived in the other two, so I was basically without Moroccan neighbors. In some ways, that was a relief. At the old place, I never knew who would come knocking – our friends from next door, a sick beggar or kids off the street playing with the doorbells. Traffic noise was a big problem at the other place, too, but my new address was quieter with less truck traffic. Though it was small, I was convinced I would enjoy the new quarters.

Becky and I both admitted the increased freedom that living apart would bring. After moving, the change in my mental atmosphere was tremendous. That episode could not have worked out better. The upcoming visit with my parents and then being home over Christmas would also help.

Preparing my first meal in the new place (a pot of my potent spaghetti) was cause for celebration – after cleaning up a giant mess. A tiny can of tomato paste exploded upon opening and squirted bloodred goop all over my white kitchen walls. A blob even hit the ceiling. The mess looked like a scene from a Sam Peckinpah movie, the result of a bloody mass murder. I spent half an hour cleaning it all up. Some neighbors looked twice as I wiped red stuff off the windows. What a mess! I had never heard of that happening. Fortunately, I was standing clear of the blast when the can opener pierced the lid.

## My Parents Visit

With my housing situation resolved, all my attention was drawn to the fact that my parents would be landing in Casablanca the following Saturday morning.

I would travel to Algeciras, Spain's southern port, to pick up a rental car reserved for me. The price of that arrangement was almost half of a Moroccan rental car. I planned to slip away from work for a day or two to handle the task.

Work had become almost non-existent. Still, no shipment of film had been received, and Marc remained out of the country. My two small editing jobs would be finished before I left the following week. Wondering what we would be doing upon my return from vacation, I was left to presume we would work on something.

I also had to complete the moving-in process, straighten out a utilities contract and help Becky close out the papers on our former address. With all those projects, I was handling three kinds of money, travel agency tickets, housing contracts – the paperwork was overwhelming. After all that, I would really appreciate my vacation. The chance to get away from Rabat looked better every day. The break could not have come at a better time.

Thinking about my parents' pending arrival, all kinds of thoughts ran through my head, considering we had not seen each other for some 15 months. What should I wear to the airport? What would they be wearing? I could not forecast our reunion. If Allah willed it, their flight from New York on Royal Air Maroc would be on time.

Arrival Day in Casablanca came and went with less emotion than expected. I waited patiently at the end of the concourse where international flights arrived and waved my hat to gain their attention. The plane was an hour late, and both readily admitted Royal Air Maroc would not win any airline service awards. The visit was not off to the best start.

My dad was fascinated by his initial interactions with the culture – so fascinated, he appeared convinced he was somewhere in India back in 1943. As a navigator in the Air Force during World War II, he had traveled the world shuttling dignitaries and delivering military transports, flying the hump between India and China. His stories and comparisons about that place and time were nonstop. He was determined to think of Moroccans as Hindus, of all things. Dad's 35-year-old memory of Hindu appearance, personality and manner automatically became his impression of the 1978 Moroccan. I couldn't believe it! From her arrival, my mom (who worked many years as an elementary school teacher) made a conscious effort to learn new things and see what Morocco was all about – she tried to remain open-minded.

I wondered: where was their sense of adventure? My parents were veteran campers, loving the outdoors, later traveling all over the world and experiencing new things. I assumed they could think of the rigors of travel in Morocco – meeting a new and very different culture (albeit in a dusty, often dirty environment) – as an experience akin to a rustic camping adventure. Man, was I ever wrong!

Over the course of our week in Morocco, there were enjoyable moments. And, after all these years, I have made an effort to accentuate the positives of their visit.

Dad encountered a snake charmer in Marrakesh's iconic Jemaa el Fnaa square and eagerly accepted a snake draped around his neck – a priceless photo op; he smiled broadly. At a roadside stop along the coast, mom was intrepid climbing aboard a camel – something every tourist had to do – another memorable event. We drove a few hundred kilometers through several provinces. A roadside stop at an intersection was a chance to stretch our legs and notice the oversized directional road signs listing Marrakesh, Casablanca and other cities in English and Arabic – a visual footnote to the local geography and a good opportunity to pose for a group photo with our Renault rental car.

A pair of lunch stops at the homes of volunteers were interesting. Zohra, Mark Dressman's maid in Kasba Tadla, prepared a spread for us to enjoy – a chicken tajine with vegetables and plenty of couscous. With Mark translating, mom enjoyed chatting with Zohra, asking about her family and how she managed doing the laundry by hand.

We landed in Midelt for lunch another day – visiting Mark Postnikoff who demonstrated his prowess in the kitchen, serving up a delicious lamb dish with cabbage. Julie and Debbie (from Georgia) joined us. Mark's maid, Melika, served pastries she had made for dessert, along with the requisite mint tea. At both stops, my folks appeared interested and impressed to see how other volunteers lived, how they were embracing the culture and mastering the language.

Luckily, my parents experienced no problems with the food during their visit. Utensils were available at every meal, so the tradition of eating with their right hand was never attempted. I kept several liters of bottled water in the car while traveling, and we stuck to bottled drinks (opened in front of us) at restaurants.

On some days, mom – wilted by the moderate heat – seemed to be suffering through the ordeal. The beggars, street vendors and pestering kids of the city streets were not her kind of company. Certainly, the language ingredient was missing for my parents, and that fact added to their bewilderment when encountering the local populations.

Why did we go to Fes? I'll never know. After a grueling 12-hour travel day (my biggest mistake in planning), all three of us had different ideas how to reach the Hotel Marinades, an upscale lodging overlooking the Fes medina – a hotel none of us had ever seen before. We finally found it.

Reaching our room, the first thing I remember hearing was a loud voice: "There's no hot water!"

After dinner, mom read aloud about the Fes medina's uniqueness.

My father's reaction: "Why don't we skip it. I've seen enough medinas for this week!"

Our itinerary, the roads we covered, the many places we visited – all mostly forgettable. My parents didn't like Morocco. Certainly, returning to Atlanta, they would say they enjoyed it – took some nice photos and bought a few souvenirs. I knew things could only improve in Spain.

The hills of Tangier never looked better. At last, we arrived at our final point of Moroccan exposure. The ferry ride to the Spanish mainland was pure relief. My parents' mood brightened noticeably. I could only hope my real vacation would begin. Two rounds of cold Spanish beer got things off to a good start.

An overnight train delivered us to Madrid. The change in temperament was remarkable and thorough. Pure luxury for me and (thank Allah) for the folks. Everything in the hotel room worked, including the hot water. The desk people were accommodating. We had a most friendly maid who cleaned up the instant we stepped out the door. My high school Spanish was getting us through the day. For once, I felt relaxed.

The next morning, I declared a day off for me. The folks went to the Prado and took a city tour by bus. I didn't go since I had seen most all the sites during my visit to Madrid in April.

I enjoyed the entire day in the Retiro Park – one of my favorite spots in the world. My morning among the trees began refreshingly cool. The movement in the park was fantastic: rowboats, canoes, paddleboats and kayaks kept the small lake in front of a statue of Alfonso XII busy with color and voices. The surrounding trees formed an amphitheater. Church bells pealed; a Mass started every half hour in Madrid, I assumed. It was 5 p.m. The late afternoon sun warmed my back. English, Spanish and German were heard. A baby cried; a nanny struggled. Light on Alfonso was great. Lots of starch in the nanny's uniform. Three nuns were there too. Artists were sketching. The trees (and everything) were green. Somehow, I paid 85 pesetas for two beers at the sidewalk café there. Very few horns were heard. A gnat landed in my beer. My Spanish was suffering. The nanny went home.

On a Friday, we began our Spanish tour. Seven days of travel (with somebody else playing tour guide) passed rather uneventfully. I was confident we could salvage a reasonable vacation with adventures in Spain. Dad felt better already; his war stories were over.

I asked him specifically, "Did you ever visit Spain during the war?"

His negative response was my source of relief. I could relate to my dad. He was in his early twenties during the war. His past experiences carried a long way toward forming lasting impressions; same for me. I could imagine my dad telling his tennis buddies back home all about the Hindus he encountered in Morocco.

The Spanish itinerary could only have been an improvement over the Moroccan program, and it was. I was the youngest member of the group that filled the motor coach. Beyond Madrid, tour highlights included stops at the Alhambra in Grenada and a bullfight in Seville. Spanish cuisine was another feature of the tour. We enjoyed paella, assorted tapas with sangria and local beers along with pastries and other provincial delicacies.

We shared laughter and fun exchanges with the assortment of passengers in our group. The acquaintance of some interesting South Africans and Australians generated enlightening conversation. Aboard the bus one afternoon, Miriam from Johannesburg – a woman about my mom's age – was most interested in my Peace Corps work in Rabat. She was curious: how did we keep up with world news and current events?

"Did you hear the pope just died?" she asked, hoping to fill me in on the latest headlines.

"Oh yes, we can read *Time* magazines and *The International Herald Tribune* newspaper," I told her, hoping to convince her Rabat was not too Third World. "I read all about that a month ago."

"No, no," Miriam interrupted me. "That pope just died; he was pope for barely a month. We have a new pope now, John Paul II."

It was news to me.

Returning to Madrid to end the tour, my parents collected their souvenirs and headed home. My mother was filled with sniffles – as if she would never see me again. I reminded her I would be home for Christmas in a couple of months. My dad handed over about $30 in leftover pesetas – that would certainly help with my return trip to Rabat.

Reflecting on their visit, I realized we were of different generations. I accepted that and learned a lot. I packed my best effort into planning their Moroccan visit. Their overall impression of my foreign living experience was quite different than what I had originally envisioned.

I was on my own once again.

# PART FOUR
... and the Job Came Tumblin' Down

## Troubling Job Thoughts

Making my way back to home plate, I spent two days recovering from the weeks on the road. I also had a ton of laundry to do. Rabat weather had turned cooler. My new place looked great upon my return. Not much mail in my box at the Peace Corps office, but I had plenty of new material to read from the stash my parents delivered.

Less than 10 weeks of work at the office stood between me and a trip home to Atlanta.

I was cautiously optimistic that my job circumstances had improved. I learned limited funding had been given to Marc to finish two films we had in the works. That would keep us going for a while. While I was away, the Peace Corps had cancelled my job position due to the near non-existent workload, so no volunteer would replace me the following June. With my living situation resolved, I planned to develop a better office environment, if possible. That looked doubtful.

Two weeks passed, and the return to my ministry position had been a challenge. I had wanted nothing more than to complete two years of service in the Peace Corps, but my position had virtually no substance left. Following vacation, I was courted with the same promises – promises of needed materials and meaningful projects. Little had changed from the disastrous state of midsummer.

While I was away, Becky had faced day after day of boredom. She more or less walked out of the office one afternoon and began full-time work on a Peace Corps slideshow project to be used in training new volunteers. She was desperate for something to do. She traveled extensively all over Morocco on photo trips, prepared scripts and put a lot of effort into her self-initiated venture. Most commendable, really.

She returned to the office and confronted our Moroccan boss about some ideas that might involve her services in the near future. The boss promised arrangements for new projects and set up a meeting with Becky the following day to disclose them. Becky waited all that next day. Not once was the promised meeting initiated or mentioned.

As before, arrangements for our work remained unheard of and, in some cases, fictitious. Much the same situation existed between me and Marc. Cases of film had been acquired, he had told me – enough to shoot every day for a year. So far, not one can of film had appeared in the office. Our scheduled trip to film in Fes was routinely delayed, then forgotten. I sat around, ready and eager to shoot, but it was impossible to make movies without film in the camera.

How long I could go on, I honestly didn't know. The situation was demoralizing and frustrating. My last day out with the camera – with film in it – had been back in early July. I was proud to report that the Ministry of Agriculture owned the cleanest camera in Morocco.

What could Becky and I do? We had discussed the situation at length. Both of us wanted to complete two years of service, but the bleak prospects in the daily work setup didn't encourage us to press on. I read newspaper clips from home about what people were doing in my profession and wondered if I could be part of that, rather than face eight more months of idleness, assuming things continued as they were.

Both of us committed to give the ministry a fair chance to supply us with materials and work. Until our Christmas departures for Atlanta and Denver, we were hopeful – though not overly optimistic – that some big changes might occur. Our strategy was to re-evaluate the situation when we returned in January and individually make decisions to stay or to leave. I had prepared my resumé, including my work there, and planned to talk to people in the business in December. I had no predictions what the chances were of landing the kind of position I wanted during a three-week holiday period. Primarily, I wanted to research the level of film production activity in the Atlanta area and look into possibilities of other foreign employment or positions that could use my language ability.

## Halloween Happiness

Feeling the doldrums, I knew a trip out of town would cheer me up, so I hit the road. Destination: the annual Peace Corps Halloween Party, held at the home of Ag mechanic Joe and TEFL volunteer Lou in Beni Mellal. Eight volunteers were working there at that time. A large group of about 55 showed up on Saturday, October 28, for a wild costume parade, great food and fun times.

I decided our getups only enhanced the everyday circus atmosphere of the souk bus rides into the town. The local population was dazed – so many Americans climbing off buses and running around town dressed as witches, clowns and other odd characters.

"It looks like an invasion!" a costumed ghoul quipped.

One guy arrived as a mummy, wrapped up in ACE bandages. Patty, Maura and Debra walked down the street, dressed as angels complete with halos, and announced themselves the Angels of Azrou.

Inside Joe and Lou's house, the kitchen was a hub of activity where we found a tub of sangria and assorted pizzas baked in the ferran down the street. It was a popular spot for the hungry crowd. Joe's large living room and the rooftop terrace provided plenty of room to circulate, catch up with friends and meet a few new faces. Lou played disc jockey, shuffling cassette tapes featuring the Rolling Stones, The Police and Bruce Springsteen.

Our assembly was a combination of volunteers from our class, rookies from the new group and a few who had extended for their third years. Lots of turbans and togas. Connie, who won the last costume contest as the Statue of Liberty, arrived at the party as Dorothy from *The Wizard of Oz*, toting two bottles of Doumi Rouge, the cheapest, vilest excuse for a red wine – so cheap it was sold in plastic bottles. She definitely looked the part in her pinafore dress made from blue and white gingham fabric and shoes she had painted red. Eric was there as the Hunchback of Notre Dame. Sally was dressed for a pageant with her veil and a Miss Morocco sash. Reprising my tourist attire, I collected plenty of photos. Our host Joe played the jet-setting playboy in his black silk shirt and jeans.

The party proved to be a news-gathering opportunity, with plenty of updates not covered in our monthly newsletters – especially regarding job situations. Two of the engineers working in Fes reported they, too, had little meaningful work. Some TEFL teachers expressed their frustration with the frequent strikes students would spring on them, often protesting for the most inane reasons.

Also much discussed: Peace Corps Director Carolyn Payton's recently circulated memo strongly suggesting country directors end the policy of approving volunteers' requests to extend their service for a third year. Apparently, Washington felt those extending their in-country stay were reducing opportunities for new recruits to have the Peace Corps experience. Volunteers I knew countered that they had put in the time and effort to learn the language and absorb the culture, so they should have earned the priority to extend their service to Morocco.

Months later, Mike Kendellen, Steve Long, Tinker and several others did, in fact, extend for a third year. They transitioned from their TEFL duties into social services programs, aiding the handicapped and those afflicted with polio.

Visiting the home's Turkish toilet, I found some interesting reading material. On the back of the bathroom door, I noticed a Countdown to Departure calendar – for tracking the number of days until we would leave Morocco, with the caption:

> NOTE — The following people
> will NOT be at the airport to greet you:
> 
> | | |
> |---|---|
> | Elvis | 8/16/77 |
> | Bing Crosby | 10/14/77 |
> | Charlie Chaplin | 12/25/77 |
> | Hubert H. Humphrey | 1/13/78 |
> | Morris the Cat | 1978 |
> | Karl Wallenda | 3/22/78 |
> | Pope Paul VI | 8/6/78 |
> | Keith Moon | 9/7/78 |
> | Pope John Paul I | 9/28/78 |

Visitors had scribbled in the margins the names of assorted relatives and acquaintances who had also passed on.

That event was worth the rugged six-hour bus ride to get there. Well after midnight, partygoers found quiet places to crash among the four houses of local volunteers. Some headed for one of the two hotels in town. It was a bit too chilly to sleep under the stars on Joe's rooftop terrace, so I plopped on a banquette in his spare room.

Sunday started late. A bunch of us collected ourselves at a café across the street from the souk bus stop, grabbing a quick breakfast of pastries and coffee. Everyone prepared to head home to points north and south. Tales of the night before were circulated with hopes for similar future gatherings. We agreed the party was a welcome breather from our often-mundane daily routines.

Rich, Melanie and I found seats on a noon bus bound for Casablanca. From there, Rich and I hopped into a grand taxi shuttle heading for Rabat.

## Seasons Change

With several important Moroccan holidays coming up, our workload continued to be light. First, we got a day off for a national holiday commemorating the third anniversary of the Green March. Still, no film had been delivered, so I focused on small editing projects.

The Muslim feast of Aid el-Kbir and Morocco's Independence Day both landed in November. Winter was on its way – our first real rain tipped us off. It was still not too cold in Rabat. Places inland – Midelt and Azrou – were turning cold, and the High Atlas Mountains near Marrakesh already had snow.

Robbie Hare traveled to Washington, D.C., to deliver her baby. Before she departed, I stopped by her house, and she gave me a haircut. I recapped the Halloween party and shared how cooking meals for one was challenging. Robbie assumed correctly that I missed Becky's cooking. She was excited about the new addition to their family; Emmett would soon have a little brother or sister. The visit turned out to be our last time together in Morocco. I would fondly remember our strolls through the medina shopping as well as the many great meals and celebrations she hosted at their house.

Stopping by the office, I learned Paul and Emmett would be on my flight December 8 – on their way to join Robbie in Washington. That news earned me a free ride to the Casablanca airport in a Peace Corps staff car.

Saturday was my big cleaning day. I did three tubs of laundry and cleaned the apartment top to bottom. I was getting better on windows and didn't miss having a maid every week.

## Washington Comes to Morocco

I was one of 35 volunteers invited to a meeting of Peace Corps officials from Washington. The conference was held at a resort hotel in Mohammedia, on the coast just north of Casablanca.

When my parents visited in September and met Paul Hare at the office, he mentioned that the upcoming event would be a waste of money. In addition to bringing all those people from Washington, the Peace Corps leadership would bring 17 other country directors from as far away as the Philippines.

Talk at the meeting centered mostly around English teachers and TEFL projects. The few people there from the technical programs hardly got a word in. Lively discussions arose over the push to end third-year extensions. Not much was decided, and it turned out to be one big gripe session. They gave us a nice lunch at the resort's restaurant, and I was given a one-and-a-half-day excuse from work.

The conference set the scene for a significant turning point in the Peace Corps' administration. We learned weeks later that the ongoing friction between ACTION director Sam Brown and Peace Corps Director Carolyn Payton came to a head during the conference. It was no secret that Brown and Payton didn't see eye-to-eye on many policies. While at Mohammedia, tales of Brown's midnight door-banging at Dr. Payton's room – complete with his angry pleas for her to resign – were graphically detailed in a front-page article, "The Peace Corps is Far from Peaceful," by James Perry in the January 16, 1979, edition of *The Wall Street Journal*. Perry called it the "Showdown in Mohammedia." Back in Washington, Brown asked for Dr. Payton's resignation. Her chief deputy and three others were either fired or resigned. Sam Brown was left to put the pieces back together, hoping to move the Peace Corps in a new direction.

Following the conference, the one official in charge of Morocco, Tunisia and other North African countries stayed another week. Paul Hare hosted an elaborate dinner at his house for all Rabat volunteers and office staff to meet the desk officer from Washington. The dinner was a chance to gain some perspective about what actually took place at headquarters. The officer was also a main contact between stateside recruiters and in-country program directors.

## The King Goes to Washington

I did most of my Christmas shopping the week before Aid el-Kbir. Prices were great because families needed money to buy their sacrificial sheep, so that was the best time of the whole year to shop – like Black Friday. I negotiated some outstanding deals.

Office activity remained light. Talk among our Moroccan co-workers centered around King Hassan II's two-day visit to America. A secretary came in from down the hall and announced to Becky, "I saw pictures of your country on TV last night!" The week's newspapers had been full of pictures and background articles covering things related to the king's visit – U.S. history, geography and Washington's monuments.

During the king's appearance before the National Press Club, he was asked about his impression of the Peace Corps in Morocco, among other things. The king said it was "America's problem, not his problem." We could not believe it! I didn't think he realized what we were trying to do there. Maybe he misunderstood the question.

I listened to the official speeches of President Jimmy Carter and King Hassan II on the radio. Surprisingly, the king spoke reasonable English. President Carter read a prepared address he obviously hadn't seen before and didn't sound overly excited about his visitors. Turned out, Morocco's minister of agriculture was also in Washington with the king, along with the crown prince – two subjects I had filmed at official events. It was great to hear some English on the radio. A French summary of the speeches followed the English versions.

Mail had been really light. I had tried to write more (to receive more) and thought the stack of postcards I sent while in Spain might generate a little return mail. So far, not much response. Everybody must have been busy; I wished I could say the same.

## The Decision

After much thought about the state of my virtually nonexistent job and the possibilities I could undertake elsewhere, I began preliminary discussions with Paul Hare concerning my departure from Morocco.

I believed I had completed my function as a cinematographer for Morocco's Ministry of Agriculture. The absence of vital materials made the position useless and my time wasted. I could be doing so many other things. The countless personal benefits – the language and cross-cultural experiences – were priceless to me. But without the foundation of a purpose for being there, extending those benefits was unreasonable. I had a difficult time of decision ahead.

One Monday evening, I stopped by the Peace Corps office and summarized my situation and feelings before Paul Hare. He was well aware of the situation at our office. Paul also had a bunch of volunteer engineers complaining about their lack of meaningful work. I wanted to lay my cards on the table and formulate an agreeable exit plan. Paul wanted to speak first with Phil Hanson about my situation.

The following morning, Phil called me at work. With some English-speaking workers around, I couldn't say much about my problems on the phone. We arranged a 5:30 p.m. meeting at his office.

At the same time, Becky presented her paperwork excusing her from the ministry office to undertake another photo trip for her slideshow project on behalf of the Peace Corps. The two Moroccan bosses who had to approve her papers gave her a brutal, almost cruel grilling about the purpose of the trip and the time she would be away from the office. This would be her second trip for the project. She was going since no work had appeared at the ministry office, as promised.

"Who do you work for, Peace Corps or us?" asked Mr. Jebbor, our supervisor. Jebbor declined her request, but Ben Saiid, the senior boss, reluctantly approved her departure.

We left the office at lunchtime, and Becky went to pieces. We had both felt the same way for so long about the countless problems at our office, but Becky became much more emotional about it. She was really shaken up and cried all the way home.

"It's all so pointless!" she told me. I heartily agreed with her assessment.

I hated making decisions. I knew this was the end of the line for me but couldn't thoroughly convince myself. That 5:30 meeting was staring right at me. After work, I took a long walk around town. On my way home, I realized something had to give and formulated my decision to leave Morocco by the end of January.

Phil was ready for a serious meeting. "Would you like some coffee?" he asked. Phil only offered visitors coffee when the going was rough. A week earlier, Becky had been given the same coffee opener. Phil knew all about the bad scene between Becky and her bosses that morning. I expressed my disgust.

He supported my decision and didn't blame me for wanting to move on to better things back home. His official dealings with our ministry had been terrible lately. No replacements would be coming. Phil was content to effectively conclude business with the Ministry of Agriculture, for the simple fact of their lack of cooperation.

We talked. Phil knew what I was thinking but was a little surprised at my definite plans: I would complete my service to the Ministry of Agriculture on November 30, giving them an immediate two-week notice. I would take my Christmas leave as planned.

When Becky first proposed her set of seven slideshows for the Peace Corps office, I was part of the deal to provide title slides, maps and charts for those programs. I had already started on some of the work. I planned to return January 2 to complete it and estimated the project would require another month's work.

Upon completion of that project, my Peace Corps service would end, and I would return to the United States – probably around the first week of February. I proposed my plan to Phil, and he approved it.

I let out a huge sigh of relief when Phil accepted my plans. It looked like everything would work out OK. His only caution was for me to not drag out my work on the slideshows. We briefly discussed what I would do back in the States. I shared my possibilities and confidence that I could find a good position.

Becky would likely leave her ministry position when she returned and learned my plans. Both Paul and Phil understood the problems Becky and I faced. We had kept them informed of the snowballing situation over the previous months. Throughout my time in Morocco, they had been great sources of understanding and encouragement.

Our business was concluded in 30 minutes. We stood and shook hands; our meeting was over. A thought erupted in the back of my mind: it took me six weeks to fill out all the paperwork to join the Peace Corps and only half an hour to talk my way out of it! Remarkable.

To endorse the no-hard-feelings result of the meeting, Phil invited me to his house later for a drink and pizza. After all, we were neighbors. A giant vodka-tonic had been on my mind anyway.

An hour later, I approached Phil's house and knew right away I was at the right address – Barry White was playing on the stereo. When I arrived, Phil turned off the music and told me his wife, Anissa, was out for the evening with girlfriends.

The evening toast – "Bye-bye, Richard," I thought of it – was uneventful. Phil and I drank, enjoyed pizza and looked at some slides of his recent trip to Spain. Only one mention of our earlier discussion arose.

"Are you really sure about this thing now?" Phil pressed. I told him my decision was final. The subject was dropped. He advanced a slide.

By Thursday, I was set to inform the ministry office and my Belgian supervisor of my decision. I had no binding contract, so my departure posed no problems. Marc knew I had been unhappy with the job but was surprised to hear I would be terminating.

"You are terminating?" he questioned me in his best English.

The real shocker hit when I informed Marc that no replacement volunteer would follow. He was visibly taken aback. He accepted my plans for pulling out and only asked that I give a letter of resignation to my Moroccan boss as soon as possible. I had planned to wait until the last minute, but his idea was more polite and should calm any big waves between co-workers, I thought. So, in my intermediate French, I wrote:

>Mr. Jebbor:
>
>For your information: I'm going to terminate my service to the Ministry of Agriculture, Audio-Visual Bureau, on November 30, 1978.
>    I prefer to leave for the United States and look for more interesting work in film production. In the office here, there is not sufficient material to make films. I have waited since the first week of July to use the camera. It is not possible for me to wait any longer. Thank you for your understanding.
>
>Sincerely,
>Richard Wallace

I had to type the letter twice. My first attempt was erred by interrupting co-workers who had already heard I was leaving. I convinced one Moroccan that two years had passed. I really didn't want to talk about it. The second try was readable, and I took it directly to Mr. Jebbor.

He already knew of my decision. Seeing it in writing only brought a French response of "All right. Thank you." My official chores were completed.

I felt as if I had aged two years in the past two weeks. The strain of the decision had been significant but was now settled. Changes were on the way, and preparing for those changes brought hints of excitement between yawns. I asked Nurse Dolores what could be wrong since I had been sleeping eight to 10 hours a night and still felt tired. She offered a vitamin supplement. Arriving home late that evening, feeling exhausted, I knew something was wrong – I couldn't even muster the strength to open the bottle of vitamins! I hoped it was just an expected end to a pressured period.

Meanwhile, Rabat was all lit up for Independence Day, November 18. All the lighted decorations used the national colors, red and green. They reminded me Christmas was right around the corner.

## And Now for the News

Explaining all the recent developments to the folks back home required some strategy. Letters had to provide the background for my decision and what it meant moving forward.

I laid out the facts: I still had no film to shoot. I had edited and re-edited all our existing films. The two Moroccan bosses had launched a new campaign of daily harassment. The job had fallen apart since I returned from vacation. Plus, I knew there were a hundred better things I could be doing.

In addition to the issues, I identified numerous benefits to making the move. For one thing, I wouldn't be lost in the crowd of June graduates during job-hunting. I had felt unemployed those last six months and couldn't wait to pick up a camera and make movies again. The total experience in Morocco had been priceless, but my basic premise for being there was no longer valid. My decision would allow me to get back into the full swing of my profession.

End of story to the home folks. I was satisfied with putting my feelings down in writing and spelling out the details behind my decision and hoped they would understand.

Paul Hare went out of town for the weekend, so I offered to house-sit again. His son, Emmett, was staying at a friend's house. I did my laundry in their machine and had friends over for a cold beer and a big pot of chicken paprika.

Upon his return, Paul posted an invitation in the monthly newsletter for a Thanksgiving party at his house. He did not disappoint. Like the feast the previous year, plenty of familiar American food was shipped in for the occasion. I also got to see people I had not talked to in months.

The gossip mill included news of my pending departure. I explained to Larry, the surveyor, and a few others of my decision to leave; all were understanding and supportive. Many of the engineers had also been frustrated with a lack of activity in their offices.

Toward the end of the week, Becky and Chuck, my engineer buddy stationed in Fes, came over for spaghetti. The dinner was my first social interaction with my former roommate since our split.

In two short weeks, I would be flying home for the holidays.

## The Final Day

I had long wondered what my last day at the ministry office might be like. The beautiful, warm late November weather resembled June and my vision. Activity for the day would be typical of the preceding days – that held true. I completed a small editing job I had started two days before.

Beyond that, similarities between my well-remembered dream and the true course of the day did not exist. I sat at the editing table, making final splices for a short film about driving a tractor. I wanted it completed and in the can when I left.

Marc rushed in, remarked that it was my last day and asked me to show him where I had stored things. A tour of all the film cabinets took only a few minutes. We exchanged addresses, and he turned and walked out. That was the last I saw of Marc, a guy I admired for facing the daily problems of dealing with the ministry over film production matters. Marc did all the legwork, arranging production and materials; all I did was use and maintain the equipment. Marc never fully understood why I left – some personality differences existed between us – and he was left to run the show on his own the best he could. His contract expired six months later, and he would be rid of the headaches and associated problems too.

By noon, I reached a good stopping place, locked everything away and went home for lunch.

Returning to the office, I recalled my first day in that room – sweating like crazy on a hot September Monday, all dressed up in a coat and tie to make that good first impression for my bosses that the *Peace Corps Handbook* talked about. On my last day, I was dressed comfortably in my plaid flannel shirt and faded corduroys.

Hardly a soul remained around the office on my last afternoon. I was all prepared with little parting speeches for my co-workers, but nobody was around to hear them. That happened often – a secretary to the big boss would quietly pass the word that Mr. Saiid had to attend a meeting or would be out of the office for the afternoon, so many would not return after lunch.

I gave two shirts to Jamal, the graphic artist. The shirts had to be 10 years old – I remembered wearing them in high school – but Jamal always remarked how much he liked them. He was excited to receive the package.

By 5:30, my final project was complete, and I was all set to walk out the door. Jamal and Mohammed were the sole recipients of my au revoir. I caught a taxi into town. My departure was different from what I had in mind – more low-key. My experiences with Morocco's Ministry of Agriculture switched to my memory file, and my anticipation of leaving for the United States the following week occupied my focus.

I had several things to handle before leaving. Luckily, my Christmas shopping was completed. Packing everything for travel would be quite a project, though.

The holiday season got off to an early and impressive start. All Rabat-area volunteers received an embossed invitation from our new ambassador, Richard Parker. He had just arrived, replacing Robert Anderson. The ivory note card read:

> Ambassador and Mrs. Parker
> invite you to an Open House
> and Christmas Carols
> Friday, December 22, 1978
> 18:30 to 20:30 hours

The address to the ambassador's residence was tucked into a lower corner. I was glad the new man in charge remembered the Peace Corps crowd, but I had other plans.

## Happier Holidays

My long-awaited return to Atlanta was most interesting. The flight was extremely long and tiring – totally unlike my return flight from Amsterdam and Kilimanjaro four years before. I enjoyed the company of Paul and Emmett Hare on the flight into New York, then traveled to Atlanta with two empty seats beside me.

My dad, brother Bill and college roommate Ray greeted me at the airport, and I had something for everyone to carry. My carry-on load featured two large Moroccan cooking pots of heavy stoneware. First impressions revealed little change in the two people I had not seen in 18 months. We went straight home and talked until 2 a.m. Quite a long day.

Our house was decorated like a palace for Christmas. All the little luxuries – TV, telephone, carpets and central heating – that I had done without for so long surrounded me. I spent the first few days hanging out around the house, talking to people on the phone.

Rested, I went to Bill's house near Stone Mountain where my older sister Diane joined us. There, I met my two new nieces, Melissa and Natalie, and observed how much my third niece, Allison, had grown. The house echoed with the throbbing hum of happy noise from the three little girls. It was a fun family reunion, minus my younger sister who had recently moved to Wyoming.

We sat down to dinner, and I fielded a few questions about the kinds of food I ate in Morocco. My current make-do-or-do-without lifestyle surprised some family members. They couldn't imagine life without central heating when it was 40 degrees outside.

The first full week at home was spent on my job search. A new resumé was printed and sent to contacts I knew in local film production. I lined up interviews with TV news people and the Associated Press, where I had previously worked. Everybody showed interest in my background, but nobody provided a firm job offer; the unemployment rate was edging up around 6 percent at that time. With plans to follow up, I remained optimistic.

Throughout my stay in Atlanta, I was invited to friends' homes for dinner to share a slideshow about my experiences, using my dad's projector. My presentation was perfected after two or three tries and became easier; I kept the same set of slides together for all the shows. I enjoyed reliving some of my experiences. A picture was worth a thousand words when describing my lifestyle over the previous 18 months. Even with the pictures, many in my audiences could not fully comprehend the culture or my living environment. The top comment on my photos came from Fulton County Superior Court Judge John Langford, with whom I had reached the summit of Kilimanjaro. I showed him and his family a typical scene of dozens of mules fenced in while their owners shopped at the nearby souk. The Judge remarked, "Reminds me of the Dekalb County Courthouse" – his cross-town, often rural-oriented counterparts. We all enjoyed a good laugh.

One afternoon, I was visited by Debbie's parents from Rome, Georgia. I delivered a cassette tape Debbie had prepared, along with some small Christmas gifts from Morocco. They were most appreciative that we had a chance to get together. I shared a few photos of Midelt with them. They handed me a cassette tape of their family's Christmas greetings to take back to Debbie.

Christmas Day arrived. My grandparents had come from Memphis. Christmas dinner was a banquet for a dozen people. Everybody understood and supported my reasons for leaving the Peace Corps four months early. My Moroccan Christmas shopping was appreciated. Bill and my dad got a big kick out of the smell of their leather belts made in Fes. Scarves made by the feet of Omar in Marrakesh made nice gifts for Mom and my sister Diane.

The last evening of my grandparents' visit, I cooked my Moroccan specialties for my family, featuring my tried-and-true recipe for kefta tajine with tomatoes and eggs. Though hesitant at first about eating it with their hands, they all grabbed the bread and dug right in, enjoying the novelty of it all.

As we rang in the New Year, it looked like 1979 would be a year spent in transition between Peace Corps living and the American way – assuming I did not accept another international position.

## Back to Morocco

On the first Wednesday of the new year, I began the homestretch of my Peace Corps career. My return trip to Rabat was rushed and uneventful. Most all volunteers reported that glad-to-be-back feeling when they landed in Casablanca. I was in limbo, feelings-wise, since I only needed to manage 30 more days in the Third World. At that juncture, I was glad to see the conclusion of my Peace Corps work approaching but indifferent about my social, family and employment prospects upon my return to the United States. The coming month in Morocco would, no doubt, realign my thoughts into a living pattern I could tolerate.

I was surprised to see the rich green of surrounding farmlands as the plane landed in Casablanca. Apparently, a lot of rain had fallen, and I surmised the winter rainy season had gotten off to an early and potent start. Airport crowds and customs slowed things up, but I was fortunate to run into a U.S. Embassy driver waiting to pick up some VIP diplomat on my flight. His passenger didn't make the flight, so I enjoyed a staff car shuttle to my door in Rabat rather than two Moroccan bus rides with my light luggage load.

The driver, though, had some official errands to run in Casablanca, so we took the indirect route through the city. We hit the fish market, picked up a spare part for an embassy staffer's washer and took delivery on a replacement felt for another's pool table. Shortly after noon we were cruising on the coastal road to Rabat, then delayed a bit to change a flat tire. By 1:30, I was in my apartment. Everything was as I had left it – with a fresh coat of dust. So far, my reunion with Morocco was going great.

Later, I collected my mail and my last living allowance from the Peace Corps office. I learned that Paul Hare was leaving his position as Country Director; he had accepted a State Department job in Washington. The move had been in the works for some time. Paul was due back the next day to clean up paperwork and would return to

Washington two weeks later. His leadership and close friendship had been essential to my enjoyment there. I also learned that Robbie had a baby girl December 23 and named her Jessica; both were doing fine.

Phil Hanson would assume the role of Country Director, but his five-year term limit working for the Peace Corps would be up in June.

I took a break and sat alone at an empty desk to read a letter from Dan, my college film production partner at SIU. He wrote that he had left his job as an Olan Mills portrait photographer in Connecticut and headed for California – a move we had talked about making jointly after my Peace Corps service. Now, joining him there looked enticing, but I preferred to pursue my Atlanta prospects before running off to the West Coast. So much could change with the right job offer. I also needed time to produce a reasonable portfolio of my Moroccan photographic work.

My buddy Amin, manager at the corner hanoot, was amazed I had gone all the way to America and back in three weeks. He reported that butter was unavailable for another week or so, explaining that the foreign supplier (Holland) wasn't getting paid for shipments. I knew how that story went. For our brief conversation, I turned the French back on and realized it had not deteriorated terribly during my three-week sabbatical.

Mark Postnikoff and I planned to travel to his town of Midelt on one last swing across Morocco whenever he returned from the States. I was looking forward to it.

While waiting for Mark, I lined up materials to work on Becky's Peace Corps slideshows and prepared to work at home. I would like that – no more city buses.

Finally, Mark arrived around 10 p.m. His flight had been six hours late landing, and TWA lost one of his bags. We exchanged lots of what-I-did-in-the-U.S. stories. Bright and early Saturday morning, we were off to Midelt. We took a grand taxi to Meknes and enjoyed a great lunch at one of my favorites.

Meknes functioned as a key transportation hub, linking towns throughout central Morocco. The nonstop activity in front of Bab El Mansour, the 12th century Islamic arch, would never leave my mind. A jumble of buses, taxis, scooters and bodies mingled freely – with the full range of sound effects. The light was not ideal. I don't think I owned one decent image of that place.

We returned to the bus station and a 2 o'clock bus to Midelt, passing through Azrou and the Middle Atlas Mountains. I was excited about seeing my first Moroccan snow up close. Above Azrou, fields remained covered with melting snow from a few days before. Mark was relieved to be on the last leg of his extended journey.

With the cold weather, Berbers were wrapped in vibrant layers of color. By 7:30, we arrived in Midelt and managed to get Mark's luggage load to his house intact. We enjoyed a late-evening reunion with Debbie, Julie and the four other volunteers living there. Debbie was excited to receive the package I had brought from her parents. Following a hasty "Thank You," she rushed off to load her cassette player and listen to delayed holiday greetings from home.

Sunday morning was another early start, heading to Midelt's weekly souk. Very high winds intensified the cold. I held on to my hat while my cameras battled blowing dust and sand – a real mess.

We walked back into town in time for church at the Room. Though a Catholic church was built there, with a priest and French nuns, during cold weather only a small side room was used. Some American walk-in closets were bigger than the space in which I, two other volunteers, four nuns, two others and a priest celebrated Mass that day. Certainly, the congregation had no trouble hearing the sermon.

Later, walking around and shopping, we saw handicrafts and local sights. The color of the wardrobe remained most impressive – bright yellows, reds and greens. I hoped my photos would capture the colorful display. I tried a "hot" shower that afternoon and almost froze solid. After enjoying a big meal of Moroccan flavors, we rang in the New Year one week late with some small bottles of champagne I had brought from the States.

Monday morning launched another series of travel days. I hoped to stay the night in Azrou. On my way back to Rabat, I spent most of the day trying to get out of Midelt. Reports of flooding just south of Midelt were apparently preventing northbound buses from reaching us and going on to Azrou. Lunch with Mark and other TEFL teachers was followed by a hopeless hitchhiking effort. Finally, I boarded a 4 p.m. bus headed for Azrou, facing the angriest clouds I had ever seen on the horizon.

Azrou sat in the heart of the Middle Atlas Mountains, and thoughts of being stranded in a snowdrift with 60 Moroccans – no matter how colorful their outfits – did not thrill me. The clouds appeared packed with snow. Worry, worry – somebody told me it contributed to baldness.

Everybody on that bus was bundled up – our load looked like a circus wagon full of clowns – the color was brilliant. It had always been said that that kind of third-class bus ride resembled a three-ring circus. True, our version had the standard number of screaming kids, chickens and old malodorous men. Travel in Morocco became more sensational with every excursion.

# The Angels of Azrou

The bus made it to Azrou in record time, by 7 that evening. It was warmer than in Midelt. Not a single snowflake delayed our trip. I walked into Patty's home in time for a small feast prepared by Fatima.

Fatima recalled previously meeting me (and my red hair) but Patty reintroduced me anyway. Always smiling, Fatima wanted to know all about me – where I came from, was I an English teacher too? Maura and Debra delivered the details in Arabic, laughing and carrying on with assorted stories, impressing their maid and tutor. I noticed Patty had acquired a cat, appropriately named Tajine.

After the excellent meal, we retired to the living room to enjoy hot tea and time catching up; I had not seen the Angels of Azrou since the Halloween party. Debra was still getting her feet wet teaching English at Lycée Tarik. I recapped my job's disintegration and how different it was living solo. Maura shared about visiting Didier in Paris over the Christmas break; Patty had spent the holidays in Spain. I mentioned my parents' recent visit and what a misadventure that was. Patty insisted she could top that. Debra uncorked a bottle of wine, and the evening was left to storytelling.

"Oh yeah, I went through that with my mother's visit," Patty launched into her story. "I tried to tell her no, but – oh, yes – the Baptist librarian from Tupelo, Mississippi, just had to come and visit me. Remember, Richard? I dyed my hair as red as yours to celebrate her arrival in Casablanca. She was shocked! The first of many surprises, I know. We made it to Azrou. I took her shopping with me. She got all upset about me arguing with my tomato guy. I always went at it in typical Moroccan fashion – lots of yelling and hand gestures. When my mom realized the scene was all about a 5-cent tomato, she kind of freaked out."

"And all the flies on the meat? Mom was horrified," Patty laughed as she continued.

"A few days later, we got the idea to stage a Moroccan wedding with my mom as the bride. Some of my students came over. They dressed her up like a bride with the ceremonial hooded gown, put her on the platter and danced, carrying her down the street. Fatima thought they were going to kill her. Mom didn't think it was too funny at the time. She was here about a week … and so happy to get off this continent." Patty said, laughing harder.

Maura jumped in for the next tale.

"Hey, it's no secret I'm obsessed with toilet paper – we just can't find any decent toilet paper here in Azrou. Lately, we've been using pages torn out of our old *Time* magazines," she explained. "One weekend, the three of us took off to Rabat for a weekend of civilization – and to round up some decent toilet paper."

Debra chimed in. "It really was a weekend I'll never forget. I wrote a letter to my mom all about it."

### one volunteer remembers...

Hi Mom:

You'll never believe this one: As I mentioned, we (with Patty Balch and Maura Murray) decided to go to Rabat. We did, and our usual mode of transportation – hitchhiking – paid off really big this time.

The guy who picked us up was a Spaniard doing business in Morocco. He's in the wastepaper business. Some sort of recycling wastepaper is involved. Anyway, he speaks perfect English and during the two-hour ride we talked a lot about Morocco, Peace Corps, what we do here, etc.

He was very interested in our lives here and, in spite of doing business in Morocco for 10 years, he does not know a whole lot about it. He comes to Morocco and leaves after two days and only stays in very nice hotels.

Anyway, by the time we got to Rabat, we had chatted quite a bit. We invited him for ice cream since he had been so nice; he was on his way to Casablanca for a flight to Spain today. He stopped and had ice cream and asked us when was the last time we had enjoyed dinner at a restaurant. We told him that it was about a month ago ... then he invited us to dinner! So, we (naturally) accepted. Then, he wanted to know where we were staying, but we knew he wouldn't want to stay there, (clean, but cheap and simple). So, we said no, you go to the nice hotel, and we will meet you for dinner. Then (the story gets better), he said no, you come and stay at the good hotel and I will pay.

So, we all trekked over here, (see letterhead: Hotel de la Tour Hassan). We got our room, and he got his own. I don't know why, but they gave us this big apartment [a suite] instead of a regular room. We all got ready – thank God we had brought some good clothes – and went to dinner at this great restaurant. I did not even know it existed here. They had the best steaks; I could not believe it. We all pigged out, and then he took us to a disco!

And all of the time he never acted like a weirdo or expected anything from us. It was definitely our best experience with hitchhiking so far.

We came back to the hotel at 3 a.m. ... he went to his room, and we came to ours. Then this morning, we had breakfast with him, and he left to catch his plane in Casablanca.

We are still in our apartment [suite] here. It's so nice ... we want to stay as long as possible. We are going to the beach today and tonight we will stay at our Peace Corps hotel. Anyway, mom, as you can see, we meet some good people over here.

Debra Snell
TEFL Instructor
Azrou

"I figured he was after Debra and suggested she take one for the team," Patty told me, laughing.

"No, no, he really was charming and did not expect anything in return!" Maura added. "Of course, while we were at that fancy hotel, we collected all the wonderful toilet paper we could."

When the subject of letters came up, Maura switched gears.

"We spend a lot of our spare time writing letters. We heard President Carter might be visiting Morocco, so we sent several letters inviting him to our house and asking him to please bring us Snickers bars and peanut butter. The White House was obliged to respond to every letter, you know."

I learned Maura and Patty were going to great lengths to boost Debra's spirits through her early struggles teaching English.

"Debra was really missing the Thanksgiving Day parade she watched every year on TV," Maura explained. "So, one Saturday, I said, 'Let's make a TV!' It's a fact – with time on their hands, Peace Corps Volunteers become increasingly resourceful, you know. We found this giant piece of carboard; we cut out a big opening like a TV screen, used some markers to make the knobs. I made an antenna for it too. One of us would peek through the opening; we took turns announcing the different floats and bands, describing the action – even threw in some Broadway sound effects. Two local boys came to the door and joined us – nice kids, Mohammed and Mobarack, about fifteen or sixteen. We told them it was an American holiday; they wished us 'Happy American Holiday!' while we all watched this cardboard TV. Everybody clapped when these imaginary floats went by. Fatima joined in – she just rolled her eyes. The boys got a kick out of watching American girls act so silly. It was pure fun."

Two wine bottles were empty as story time wound down and midnight approached. The Angels of Azrou were due in their classrooms the next morning. Lights out. The town's quiet encouraged my slumber.

Tuesday was Azrou's souk day, so wandering through the makeshift stalls occupied my time while Patty, Maura and Debra taught. Azrou was packed with Berbers from the surrounding mountains. For many, it was their weekly opportunity to buy foodstuffs, vegetables and other supplies.

Colorful carpets were everywhere, laid out on the bare ground, under perfect skies – quite a sight – more vivid photos. A carpet merchant asked me to take his picture while he and his father proudly held up their best merchandise. I complied, then waited for the usual plea for a donation. I was shocked when the man pulled out a roll of bills and wanted to pay me to send him two copies of the picture. I jotted down his address and agreed to send him two prints. It was worth the experience ... a Moroccan wanting to give me money – unforgettable.

After a quick lunch at Azrou's answer to Burger King, I was off on a 2 o'clock bus to Meknes, transferring to a grand taxi and reaching Rabat around 6:30.

### one volunteer remembers...

How did we teach English? After 30 years teaching TEFL and ESL at Georgia State University, I still can't answer!

Arriving in Rabat, we had a three-week TEFL training stage near the end of the summer and that was it.

Landing in Azrou, my first day in the classroom at Lycée Tarik, I think I almost had a nervous breakdown. Maura and Patty had to talk me down, assuring me I could do it.

We had no books for the students or a Teacher's Manual. We were on our own to develop lessons and figure out how to teach without materials. For the first-year class, we used a book we had been given during training that included the most popular TEFL dialogue, titled "Is this your handbag?" We would act it out for the students:

Person A: "Hello!"
Person B: "Hello!"
Person A: "Excuse me, is this your handbag?"
Person B: "Pardon?"
Person A: "Is this your handbag?"
Person B: "Yes, it is. Thank you very much."

It became permanently implanted into our minds during training. Constantly hearing "Excuse me" and "Pardon" would send us to the floor laughing like crazy!

For late-night entertainment at home, hoping to laugh a bit among ourselves on the coldest nights, we made silly jokes out of that sample conversation ... about everything! All the TEFL volunteers did.

During my second year in Azrou, I did get a set of 20 textbooks with professional development money from Peace Corps and used them in my second-year English class. Those were very helpful.

The winter months at Lycée Tarik were cold. The classroom windows were often broken; snow would blow into the classroom. Picture students under their djellabas trying to stay warm. I couldn't see their faces!

The blackboards were often broken and there was no chalk provided by the school. Copy machines were unheard of, and

> the mimeograph was working only occasionally. Students were supposed to have a copy book, a small notebook for their notes. The conditions were unimaginable compared to today, but we just got used to it.
>
> In fact, in 2005-2006, when I was at the university in Beni Mellal on my Fulbright (Scholarship), conditions were only slightly better. There were no books. Strikes were common, and students would walk out or stand outside my class yelling and making noise so it was impossible to teach. The students who would come to class would leave because of the pressure to strike. It was very hard conditions to teach, but I did it ... I had brought my own chalk!
>
> Debra Snell
> TEFL Instructor,
> Azrou

## The Homestretch

Back in Rabat, I dropped by to see Becky who'd returned from Denver. She had moved into a large house shared by TEFL teachers Michael and Allen with Greg, the TEFL program coordinator at the office. The spacious house was well furnished, with several bedrooms surrounding a central salon. I had visited the place for a volunteer's birthday celebration the summer before. The layout was ideal for entertaining.

More stories to share. Becky's homecoming was tempered by her parents' pending divorce. Like me, she had spent most of her time catching up with friends and family and explaining to all what life was like in Morocco. She was reunited with a white Christmas.

The next day, I collected some vital food supplies to restock my kitchen pantry, while getting reacquainted with my friendly corner grocer. It was back to work. I was set to finalize my departure plans, targeting February 2 and planning to coordinate the necessary projects for the Peace Corps training programs that Becky was producing.

Later that afternoon, I walked over to the Peace Corps office to find my mailbox empty, void of any welcome back messages. Staffer Linda had little new gossip to share.

The next morning was spent rearranging my furnishings for the work-at-home routine. Becky came by to discuss production plans. The dining table she and I once shared made an excellent surface for laying out and producing the graphics she needed. We decided to devote extra time over the weekend to get a few steps ahead in production.

Saturday became a full workday at home. Becky arrived, and I made a big pot of soup. She worked on her scripts while I outlined needed title slides and other graphics. Things were really shaping up, but a lot of full-time work remained. I would stay busy.

Our Sunday afternoon together started the process of editing the many slides Becky had collected from her photo excursions to various regions of the country. More details, more work – lots of ideas flew around during our collaboration. We called it a day around 4:30.

That evening, I considered the logistics of moving out for good. Everything had to go. My landlord came by, and I explained my February 2 departure and his upcoming vacancy. He was nice about it. He reminded me to drop the keys by the real estate agency. Taking care of that matter was a great relief. Some landlords could be picky about advance notice; the guy knew he would have no problem renting the place.

The weather remained so agreeable, Monday kicked off with a walk all over town. I dropped off my roll of black and white film to be developed so that I could send the Azrou carpet merchant the two promised prints. Then I stopped by the embassy and placed an ad in the embassy's newsletter for things I needed to sell. A final swing through the Peace Corps office was a waste of time – my still-empty mailbox was collecting dust.

Tuesday, Tinker from Kasba Tadla arrived in Rabat to get books from the Peace Corps library, so I gave her a pantsuit for her maid that mom had sent back with me. I could imagine Zhora wearing it while cooking or washing clothes. She would wear it everywhere, I was sure.

### one volunteer remembers...

I decided to extend for a third year. Anita, a volunteer I knew in Casablanca, contacted me about assuming her position at a center for handicapped children, which was run by the Save the Children Fund (SCF), a British organization. Most of the kids there had post-polio syndrome with varying degrees of residual paralysis. At the time, polio was still common in

Morocco, and more prevalent in the cramped quarters of the Casablanca slums. Efforts had been made to establish a nationwide vaccination program but had been hindered by corruption in the Ministry of Health.

My job was to administer a program of sponsorship, whereby Brits would "sponsor" a child by sending monthly stipends. I was to identify worthy candidates and translate the correspondence that was shared by the sponsor and child. My first order of business was to do home visits to all the existing beneficiaries. The program had been administered by a Moroccan fellow and, unfortunately, I found that a number of the sponsored kids were actually his own friends and relatives who did not need the help. My unannounced home visits sometimes led me to well-appointed middle-class apartments. I had to remove these kids from the program and was then able to identify kids who were at risk of having to leave school to work unless their families received a stipend. Most of them lived in the bidonville (industrial slum) next to our center and were handicapped or had a widowed mother.

There were also other projects underway in the center. We had an elementary school, a workshop to build the necessary leg braces and crutches, physical therapy and a trade school for the older kids who weren't able to pass the academic tests which would have allowed them to move on to regular high school. It was a good place run by kindhearted Brits who spoke very rudimentary Arabic and tortured French. Mary Browne was the nurse, and she was a marvelous person who had given her life to SCF. She had been in the 1940s airlift to Berlin, had PTSD from a traumatic evacuation as the Americans retreated from Da Nang in Vietnam, served with the Tamil Tigers in Sri Lanka, worked in Egypt, then Upper Volta before it became Burkina Faso.

Living in Casablanca, my social world was no longer the fun volunteer circuit of the Tadla plain. There were numerous old British ex-pats and bizarre evenings at the Churchill Club. It was a bit rough to go from being embraced as a teacher in a small town to being just another Nazrani in the big city. However, the kids at the center were wonderful to work with.

There were two sweet little boys who had been abandoned on a street corner, left on the same piece of plastic. They were best friends who lived in an orphanage nearby and came to the center every day. Nasser had a flail leg from polio, and Abdelwahed had arthrogryposis – instead of hands he had tapered forearms that looked like flippers. They kept getting recurrent cases of scabies at the orphanage, so we would scrub them down and treat their infestations. We had put together a small lending library for the kids, and these boys loved to have a story read to them. They would pick out a book and crawl up in my lap, and on numerous occasions they shared their raging cases of scabies with me ... the itchiest itch that ever there was!

In the summer, we would load up a group of kids in our clunky old bus and go camping by the sea. A British member of the Lion's Club had donated his beach house to our center, but it was confiscated by an official in the Ministry of Health for his own family. So, we just set up tents and camped by the sea. One of my favorite memories was swimming in the Atlantic like sea turtles with the kids clinging to our backs. For most of those kids, this was their only chance to get out of the city and to have the freedom of movement in the water. Many had flail limbs that were just skin and bone. Most were unable to walk and couldn't propel themselves. They looked forward to their seaside adventure each summer.

I would take groups of kids to the university hospital for eye exams, playing dumb at the entrance when the gate keeper implied that I should offer him a bribe. There was a kindhearted soldier who kept an eye out for our motley crew. He always came to our rescue and shepherded us past the greedy gate keeper. He loved to scoop up the kids and carry them to the clinic. The neighborhood social worker was an old French lady who was tough as a boot but also tenderhearted. I was toying with the idea of staying on in Morocco.

"Don't be like me," she cautioned me. "I stayed too long and now I belong neither here nor in France."

So, I came home, retooled by doing TEFL for a year while I earned my prerequisites to go back to school to become a physician assistant. My time with the kids at SCF was the impetus for me to go into healthcare.

Peace Corps in Morocco was a formative experience, full of serendipitous encounters that revealed the best of people's generosity and resilience but also offered a window into the worst examples of greed and misogyny.

Tinker Goggans
*SCF Program Administrator*
*Casablanca*

## Paperwork & People

I started on all the paperwork needed to exit the Peace Corps, papers similar in bulk to what was required to gain acceptance. So that the office could make ticket arrangements, I submitted my travel itinerary to depart on Friday, February 2. If all went according to plan, the one-way trip would be a rerun of my December journey.

A relaxing, low-key weekend followed. Laundry was my only accomplishment. While collecting the wash on the rooftop clothesline, I enjoyed a spectacular sunset and a tall glass of wine. A few hours later, the full moon rising over the Grand Mosque down the street created the scene for some of my most memorable photos.

I took a half day off from my artistic efforts and visited a few of my favorite merchants in the medina. With my departure less than three weeks away, my purchases included a nice ceramic soup bowl set and some small brass plates.

Early Monday morning, I decided there was time for one last-minute excursion to Casablanca. My main reason for going was to recover Mark Postnikoff's lost bag, which was being held by TWA at the airport. I was also considering buying a nice leather coat in town.

By 8:00, I was rolling down the coastal highway in a grand taxi, accompanied by one Moroccan and four Senagalese sailors on shore leave; all four spoke pretty good English. Stories of their maritime adventures covered several kilometers. Entering Casablanca, the thump-thump-thump of the city's brick streets was pure excitement for me. I would never get tired of that place – palm trees and the garish French influence in most of the older buildings. Our taxi arrived in the city's center, and I bid farewell to my sailor chums. It was a short walk over to the bus station where I could catch a shuttle to the airport.

The Casablanca airport was its usual mess of people, police ... and problems. I located the TWA baggage office and recovered Mark's lost bag after weaving through crowds of tourists. Once I exited the terminal, I thought surely the return shuttle bus between the airport and Casablanca would be running on schedule ... but it wasn't. I waited over two hours. I passed the time with a group of four American tourists, giving them my basic Welcome to Morocco message. We covered food, clothing, weather, a full lesson on the strange money system and even bus schedules to Marrakesh. A chorus of endless questions came from them. Wide-eyed and all ears, they were most interested in my suggestions – sort of fun, actually. The little things I had learned by living there appeared to them as potentially life-saving instructions.

A shuttle finally arrived, and we all relocated to the center of the city. A quick goodbye and I plopped myself into a grand taxi for the return ride to Rabat. No time for coat shopping; I had agreed to meet with Becky that evening about our work in process.

The evening was spent conferring with Becky and recounting my hectic mission to Casablanca. She had experienced a memorable day herself at the ministry office. Phil Hanson paid a visit to her Moroccan boss and discussed the pitiful work situation. The final negotiated result was that Becky agreed to work three days a week at the ministry and have two full days available for her Peace Corps projects – with the understanding that if an important assignment came up, the ministry work would have priority. Becky was relieved with the new arrangement.

As the week wound down, I made more progress on graphics for the training programs. I took a break after lunch and walked over to the Peace Corps office. The secretary was already fielding several calls about my items listed for sale in the latest embassy newsletter. In no time, both my electric blanket and work table were sold.

The week was ending on a high note: a big farewell party for Paul Hare at his house. The entire Rabat crowd was there, plus a few from the embassy. It was a real all-American fiesta. Lots of food with plenty to drink. My departure seemed to have gained respectability since Paul was leaving too – sure made it easier to talk about – as if we were in the same league, though we certainly were not.

Mark Postnikoff had traveled all the way from Midelt for one last visit, his bag and a chance to buy some items not available in his town. Attending Paul Hare's sendoff celebration was a bonus and the chance to savor American beer and party food. Mark had established himself as one of Peace Corps' most accomplished chefs and counted his homemade mayonnaise among his top culinary achievements. For Saturday's dinner, we cooked up a delicious meal featuring the two-pound Hormel canned ham I had brought back from Atlanta. Trading stories and ranking our most memorable Moroccan moments, we enjoyed a fun evening. Another farewell. Mark had all day Sunday to find his way back to Midelt.

Well after midnight Sunday, I got the urge to listen to the Super Bowl. I spent a full two hours hunting down the weak Armed Forces Radio signal. Finally, I heard about 30 minutes of the first half before the static became louder than announcer Curt Gowdy. Two days later, I bought a copy of *The International Herald Tribune* and read all about the

Steelers outlasting the Cowboys, winning 35-31. I missed seeing it on TV at home by just two weeks. I recalled telling an early departee the previous year, "If you're leaving Morocco, why don't you at least get home in time to see the Super Bowl?" I never dreamed I'd be in a similar predicament a year later.

## Final Goodbyes

My final day in Morocco was fast approaching.

Monday, I began all the necessary medical procedures to leave Morocco. The doctor's office was just down the street from the Peace Corps office. To complete the necessary lab work and examinations would require three visits.

Becky and Chuck stopped by that evening for a drink; I detected a serious relationship in the making. Becky reviewed my latest results for her slideshows. It was my goodbye to Chuck – another nice, intelligent guy, funny in his own way. He had led me on many guided tours of the amazing Fes medina.

I began working on my Peace Corps Final Report, a required document summarizing my work. My objective was to make it detailed and interesting to read. Keeping up with all the paperwork was becoming quite a job. My February 2 departure date was made official. I started to think about packing.

By Wednesday, the second of three lab days was completed. More work on my final report and projects at home. My place looked like a kindergarten – paper cutouts and art materials were strewn everywhere.

Thursday meant the final day of lab work for my medical discharge requirements. Hallelujah!

I stopped by the embassy to visit Mark Ward, a friend I had met during the theater season. His job as Program Director for the Agency for International Development (AID) was to give U.S. foreign aid money to Morocco. I gave him my resumé and inquired about any possibilities in my field with a government agency. Before I knew it, I was in the office of Morocco's Director of ICA – the International Communications Agency, formerly called the U.S. Information Service. Leslie Lyle was interested in my background and quickly handed over three names for me to contact in Washington – one was a personal friend of his. My interest in future work with the government was renewed, but only if the right program with travel was available. It proved to be an enjoyable morning networking on the international job-hunting trail. I made a good presentation. Talk of language abilities, foreign experience, travel history and a specialized skill could possibly work to my advantage. At least, that was my thinking.

Rich Eckert and his co-worker, George, came over for my routine spaghetti supper. Rich had a six-pack of American beer (not cold) stuffed in his coat. I had no idea where he got it. Rich and I recalled our first weekend trip away from the lycée during training, our train trip to Asilah and gorging ourselves on the great seafood there. George was wrapping up his third year of service and was having mixed feelings about leaving the country in June. His post-Peace Corps career plans remained undecided. I was glad to see Rich was much more satisfied in his new position working with George in Rabat. He was content with wrapping things up and heading home in June.

---

*one volunteer remembers…*

Just before we left Morocco, George and I went down to the Café Renaissance on Mohammed V in Rabat for coffee. We ran into other PCVs finishing their term. A little later, more exiting volunteers showed up. We decided to have breakfast. By the time we finished breakfast, it was nearly noon. So, we started drinking beer. Then, before you knew it, it was 2 p.m., so … we ordered lunch. After a few more beers it was nearly 4 p.m. We all reconvened at the "hole-in-the-wall" restaurant (El Bahia) in the medina that evening.

I just remember feeling so proud for what so many of us had accomplished. Two years away from all our friends and family and support networks, immersed in another culture, isolated; and yet we found a way to do our jobs and make some sort of positive contribution.

It was not the size of the accomplishment but the realization of the goal that was the reward. I feel that what I learned about myself and the world around me was the reward. Whatever little good I did while I was in Morocco was the icing on the cake.

Rich Eckert
*TEFL Instructor in Settat*
*Clinic staffer in Rabat*

## Last Visits & Loose Ends

With just a week left, I enjoyed a visit from Larry Berube, the surveyor from Beni Mellal. It was a great surprise to see him at my door. Like Mark, he had come a long way to visit me before I took off – Larry also needed to buy soy sauce. He was living with a Japanese Peace Corps-like volunteer and had become hooked on rice dishes and soy sauce.

We hit the streets. The night was spent with an assortment of potent potables at a variety of locales. Our attempt at a late-night walk home was interrupted by a policeman in front of the Grand Mosque, of all places. He asked for our identity papers (green cards). Luckily, we both had them, but mine had expired in August. I had never been stopped before. If anybody ever looked at it, they never noticed the date it was issued. That little guy did. He was not happy with us. Somehow, a string of my most coherent French came out – explaining our work in Morocco, our jobs with ministries (for his government) and that we were nice Americans. I promised to run right down to the station on Monday morning and renew my papers. He smiled. We smiled. A few handshakes and we were liberated. A unique experience, one week before my departure. Larry headed for his hotel. I almost ran back to my place and couldn't wait to lock the door behind me. What a day!

Sleeping in on Saturday, I got a late start on a full day of work with the slideshows. Becky dropped by with more ideas requiring my time. Finishing everything looked like a tight fit. I planned to go about my moving-out business and work on the project in any available time.

Other volunteers were in town for meetings and business, so a bunch of us got together for dinner at our favorite Spanish restaurant in my old neighborhood near the ocean. Walking over there was an experience. It was my first trip back since September. Lights shone from the fourth-floor place Becky and I shared – a strange sight. The bar/restaurant contained its usual noise, smoke and crowds, but the paella dish was superb. More goodbyes: to Robin, my guide for my first weekend stay in Morocco in Kasba Tadla, and to Mark Dressman, who was also in that group and ended up teaching English there.

A low-key Sunday followed. Moving day. A guy picked up my remaining furniture. He was setting up his new place in nearby Kenitra. Most everything went out the door, and I suddenly became wealthy.

Larry showed up after loading up on soy sauce and before heading back to Beni Mellal. He demolished me in chess; we joked about Friday night. Larry was thinking about taking a job in Saudi Arabia after his Peace Corps stint was over. A real character. Another farewell.

Later, Patty and Maura dropped in on their way home from Casablanca. The pair posed in front of my world map for a keepsake photo. While we shared a bottle of wine and some cheese, they scooped up leftover odds and ends, including the glasses we were using. Patty wanted my world map to explain to folks back in Azrou exactly where Tupelo, Mississippi, was located. Maura claimed any toilet paper I could spare. More hugs, more goodbyes – I was getting good at those.

Between visitors, I completed more work for Becky's programs.

With my newly acquired wealth, I treated myself to dinner at the Café Renaissance, our old hangout in town. Many a memorable hour was spent in that place. Possibly my last visit. The waiters recognized me; I seemed to be their only red-headed customer. I had a great view of everything with a seat along the back wall. My usual order of roasted chicken, spiced to perfection, with fries *(poulet et frites)* was quite satisfying. I knew what the bill would be but asked anyway, paid and left. I would remember the Renaissance well.

Monday started a new week, introducing beautiful weather in Rabat. Back to work. Only my large table and two uncomfortable stools remained at my place. The last buyer decided not to buy my kitchen supplies, so I could still cook. I had spent an extra-firm night on my makeshift bed – my bedspread and djellaba laid out in a pile under my sleeping bag.

Utilities were wrapped up. Some of the nicest Moroccans I had ever met came by – one to read my meter, another to remove it, then another to add up the bill. The pleasantries abruptly ended when the final tally was determined – the cashier had to pay me money. My deposits exceeded my final bill. He was not happy. I collected my dirhams and gave him a polite smile.

More cash to spend. I hopped into a familiar medina shop and quickly spent $50. A staff worker from the embassy picked up my large table, the last of my furniture, so I spent the night at Becky's new residence. I was beginning the final stage of leaving.

### one volunteer remembers...

After two years, I decided to stay for a third, reasoning that I'd spent the time and effort to learn Derija and the culture. But the head of ACTION was Sam Brown, the peacenik turned bureaucrat, and he frowned on us generalists, insisting that extensions be based on addressing basic human needs. After casting about, and with the assistance of the Rabat office and Dave, a volunteer who worked as a physical therapist in Marrakesh, we came up with a plan.

At the time, polio was endemic in Morocco. But with massage and kinesitherapy immediately administered after diagnosing the initial fever, palsy in the limbs could be mitigated. Dave and I met with the Minister of Health in Rabat, who was also a teaching physician at the medical school. He invited us into his office and made us espresso while we pitched the plan to have me trained and deployed back to Midelt to not only return to my teaching duties, but also to report to the local hospital every week and provide therapeutic treatments. He appeared to be impressed that we spoke to him in Derija and gave his approval to our plan.

Dave was leaving Morocco at the conclusion of his two years, so I was to be trained in Tetouan by a physical therapist named Sally. This turned into one of the most impactful and strangely wonderful summers of my life. Sally worked at a *Centre des paralytiques* (Center for Paralytics). It was a sort of summer camp for maladies – from deaf-mutes to patients afflicted with cerebral palsy.

Every day, we would take the kids to the beach. They were thrilled at the chance to swim in the Mediterranean, stripping off their braces as they crawled to the surf. The able-bodied patients would swim first and then form a human chain to keep those less able to float safely. With some of the most disabled, we would motorboat them around in circles, hearing their squeals of delight at the sensation of the water slipping over their twisted frames.

After the swim, they would form a circle and their show would begin. The first act was always the deaf-mute boys enacting Kung Fu fights, nasally snorting their cries as they whirled and kicked the air. Then more singing and dancing. The final act was me singing *Muhammed shibani* (Old MacDonald), the kids calling out the names of the animals. Then we would sing *A'ndi Allah fi al-telifun* (I got Jesus on the mainline, tell him what you want), and the kids would holler their wishes into the midday sunshine. Naturally, by this time, we would have dozens of onlookers gathered to see the performances.

One day, while I was walking through the souk, someone tapped me on the shoulder and asked, '*Muhammed shibani?*' Unforgettable.

The school year began back in Midelt, I returned to my teaching duties and started my weekly visits to the local hospital. Gradually, people who knew me in town stopped saluting me as *Usted* (teacher) and began addressing me as *Tabib* (doctor).

I began to be summoned to different houses for all sorts of reasons. I was supposed to teach a household member how to perform massage and physical therapy, but people preferred to have me perform the treatment.

One case was a long, skinny black man who had fallen a hundred meters down a mine shaft. He was put back together in the hospital but had received no follow-up therapy. Instead, he had languished in his bed for several years and had long bedsores on the backs of his lower legs. I began to massage his legs with his wife and six daughters looking on. Then I started pressing on pressure points on the sole of his foot. Suddenly, his toes began to wiggle, drawing gasps of astonishment from everyone in the room. Immediately, he began to try to shoo all of the females from the room.

With the women no longer present, he spoke to me quietly. "You know, my toes weren't the only thing that began to wiggle." He confided to me that it had been some time since he had been with his wife. I told him that I would be happy to teach her, but he cut me short.

"You foreigners don't understand. Here a man doesn't ask a woman to help him."

He later asked me for power pills, long before the days of Viagra. Remarkably, this case was my only true success as his youngest daughter, after observing me, began to massage her father's legs.

"Only up to my knees," he said. "I take it from there."

Steve Long
*TEFL Instructor
& Physical Therapist
Midelt*

# Final Hours

The previous week, I had preplanned Tuesday as my final photo and shopping tour of the Rabat medina. I wanted both the early morning light and the favorable price that went along with the good fortune of being a merchant's first customer of the day. Turned out to be a beautiful day in Rabat. I walked the length of Mohammed V, the main avenue that bisected the medina. To avoid the look of a tourist, I toted my camera equipment in a well-worn straw bag.

That excursion was pure fun. No rush to get anywhere. The medina was in full swing. I stopped at will to photograph local activity. I even paid a man to take his picture. He made a unique sight, elderly and ragged, sitting on the sidewalk selling a single product – snails. He had a large burlap bag of snails in front of him. I recalled seeing a similar character during my first medina experience chaperoned by Wally before we started training – could this have been the same man? He was most cooperative and didn't try to smile uncomfortably as some paid subjects did; he was very natural. With all my picture-taking through the medina, not a single sign of protest. Photography in Morocco could be fun, I discovered, under such circumstances.

By 10 o'clock, I was at the door of the local Artisan's Cooperative, a government-sponsored shop of top-quality handicrafts. I had bought items there before and escorted other volunteers there. Farouk, the owner, recognized me. I explained my upcoming departure and search for a nice carpet to take home. I was the first customer of the day and, before long, found myself knee-deep in thick carpets. With my wealth, I decided to purchase two carpets and worry about packing them later. Bargaining was quick and easy.

Out of both film and money, I dragged my load to the Peace Corps office and waited for a ride with Greg, the TEFL staff person who shared the house with Becky.

I spent the remainder of the afternoon at my apartment, packing. Until I found another duffle bag, the two carpets posed a problem. Eventually, everything fit somewhere.

That evening, Becky and I enjoyed one of our favorite restaurants for dinner – the Café Français, known for crepes. Mostly, we talked about the good ole days. Lots of good memories. It turned out to be our last time together in Morocco.

I completed my final apartment cleanup on Wednesday. I turned in two gas bottles for my $25 deposit and told Rahim, my hanoot storekeeper, that I was leaving for the United States. We exchanged addresses. I knew he would never write, though he promised to do so. He and his two sons grouped together for a photo right behind the orange juice and the scales used to weigh my butter. He was a Berber, typically shy. I gave him some U.S. pennies and a Kennedy half-dollar – he acted as if I had handed over pure gold.

The evening was spent hauling the last of my luggage to Becky's house. In the meantime, and through a grand mix-up, Becky had to leave for a meeting in Fes the next morning, so our goodbyes had to be made on paper. I had a feeling that would happen – both of us had been running around like crazy. A disappointment ... I had speeches prepared and everything. Becky left me a thoughtful note, wishing me the best of luck.

Time was running out. I spent the remaining hours completing the artwork for the slideshows. The house was cold. I drank a lot of hot chocolate. Thirty-six hours left in Morocco, I thought.

Thursday meant my last full day in the country. I turned in my apartment keys and handled final paperwork at the Peace Corps office. I picked up my plane ticket and said goodbye to the office staff. Phil Hanson, originally my program advisor and now Country Director, was short on words. I figured he was either really busy or just relieved to see me go.

Walking out of the office for the last time, I felt like I was halfway to Atlanta. A big relief. All the thought, time and work spent on my decision to leave was finally materializing into the actual event.

By 6, my required work for Becky was completed. I suddenly thought of all the little things I would have liked to have done in Rabat before leaving. There were so many, I forgot the whole idea and just killed time.

A few people dropped by. We popped the cork on a bottle of champagne. Ironically, some of the folks who came by were the same ones I first met when I got off the plane in Rabat back on June 29, 1977. Now, they would be the ones to see the last of me in Morocco.

## Departure Day

Friday, February 2 was my designated departure day. Considering the circumstances, I had slept well. Up by 7, I was ready for Mustafa, the Peace Corps driver, to come by at 8. I wrote a final note to Becky and drew a keepsake sketch for her.

The note outlined our experience together, my obvious blunders and shortcomings, her notable strengths and unlimited energy. Since she had met the real Charles in September, I closed with a remark about the Charles/Richard confusion at our first meeting in Atlanta.

My departure from Rabat was on time, uneventful and fast. For the last time, I explained my early departure to Mustafa, how much I had enjoyed Morocco and all my plans for the future. I sounded like a broken record.

All the worry about customs and passport checks at the airport was relieved by the total absence of problems there. I opened a suitcase for the agent's glance, but the two bulging duffle bags hopped aboard the plane unopened.

I became nervous waiting to board. Finally, feeling lucky and relieved, I sat in my window seat. My bulky carry-on load was manageable. I made a point to observe a local Moroccan for the last time — a member of the ground crew. He drove away in a service truck; we rolled down the runway. Ideal flying weather.

Gaining speed and leaving the ground, I stared out the window, memorizing the surrounding rural terrain, the sights and lasting impressions of my former home:

A second-class souk bus packed with color, kids, sheep, chickens, smelly men, covered women.

The rustic, ramshackle, chilly houses – residences of proud, independent people, generous with their hospitality and welcoming to foreigners.

Muddy fields, a shepherd and his flock.

A wiry figure urging a stubborn mule hitched to his plow.

Makeshift carts fashioned on rear auto axles, pulled by anything with four legs.

Cows, donkeys, horses planted to a spot in the fields with their front legs tied together.

Dogs ripping through the day's early store of garbage on the roadside. The slogan "man's best friend" never existed there.

Well-built roads navigated by slow scooters and some of the world's worst drivers.

Sugar beets, potatoes, cotton and all my former film stars.

The base of my discoveries – personal and otherwise – plus the land of friendships, hardships and accomplishments.

All diminished to microscopic bits, and the Moroccan coastline introduced the Atlantic. The enclosing cloud cover sealed my final impressions of the view.

The experiment was over. The experience and productivity of my future would be the only measure of the worth, in knowledge gained, of this treasured past.

*Kulshi la bes!* (Everything is fine!)

# Epilogue

My Peace Corps experience ended four months short of the standard two years. In my case, leaving Morocco in February rather than in June provided ample time for my readjustment to civilian life in the United States, consumed with the hunt for full-time employment.

I made a road trip to Washington, D.C., and followed up with the contacts collected from my embassy friends. Some interesting meetings resulted, but I discovered I was not cut out for a career with Uncle Sam. Paul and Robbie Hare invited me to their home for dinner one evening, and we enjoyed sharing our favorite memories of Morocco.

During the early days of May, I heard from Dan, my college film production partner. He convinced me to join him in California. I spent nearly a month in Los Angeles showing off my portfolio, applying to more than a dozen production companies and all the major studios. With no takers for my film production skills, I realized I was not destined to land the job I wanted in Hollywood. My mother appreciated me making the effort. Back in Atlanta, scanning the classifieds, I noticed an ad for an "Audiovisual Specialist" to work for a trade association based in New Orleans. Going the industrial/commercial photography route sounded promising.

By June 15, I began a 38-year career with the Southern Forest Products Association, a nonprofit trade organization representing lumber manufacturers. Producing slideshows for the field staff and membership meetings evolved into media and public relations work, several film and video productions, developing publications for the building trade and various writing assignments.

In 1984, I married Pam King, a widow with a three-year-old daughter, Lisa. The next year, our daughter Karen was born. Family life included summer vacations all over the country. We survived our flooded home following Hurricane Katrina and relocated to a small country town 40 miles north of New Orleans, fortunately living above sea level for a change. Both daughters finished college, married and became school teachers; the girls have blessed us with three grandchildren.

As the years passed by, I've read with interest how world events have impacted Peace Corps Morocco. Since its programs there began in 1963, more than 5,200 volunteers have served the kingdom. As of early 2020, some 260 volunteers were serving there, primarily in youth development programs.

In 1991, 380 Peace Corps Volunteers were evacuated from six Islamic countries – including Morocco – following Iraq's invasion of Kuwait. Then, in April of 2003, the Peace Corps program in Morocco was again suspended due to events in Iraq. After both interruptions in the programs, volunteers eventually returned to service.

I've enjoyed maintaining friendships and correspondence with many members of the 1977 volunteer class. Where did they end up? After serving in the Peace Corps …

Becky Mangus married Chuck Dammers. They made their home in Maryland, raising two sons. Becky worked in the communications field, including: photographer and graphic designer for ACTION, executive director of the International Photography Society, production manager for a publishing company and owner of her own marketing and graphics design firm. In 2002, with a partner, she purchased a local business newspaper and became its publisher. She sold the paper in 2018 and continues to work with marketing clients. She enjoys being grandmother to five. Chuck has worked as an engineer – first in transportation and later with stormwater management capital projects.

Paul Huntsman eventually found his dream job in Hollywood, compiling an illustrious, award-winning career in audio production. He worked as the supervising sound editor on dozens of major motion pictures, credited professionally as J. Paul Huntsman. His impressive profile at IMDb.com lists 67 credits for his audio work. Sadly, Paul died in 2008 following a battle with brain cancer; he was 55.

Maura Murray married Didier Moity three times – in Morocco, in Oklahoma and in France. Living in Paris, Maura taught English as a

Second Language (ESL) for a telecommunications corporation, later transitioning into advertising and communications. After raising three children, she retired and launched her own business as an English public speaking coach. Didier also worked for the telecom as an electronics engineer. Today, they are both retired and involved with community service activities for job placement and human rights organizations.

Patty Balch married Louis (the Georgia Tech engineer) after her second year of medical school at the University of Mississippi. Her residency took her to North Carolina where they raised three boys. Patty's career in medicine included teaching and many years in private practice. Now retired, she has enjoyed traveling the world and volunteering for international medical missions, such as treating refugees in war-torn Syria.

Debra Snell relocated to Atlanta, taught ESL for a few months, then worked eight years for insurance companies. While working, she completed her master's degree at Georgia State University, later accepting a position to teach there in the Department of Applied Linguistics. In 2005, she was awarded a Fulbright Scholarship and returned to Morocco to teach. On January 9, 2006, she joined some friends to visit her maid, Fatima, who had served countless volunteers over many years in Azrou and was very sick. Debra recalled: "My entourage got to Fatima's place, and I discovered she had been in a semi-coma for three days. I leaned over, kissed her and told her who I was. She opened her eyes and looked at me for a few seconds. Then, two minutes later, she died. She was buried later that day." For Debra, the year 2020 marked 30 years of teaching and her retirement.

Mark Postnikoff realized that "… after Peace Corps, life was never viewed again in the same manner." He married and raised five children, four of whom served in the U.S. Navy. He worked many years for the federal government, retiring in 2012. Mark relocated to Alabama, earned his real estate license and remodeled several homes. He "enjoys every minute of life."

Mark Dressman spent a year getting a master's degree in education, then taught on the Navajo Reservation. He returned to graduate school at UT Austin, earning his Ph.D. in curriculum and instruction. Teaching posts included New Mexico State and the University of Houston; he later joined the faculty at the University of Illinois. In 2005, he began annual trips to Morocco, making contacts with faculty at universities and eventually with the Fulbright Commission. In 2014, he received a Fulbright grant to study English education in three Moroccan universities. He retired from Illinois in December 2018 and has most recently worked as Professor and Chair of English at Khalifa University in Abu Dhabi, UAE.

Steve Long married Rosita in 1982. He taught ESL in Jeddah, Saudi Arabia. His family grew to include two children. Returning to the States in 1995, Steve worked in advertising and joined a multimedia company making interactive CDs. By 2000, he had started his own company to revise advanced-placement materials. He returned to Saudi Arabia in 2005, becoming a technical writer until his retirement in 2018.

Rich Eckert worked two years with ACTION where he met his wife. After grad school, he worked as an accountant/controller, then as a risk management professional. Twenty years defined his career and reputation as a stock analyst. Now retired and living in California, he's busy with gardening, some volunteer work and ushering at major league baseball games.

Denise Schickel returned to California and, with her interests in holistic health practices, attended massage and yoga school. She later entered grad school, earning her master's degree in organizational psychology. Denise then completed a Ph.D. program at Walden University and was awarded her doctorate in industrial/organizational psychology. Recently, she published a book, *15 Steps for Self-Care for Baby Boomers*.

John Schroeder and Debbie Beck married in Gibraltar during their 1979 spring break. Debbie taught English as a Foreign Language (EFL) in Bergamo, Italy, (hometown of John's mother and birthplace of their daughter). They settled in Oregon; both taught English for several years at Southern Oregon University. John retired from teaching in 2003. Debbie transitioned to administration at the university. Today, both are enjoying retirement.

Tinker Goggans continued her career in healthcare, working as a physician's assistant in pediatric neurology in Texas. She retired in July 2018. Tinker and her husband moved to her hometown and stay busy remodeling their home, built in 1927.

Piotr Kostrzewski entered the leisure travel industry, arranging and escorting customized travel programs, including trips to Morocco. He reports: "I go back to Morocco at least once a year; generally, the trip is a grand tour of all the prime highlights."

Terry Lajtha worked as a film editor on science documentaries for kids – films featured on the educational PBS show *3-2-1 Contact*, among others. She worked for the National Geographic Society as a film editor, then editing independent documentaries about social issues. Her recent update: "I have two grown kids who inherited my love of travel and languages. I am currently studying my seventh language – Czech!"

Mike Kendellen began a 35-year career in international humanitarian and development work. He worked in Asia, the former Soviet Union and the Balkans, directing refugee assistance programs. Mike became involved in the global landmine problem, working for the International Campaign to Ban Landmines, winner of the 1997 Nobel Peace Prize. Since retiring in 2014, he has published two memoirs: *Making It Happen,* an account of his Peace Corps service in Venezuela (1974–76) and *Don't Go Out After Dark,* about delivering aid during a war in Tajikistan. His third book on 10 years with the Vietnamese boat people is due in 2021. He dabbles in amateur photography and lives with his wife, Barb, in Washington, D.C.

Trish and Ed Henderson landed in Vancouver, Washington, where Trish taught middle school and continued in that field for 35 years. Ed worked years developing the National Society for Tax Professionals. Today, they are both retired, spending time traveling and being grandparents.

Larry Berube worked many years as a painter and carpenter. Twenty years ago, he returned to college, earning a bachelor's degree in writing. Larry began writing poems about his life experiences and published many of them in a memoir, *Nuns, Nam & Henna,* which received the 2018 award for Best Book of Poetry from Peace Corps Writers. He retired to Florida where he continues writing poetry.

Phil Hanson launched his diplomatic career in July 1979, working for the State Department as a General Services Officer in Ouagadougou, Upper Volta (now Burkina Faso). In 1981, he was promoted to Director of the Joint Administrative Office of the American Mission in Lomé, Togo. Tragically, on June 25, 1981, Phil died in a plane crash while traveling between the two cities. He was planning to join his wife Anissa and their 10-month-old son, Neil, in Rabat before heading to the States for home leave. Our entire volunteer class was deeply saddened by the loss. Phil was only 35.

Paul J. Hare continued his Foreign Service career at the State Department in Washington, serving as Director of the Office of Southern African Affairs. In 1981, he was posted to the embassy in Israel as Counselor for Political Affairs. On May 20, 1985, President Ronald Reagan announced his intention to nominate Paul as the next U.S. Ambassador to Zambia; Paul served there as America's top envoy for three years. He retired from the Foreign Service in 1991 and became Vice President of the Middle East Institute based in Washington, D.C.

From 1993–1998, he was appointed by the Clinton Administration to be the U.S. Special Representative for the Angolan Peace Process. Subsequently, he was President of the U.S.-Angola Chamber of Commerce until 1998. He authored two books: a biography of his father, Ambassador Raymond A. Hare, titled *Diplomatic Chronicles of the Middle East* and *Angola's Last Best Chance for Peace: An Insider's Account of the Peace Process*. Paul is now retired, living in Virginia.

On March 15, 2020, all 7,367 Peace Corps Volunteers serving in 61 countries around the world were evacuated back to the United States due to the coronavirus pandemic. In response to this unprecedented action, Peace Corps Director Jody Olsen noted that "… these evacuations represent the temporary suspension of Volunteer activities. We are not closing posts, and we will be ready to return to normal operations when conditions permit."

For the first time in the nearly 60-year history of the Peace Corps, the world was left without the services of JFK's ambassadors of peace.

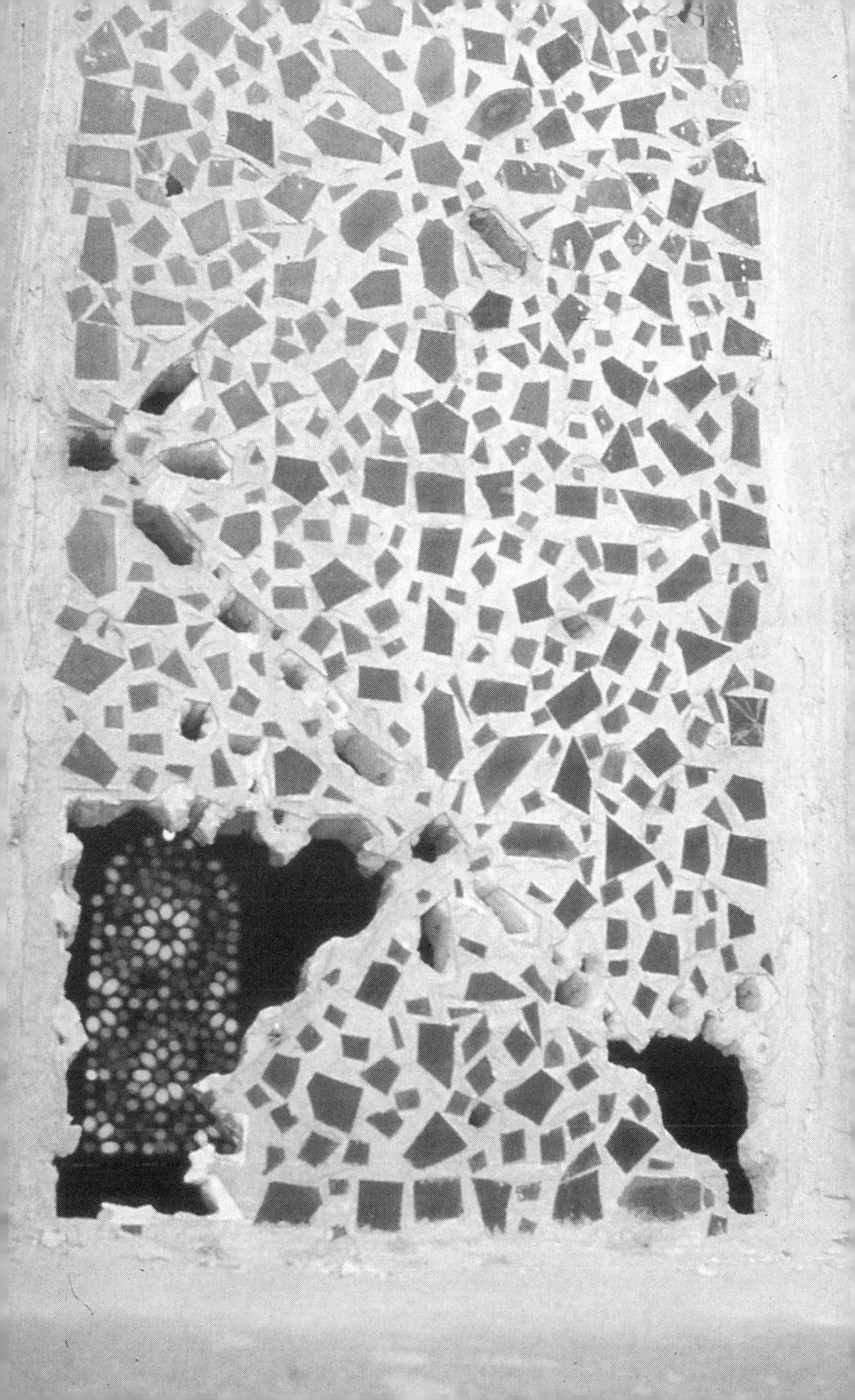

# Acknowledgments

I wish to thank the generous contributions of Peace Corps Volunteers from my 1977 Class who provided so many thoughtful, cherished recollections of their experiences in Morocco. Very special thanks are extended to Mark Dressman and Debra Snell who provided essential translations and linguistic assistance throughout my book. Mike Kendellen was also very helpful, providing newsletters we received during our service – full of insights into the workings of our Peace Corps administration, along with notable contributions from volunteers.

While writing my book, I enjoyed looking up old friends and having lengthy email and phone conversations about their Peace Corps memories, as well as what they had been up to since their days in Morocco. I have missed two opportunities to join reunions of our class, and I'm determined not to miss the next get-together; we all have so many good times to share.

Special thanks go to my editor, Joy E. Rancatore, for fielding my many questions and making my book better. And more thanks are extended to Rachael Ritchey for her expert arrangement of my words on these pages.

And finally, I want to thank my wife, Pam, for her love and support during this project.

# About the Author

Richard Wallace volunteered with the Peace Corps, serving in Rabat, Morocco during the late 1970s. He returned to the United States and, for the next 38 years, worked for a nonprofit trade organization representing lumber manufacturers. His career included producing many audiovisual programs, developing publications for the building trade and transitioning later to media and public relations work. He retired in 2017 and lives in Ponchatoula, Louisiana.

Made in the USA
San Bernardino, CA
19 July 2020